The Dynamic Enterprise

The Dynamic Enterprise

Tools for Turning Chaos into Strategy and Strategy into Action

Lisa Friedman

Herman Gyr

Jossey-Bass Publishers • San Francisco

The identifying details in the examples in this book have been changed to protect the confidentiality of the enterprises and individuals involved.

Substantial discounts on bulk quantities of Jossey-Bass books are available to corporations, professional associations, and other organizations. For details and discount information, contact the special sales department at Jossey-Bass Inc., Publishers (415) 433-1740; fax (800) 605-2665.

For sales outside the United States, please contact your local Simon & Schuster International Office.

Jossey-Bass Web address: http://www.josseybass.com

 Manufactured in the United States of America on Lyons Falls Turin Book. This paper is acid-free and 100 percent chlorine-free.

Library of Congress Cataloging-in-Publication Data

Friedman, Lisa.
The dynamic enterprise: tools for turning chaos into strategy and strategy into action / Lisa Friedman and Herman Gyr.
    p. cm. — (The Jossey-Bass business & management series)
Includes bibliographical references and index.
ISBN 0-7879-1014-7 (acid-free paper)
1. Organizational change. I. Gyr, Herman. II. Title.
III. Series.
HD58.8.F765 1997
658.4'06—dc21
                                                                97-21047
                                                                     CIP

Credits are on page 267.

FIRST EDITION
HB Printing 10 9 8 7 6 5 4 3 2 1

The Jossey-Bass
Business & Management Series

Contents

To Alex and Andy

Preface

It takes courage to go to work today. Our businesses, institutions, and governments face tremendous pressures to become enterprising. Executives, managers, and front-line workers alike are expected to deliver performance faster, cheaper, and smarter. At the same time, they find themselves in a business climate that is complex and shifting rapidly around them. Changes come from almost all directions simultaneously: the marketplace, competitors, advancing technology, and growing customer demands. These forces together create a sense of urgency in our workplaces and produce a business atmosphere that is often pressured and complex.

Furthermore, shifts no longer affect businesses individually— entire industries are in transition, so that the individual enterprise rarely has the option to remain the same. Frequently, changes take place industrywide; these changes in turn exert new pressures on and offer new opportunities to a whole set of related industries. This cascading, interactive network of change unleashes forces that can thrust our organizations into disarray right when there is most pressure to deliver high performance.

Answers that made sense in earlier times are suddenly irrelevant. Leaders and managers face challenges for which their education and business experiences provide no precedent. Previous answers for managing change (generally for managing a single major change initiative or for managing a large-scale but unidimensional change) are inadequate for working through the complexity of the multidimensional challenges faced today. Furthermore, often no other firm or institution provides an adequate or time-tested benchmark for envisioning the future.

The nature of today's changing workplace can be exciting and challenging for some but may overwhelm others. However, from all indications, current levels of change are just the beginning. Not only are changes in the workplace complex and multidimensional, approaching on many fronts at once, but they are also occurring at an *accelerating* pace. As each change enables and even necessitates a new wave of change in another area, changes build on each other and increase exponentially.

How is an enterprise to survive and thrive under such tumultuous conditions? How can leaders, managers, and other stakeholders make sense out of the many new forces affecting their work? What is needed to find clarity and guidance in midst of this chaos?

We believe that these questions represent serious challenges and responsibilities for the businesses, nonprofit institutions, and government agencies of our times. If we cannot help our enterprises find meaning and clear direction among constantly shifting priorities, our businesses and institutions will face significant troubles. We must be able to build enterprises that can integrate the multiple new impacts and forces so that people throughout the enterprise can work together and move their companies successfully forward. We call an organization with this capability the *Dynamic Enterprise*.

The Dynamic Enterprise enables rapid response to a dynamic environment. It enables its people to navigate successfully the challenges of continuous and exponential change, to turn chaos into shared strategic direction and clarity, and to transform complex change into a drive and momentum for moving toward the future.

This book represents our best thinking about tools and methods for creating the Dynamic Enterprise. Knowing that current business conditions necessitate the creation of a Dynamic Enterprise is a different story from knowing how to create it. What capabilities are needed? Who builds the Dynamic Enterprise? Who does what? How is it built?

We have found that all stakeholders need to be involved in creating the Dynamic Enterprise. To do so, they need to understand what they are facing together and need to be able to communicate with each other—throughout the enterprise—about changes ahead.

In its heart and soul, this book is about a set of practices—collectively referred to as *Enterprise Development*—that are needed to build the Dynamic Enterprise. Enterprise Development provides a common language and a framework for developing and maintaining the Dynamic Enterprise. It provides a way to focus all participants on the changing conditions they are facing. *People* build the Dynamic Enterprise. It is people who together must translate the many changes in the environment into decisions and actions and ultimately into products and services. Enterprise Development is a tool they can use to map the many conflicting forces affecting them, to make sense out of the changes they face, and to translate change into pragmatic and coordinated strategic action.

Who Should Read This Book?

This book will be of interest to readers who must deal with significant change in their everyday work lives. We wrote it with three primary audiences in mind:

- Executives, managers, team leaders, and others in leadership positions (formal or informal) who are responsible for leading their enterprises through times of change
- Stakeholders who are significantly affected by change—those who are currently involved in a change initiative, turnaround, or strategic development effort, or those who think they ought to be
- Change agents—such as performance support teams, change support teams, consultants, facilitators, and others—who are helping to coordinate, support, and move change forward

Because creating a Dynamic Enterprise by definition involves linking stakeholders throughout an enterprise, this book is intended to be helpful at all levels in an organization. The ideas presented are designed to be used (and have been used) by CEOs, executive teams, middle managers, department heads, front-line workers, strategic partners, and union leaders as well. We have worked for years to develop commonsense language that is straightforward, without jargon, so that it can be useful for guiding the profound strategic choices being made by leadership teams, as well as the concrete and pragmatic decisions faced on the front line. We struggled to find the concepts and words that would enable these diverse groups to communicate with one another about the strategic direction of the enterprise and what was needed to achieve their goals.

The book may also be particularly helpful to those who are part of an identified change initiative or strategic development effort within their enterprise—individuals who are leading companywide change initiatives, reengineering or work redesign teams, cross-functional projects, and even alliancing or partnering efforts that cross enterprise boundaries.

As a practitioner's guide, this book weaves together frameworks and practices with descriptions of actual applications. Examples are presented throughout to illuminate the application of the concepts and tools presented. Many of the tools may be familiar, but the order and combinations in which we suggest they be used should deliver new insight and confidence for practitioners to make full use of their existing competencies. Indeed, that is one of the core purposes of the book: to encourage readers to capitalize on their existing experience and knowledge. We hope to offer frameworks to help readers recognize, articulate, and integrate what they already know in order to engender confidence and catalyze action for everyone working in a constantly and dramatically changing world.

An enterprise of any size or scope can become a Dynamic Enterprise. The concepts apply to global corporations, divisions within a company, teams of any size, government or nonprofit agencies, or a sole proprietor's small business. An enterprise can even include a group of strategic partners, a network of alliances, or a supply chain or "value chain" crossing many companies.

Map to This Book

Part One contains two chapters. Chapter One describes the changing nature of the workplace, and Chapter Two outlines the kind of Dynamic Enterprise that is needed to survive and thrive in this tumultuous business environment.

Some readers, seeing the title *The Dynamic Enterprise,* may already imagine what such an enterprise is and will want to jump into the middle of the action—to learn the tools to create it. These readers may want to skip the description and examples of the

Dynamic Enterprise in Part One and begin reading the book with Part Two.

Chapter Three introduces Enterprise Development as an integrated set of tools to guide the creation of the Dynamic Enterprise. Enterprise Development maps the six core competencies needed in the Dynamic Enterprise, and each subsequent chapter elaborates on one of these competencies:

- Seeing the whole system of the enterprise (Chapter Four)
- Creating a shared vision of the future enterprise (Chapter Five)
- Viewing the past and present honestly and accurately (Chapter Six)
- Understanding the nature of the change (Chapter Seven)
- Mobilizing the three essential drivers of change (Chapter Eight)
- Implementing change to turn strategy into performance (Chapter Nine)

Chapter Four introduces the STEP Model, a framework for assessing the enterprise as a dynamic system that enables users to understand the unique relationships between the elements of the enterprise system. Chapter Five discusses how to create a broadly shared comprehensive vision and strategy. Chapter Six describes how to develop a shared view of the past and current enterprise, for it is essential to understand the starting point before embarking on a strategic change. Chapter Seven then presents concepts that aid in understanding the nature of the change required to move from the current to the future. Not all changes are created equal, and a single approach to change management is not appropriate across the wide variety of changes. In this chapter, we use business and organization life cycle models to clarify the quality and magnitude of the intended change.

In Chapter Eight, we present three drivers of change—leadership, stakeholders, and performance support—that we have found to be essential to the success of the Dynamic Enterprise. When one of these drivers is missing, failure is very likely to occur, and the particular nature of the failure can be readily predicted.

Whereas the chapters in Part Two give an integrated blueprint for creating the Dynamic Enterprise, Chapter Nine, in Part Three, focuses on implementation—how to turn designs into reality. In this chapter, we outline the six basic phases of implementation that comprise the Enterprise Development Workplan and offer our thoughts about the most crucial elements of implementation success.

Finally, in the Epilogue, we take a longer-term look at our businesses and institutions. The main body of the book relates to the unique challenges mainstream enterprises face in the immediate future. In the Epilogue, we expand the Enterprise Development framework to include a larger picture of the business system, looking farther out in time. As more work groups are examining data from a wide array of emerging changes and considering the implications for their enterprises, they suddenly face a whole new set of business challenges they are only beginning to recognize. Across many industries, leaders and teams are discovering an urgent need to create sustainable strategies and business practices that do not yet exist fully in even our most dynamic enterprises.

Perspective of This Book

This book is written by practitioners for practitioners. We each bring fifteen years of experience from our backgrounds in business and organization consulting, in facilitating Enterprise Development workshops, and in leadership coaching. The ideas presented in the book are based on our work experience and our review of business, management, and organization development practices and have evolved through continual testing and reshaping with clients.

Over the years, our clients have helped us refine the concepts. They would not accept ideas that made good theory but did not add value in practice. Long-term Enterprise Development projects helped us distinguish the most important needs for turning ideas into actions that survived over time. We also learned a great deal about the idiosyncrasies of human nature as people faced exponential change and how these human dynamics affected the very logical workplans that were set up for moving an enterprise forward. We have attempted to incorporate these theoretically unexpected but realistically recurring observations into our writing. This book, therefore, is not about the theory of creating a Dynamic Enterprise that can deal with significant change. Instead, we wrote about what we have observed to be essential for developing the Dynamic Enterprise in an actual workplace full of people under stress, who are acting as their most dramatic, creative, imaginative, political, and contentious selves.

Many of the ideas presented in this book are not new. Our concepts about vision, leadership, business challenges, organization development, and managing change build on a rich foundation of work established by a talented and diverse group of academics and practitioners. Even if certain ideas seem familiar to some readers, we hope that we have added to the discipline and practice of Enterprise Development by synthesizing and integrating these ideas into a simple and usable framework. We have attempted to link the ideas from separate business strategy and organization development disciplines while adding observations and examples from our own practice. Our hope is to provide a common language and an integrated framework and mapping process that can be used by stakeholders throughout an enterprise for facing the challenges of exponential change.

Acknowledgments

Many people have contributed to this book by adding their ideas, time, and energy, as well as their stories.

We would like to express our appreciation for the authors and practitioners whose ideas provided a foundation to our work: Peter Senge in the area of organization systems dynamics; Ariadne Beck, Wilfred Bion, and Ichak Adizes regarding the phases of organization development; Stan Davis and many others who have written about business life cycles; Peter Block, David Bradford and Allen Cohen, Marv Weisbord, and Robert Jacobs about the importance of the stakeholders' role in the creation of the enterprise, and Gary Hamel and C. K. Prahalad on focusing the enterprise around the strategic business future. Some of the earliest ideas for the STEP Model of enterprise systems were developed in collaboration with Sam Kaner. In addition, Richard Pascale provided mentoring in the late 1980s when we were first forging many of the ideas that appear here, and he connected us with several of the client projects that helped us carry these ideas forward.

Clients over the years have been wonderfully generous in helping us clarify our ideas and allowing us to use their examples. We particularly want to thank Julian Darley, Margaret Jordan, Alva Wheatley, and Charles Rickard for allowing us to use their experiences as examples of the drama inherent in large-scale change and their actions as models of how leaders can respond successfully to the tests they face.

Our colleagues at the Enterprise Development Group and at Co-Development International were very helpful and generous in sharing their insights from consulting engagements around the world. Many thanks go to Dan Doherty and Tita Puangco for successfully testing the application of Enterprise Development in South Africa and in the Asia Pacific region.

In addition, we are grateful to those business leaders and authors who have begun thinking and writing about the shift from the industrial information eras to a new, emerging era—a time of constrained resources and heightened need for our enterprises to play a significant role in sustainability and restoration. We would also like to thank our colleagues working at the Center for the Evolution of Culture, who inspired us to add the epilogue to this book.

Many individuals at Jossey-Bass provided insight and encouragement just when needed. Thanks go to Sarah Polster, who first encouraged us to write this book, and to Cedric Crocker, who provided continual clarity and focus.

And of course we want to thank our sons, Alex and Andy, for being so loving and full of life. Their enthusiasm and spirit helped give us the fuel we needed to work, to think, and to write.

We encourage readers to contact us by visiting our Web site:
<http://www.enterprisedevelop.com>

Palo Alto, California   LISA FRIEDMAN, PH.D.
August 1997   HERMAN GYR, PH.D.

The Authors

Lisa Friedman and Herman Gyr are the founders and principals of the Enterprise Development Group, a consulting and training firm specializing in strategy development and implementation for work groups facing complex change. They use the concepts presented in this book to enable individuals in businesses and institutions to create *Dynamic Enterprises*—to look courageously and strategically into the future and to build the responses to what they see into their enterprises as quickly as possible.

In fifteen years of training and consulting, Friedman and Gyr have worked with companies and institutions across a range of industries, including technology, health care, oil and gas, manufacturing, financial services, insurance, hotels, real estate, universities, fisheries, and the military. Within these groups, they have worked with individual CEOs and executives, with management teams, and with project and change teams facing a range of business and organizational challenges. This work has included the "harder" topics of business strategy, planning, and change management issues, in conjunction with the frequently needed "softer" side of change—the culture change, team building, conflict resolution, and individual coaching often required to bring the strategy into reality.

Friedman and Gyr are currently developing the Millennium Strategy Workshops to enable participants to examine their enterprises from a broader and longer-term perspective.

Lisa Friedman received her B.A. degree (1976) from Stanford University and her Ph.D. (1980) in psychology from the California School of Professional Psychology, Berkeley. She worked as a licensed psychologist for ten years before shifting to organizational and business consulting and training.

Herman Gyr began his studies at the University of Zurich, Switzerland, earned his B.A. degree (1976) at the University of Michigan, and received his Ph.D. (1981) from the California School of Professional Psychology, Berkeley.

Prologue
The Gift of Perspective

The Bushmen consider their hills a sacred, mystical place. In Botswana, where they live, in the Kalahari Desert, the land is flat as far as they can see. Mile upon mile is covered with sparse, open forest. As the Bushmen look ahead on the flat plain, they can see only the baobab and thorn trees of the African bush around them.

Bushmen have been known to journey for days to reach the Tsodilo Hills. The hills rise sixteen hundred feet from the floor of the plain, and the summit provides a breathtaking 360-degree view. Because the surrounding land is so flat, from this height the Bushmen can see the earth curve away from them to the horizon in all directions. They can see the green of the Okavango Swamp hundreds of miles to the northeast. For the first time, they can see where their camp is placed and where they live in relation to other camps and landmarks. To a people who live without this perspective in their everyday lives, this rare view of their world is powerful—it is magic.

—*Story told by Richard Rathbun*

Facing Chaos

Chapter One

Exponential Change and the New Business Environment

A world tossing and turning, restless with fresh and disturbing impulses, trying to redo itself, rethink itself, realign itself, and trying to live up to its troubled and inarticulate sense of new realities. That's what everybody's complaining about, not that the world's asleep, but that it can't sleep any longer.
MICHAEL VENTURA, *Shadow Dancing in the USA*

The price of fish dropped from $2.40 to 60 cents per pound. The fishermen's world turned upside down. How could they sustain their livelihoods? What had happened? How should they respond?

The family physician used to be an independent practitioner, who treated his or her own patients and was paid by patients or an insurance company. Now there is a complex "health care food chain" that funnels dollars from large employer groups to large networks of health care contractors. The individual family physician has to scramble to find a place in a funded network and to offer services that fit the new budget and the business plans of managed care.

A high-tech manufacturing company is growing at a rate of 55 percent annually and expects to hit $1 billion within the year. This growth rate means that "half a company" must be hired and added each year. Each calendar quarter brings new policies, new organization charts, new office facilities, new product lines, new companies acquired.

A utility expects that when deregulation hits its industry and customers are free to choose their energy providers, the company could lose 50 percent of its customers within the next several years. Market research indicates that customers choose primarily based on price, and the utility is currently one of the most expensive alternatives. Furthermore, since it has large fixed asset costs, the more customers the company loses, the higher the price charged to remaining customers would need to be. Managers whisper to each other about a "death spiral." What is next?

The managers of a retail chain know that they have to change from their outdated mainframe computer system to new client-server technology: the old system can no longer keep up with new demands. However, they realize that they should not automate their existing administrative and business processes because these are as outdated as the technology. Before upgrading their technology, they need to redesign twenty major business processes, including key financial, business, and human resource processes. All the processes are interdependent, creating a complex web of change. Twenty design teams are launched simultaneously in an effort to redefine the way the company operates.

A technology company has grown 40 percent per year and is approaching $1 billion in annual revenue. Its international sales team realizes that sales are about to hit a wall. Customers want something new, and sales managers expect revenues to plummet unless the company learns to provide it. Customers no longer want only a high-tech product that they have to integrate themselves; they now want a "total enterprise solution," customized to their own industry. It is no longer enough to have the best product. To get new contracts, the company will need to be part of the network of providers that can best solve customers' most urgent issues. The members of the sales team are the first to see this growing need. Can they get the rest of their company to see it in time?

Look anywhere. Ask anyone. Change is changing.

Try your own survey: ask people you know what is happening in their workplaces. The collage of examples that opened the chapter illustrates just a fraction of the current transformations that are occurring. Companies are growing, downsizing, or restructuring. Markets are disappearing, shifting, becoming global, expanding rapidly. New competitors are coming on the scene, often from entirely different industries. For some companies, longtime customers are becoming competitors; other companies are partnering or aligning with competitors to meet changing market needs. Work processes are being redefined, and organizations are being redesigned. People change companies, change roles, change jobs.

"Change management" programs proliferate, but sometimes they only add to the confusion because there is not just one kind of change. There is a broad spectrum of change, across almost every area of business and organization, much of it occurring simultaneously. Changes range from small incremental improvements to profound industry transformations that shake the very identity of an individual business or institution. These are dynamic times.

Three Ways Change Itself Is Changing

Change is changing in three significant ways:

- Changes are *multidimensional* and *complex*. They affect more than one system simultaneously.
- There are more changes of *greater magnitude,* involving fundamental shifts in the very definition of the work or how it will be done.
- Change is *accelerating exponentially*—it is occurring at an ever-faster pace.

Multidimensional, Complex Change

There are many *external* drivers of change in the workplace, all of which exert their influence simultaneously. The most prominent driving forces will vary for each industry, but most will be strongly influenced by global markets, cultures, and politics; shifting demographics; growing customer expectations; shifting relationships between competitors and strategic alliances; realignments in the basic industry "food chains" (who pays for what and what they expect for it); emerging technologies; and even new ways of conceptualizing work (such as shifts to lean manufacturing or emphasis on sustainable business practices)—to name just a few of the external forces that may be exerting simultaneous pressure.

These changes in the external environment set off other changes in the *internal* organizations of our enterprises. We see many instances of shifting organization boundaries (through out-sourcing, mergers, acquisitions, partnering alliances), new orga-nization structures, redesigned manufacturing and work processes, new information and communication systems, changing roles for leaders and managers, changing employee expectations, and new kinds of meeting formats. Temporary project teams are formed, where it is known from the beginning that the team will exist for only a short time. Work takes place in different and more flex-ible locations and at more flexible times. New trends such as "hotelling" (workers have a locker and use office space only when needed—similar to a hotel room) and telecommuting from home, airplane, or any other remote location act to create a flexible "work anywhere, anytime" culture.

A telling symbol of the changing, dynamic workplace is a new generation of office furniture designed with large wheels. Desks, conference tables, file cabinets, chairs, chart pads, and even com-plete cubicles are available in movable pieces that can be mixed and matched in one configuration now and another one later. It is not just that the wheels are functional. The wheels are quite large and prominent—they symbolize a new fashion. In the past, office furniture was designed to symbolize solidity, tradition, and stabil-ity. Now established designers are creating new lines of workplace furniture to highlight flexibility and mobility.

Greater Magnitude of Change

Some of these changes are small, such as incremental improve-ments in an area affecting a limited number of people. Other changes occur at the most profound levels and lead to the restruc-turing of entire industries. For example, in an age of direct con-nection and flattened hierarchies, many industries and corporate functions that served a "middleman" role are shrinking or being eliminated altogether. When new technology and business prac-tices enable customers or employees to go directly to the source of the information or goods, they find it repetitive and wasteful to go to someone who does not add value to the connection. This level of change is not simply a shift in the way work is performed but is often a basic questioning of the very purpose of the work, of whether it needs to exist at all. These fundamental pressures for change are most often felt not just in one department or one company but across entire industries.

Exponential Change

The dramatic interaction of various changes often causes others that were neither intended nor anticipated. Customers create new demands on suppliers, who in turn exert new pressures on *their* suppliers. New technology enables new work processes that in turn require new job descriptions, new organization charts, new work relationships, new meeting arrangements, new furniture. Shifting opportunities and demands create a snowball effect, where each individual change creates a growing number of related changes.

How People Experience Complex Change

In the course of our consulting and training work, we regularly conduct formal surveys to understand the breadth of changes companies are facing and how they handle these. However, informal check-ins gather much the same data in more lively and expressive ways. In our "Strategy Huddle" workshops, where work teams meet to plan their futures, we frequently question participants about the trends they are seeing in their workplaces and about their experience with change. Across a wide range of industry groups (high technology, health care, utilities, manufacturing, academia, nonprofits, oil companies, and many others), the answers have been strikingly similar. Whether we are working with leaders, middle managers, or work teams, group after group describes facing many of the same pressures: growing need to "do more with less—a lot less," "increased emphasis on quality and service," "decreased cycle time," "tougher competition," "need to become global," "more demanding customers," "decreased funding and resources," "increasing regulations," "increasingly new and complex work," "new technology," "new organization structure (recently reorganized)," and "more change everywhere!"

Though every work group is unique, each has produced a list that is quite similar. We tend to summarize these trends by connecting the ideas: "So you have to do more with *a lot* less; furthermore, it is a new, complex, and unknown 'more' that you've never done before—and you have to do it quicker! While competitors are close on your heels, you also have more regulations to pay attention to, and customers are increasingly demanding improved quality and service. You have to deliver this higher quality in work that is new to you, using technology that is new to you, with an organization structure that is new (and that you haven't quite settled into yet), and you have a lot fewer resources to do it with. Meanwhile, everything is changing around you. Is this the picture?" To date, every group has given a big sigh and agreed.

We next ask how people in the enterprise generally experience these realities in their work life. This is an open, neutral question, but we typically receive responses with a great deal of energy and emotion behind them, such as "stress," "anxiety," "insecurity," "confusion," "decreased loyalty," "increased hostility," "leave-and-stay syndrome," "no time to think," "feel overwhelmed," and "panic!"

In addition, we also often hear responses pointing to the fact that distress may be spilling over into people's personal lives, such as "emergency rooms, alcoholism, and divorce!" Everyone laughs at the moment of comic relief, but no one denies seeing these effects.

In almost all instances, the first spontaneous responses given are consistently negative. We have to ask whether positive responses exist because *none* are suggested without prompting. Once asked, participants almost always recognize the potential for more positive workplace experiences and call out ideas: "challenge," "opportunity," "excitement," "stimulating work environment," "always learning," "never bored," "sense of purpose."

We have found these informal surveys quite illuminating. They illustrate again and again that at the very time when people are being asked to deliver higher performance under more challenging conditions, many are actually feeling more stressed, confused, and even hostile. These are not ideal conditions for companies to use streamlined resources to beat the competition to the future. To accomplish a new and unknown "more" with "less," the people of the enterprise need to have more of the positive experiences— the sense of challenge, excitement, and purpose—rather than feeling confused and overwhelmed.

What Do People Need When Facing Exponential Change?

What makes the difference? What helps turn the negative experience of workplace pressures into positive motivation?

When we ask this question in our workshops, participants are again quite consistent in their responses. Obviously, the answers are not esoteric—they are fairly obvious. People want assistance for facing the challenges of higher performance at a time when everything is changing around them, when the stakes are great because the competition is everywhere and is struggling to steal their market share, and when they have less and less time to figure out new solutions for increasingly complex problems. They wish for "clarity about what is changing and why," "clear direction about where we are going," "common understanding," "vision," "strong leadership," "support to change—operational and emotional support," "adequate resources for change (not excessive)," and "more communication!"

So as not to feel overwhelmed by the pressure toward higher performance at the very time that everything is changing around them, people at work need shared and clearly communicated direction to help them navigate through the chaos. However, we have found that they rarely feel that this clarity and direction are in place. It is not a coincidence that so many groups begin by describing the negative aspects of their workplace experience. They can identify what they need, but it is not yet the norm to have processes in place that guide them and inspire confidence in the future of their companies and institutions.

The dynamism in the business environment, as well as in the internal workplace, is often anxiety-provoking and overwhelming just when the enterprise is facing its toughest challenges. However, as the quoted responses indicate, a dynamic environment can also be stimulating and full of opportunity. What kind of enterprise can connect its people to this dynamic environment in a positive and invigorating way? What is needed to settle people and connect them to their potential excitement about the future? What can help them integrate all that is new and keep their bearings in the midst of constantly shifting input? What is required to give people the clarity and shared common direction they crave in the midst of ongoing exponential change? We call an enterprise that has these capabilities the *Dynamic Enterprise.*

Chapter Two

Leveraging Chaos
The Dynamic Enterprise

*Successful competitors move quickly in and out of
products, markets, and sometimes even entire businesses—
a process more akin to an interactive video game than to
chess. In such an environment, the essence of strategy is
not the structure of a company's products and markets,
but the dynamics of its behavior.*
GEORGE STALK, PHILIP EVANS,
AND LAWRENCE SHULMAN, "Competing on
Capabilities: The New Rules of Corporate Strategy"

"What do you *know about our business?"* This question was asked of
one of the authors a few years ago at the beginning of a weeklong
strategic planning session with an association of owners and managers from large distribution centers. The inquiry came from one
of the participants, the CEO of one of the largest companies in the
group. The author's response was, "I don't know much about your
business. In the next few days, let's find out what you yourselves
know about it." The participant was not particularly happy with this
answer and sat down rather dejectedly, expecting, no doubt, that
his time would be wasted. This man, who had led his company for
several decades and was a recognized and respected leader in his
field, obviously had a good grasp of his business. He had succeeded
on the basis of deep industry knowledge (indeed, his family
had been involved in the industry for generations), and now—during what he perceived as merely a temporary downturn—he was

simply looking for an outside "content expert" to give him clear answers about what to do next. In his world, the guiding assumption was that one could outline a well-defined and rather narrow and unidimensional path and then follow it. One could "know" what to do, could project a fairly certain future; and if there was a stumbling block on the way, one could engage industry-derived expertise to fix the problem in short order.

In the traditional corporate environment where this CEO had built his success, "organizations" were typically represented by their organization charts, by the standardized arrangements of business functions, which generally existed in a hierarchical, linear, and relatively static relationship to each other. The boxes on the chart could be "engineered" to deliver relatively consistent outputs for a fairly predictable business.

However, in the dynamic environment described in Chapter One, the relatively unidimensional and functional view of planning and organization no longer holds. The enterprise is critically affected by many forces that interact in *dynamic* ways to shape its current and future form. The path forward is rarely linear and narrowly bounded; the final destination is never clear. Effective performance must be established through "discovery" rather than based solely on "knowledge" gained from past experience. Instead of finding answers in "expertise" (practices built on previous successes), answers must be *discovered* through scanning, analysis, imagination, seeing new patterns emerge, and ultimately courageous choices (courageous because these choices are made in heretofore unknown territory).

By working their way through the concepts that will be described throughout the rest of this book, members of the distribution industry association discovered that the picture of their business reality was quite different from what they had imagined as they entered the conference. The association was comprised of owners and managers of centers where manufacturers' representatives showed their goods to buyers for retail stores. In the past years, many of these companies had experienced a downturn in their business, which they had attributed to the economic recession. Many of their tenants, the wholesalers, had left their buildings, and areas of many buildings stood empty.

Building owners and managers often had a real estate background and tended to view the buildings as property to be managed. From their vantage point, if tenants left, it meant that rents might be too high for a weak economy, or that service was not appropriate, or perhaps that the location was in decline. In previous meetings, association members had focused on how these problems could be addressed. They worked on restructuring rental fees, establishing councils for tenant relations, and redesigning the interiors of buildings to make them fashionable and appealing. Some added piano players in the lobbies.

This time, as the association members began systematically to examine the changes in their external environment that were affecting them, they began to see a pattern emerging that they had not noticed before. Changes were taking place in the external environment of their customers' industry that in turn affected their customers' businesses and what they needed (or didn't need) from the centers. Larger retailers were buying smaller retailers, so there were fewer customers for their own customers. As the number of retail establishments consolidated, fewer people needed to come to their centers to meet with wholesalers.

In addition, association members discovered that technology was increasingly affecting their business. However, because many of them were not familiar or comfortable with the newer technologies, it was actually the youngest and newest to the field who had significant knowledge in this area. They noticed that several of the larger retailers (of whom there were more each year) were beginning to install computer systems that could link them directly to manufacturers. These larger companies liked this direct connection because they could establish a "pull system" for their inventory. When one item sold from a store, it showed up on the manufacturer's computer for reorder. Many of the transactions that had previously taken place in person-to-person contact at the distribution centers could now take place directly through new information technology. Technology was beginning to restructure their industry around them. They were in danger of losing their place as a vital link in the traditional distribution system.

When the group took the time to let the importance of this information sink in, it was a quiet moment. The participants recognized that a revolution was occurring in their business. Many of the owners had had family in the business for years; they had grown up in the industry. And yet if they paid attention to emerging data, they could imagine that for a growing percentage of their customers, their centers could become superfluous to the process of getting goods from manufacturers into stores.

This was not an easy truth to see—that the industry of your life's work is in decline, is endangered.

Once the owners and managers of the centers saw the patterns clearly, several could also see new possibilities in the industry restructuring. Many retail and manufacturing groups had not yet made the major capital investments in the new technology. Their own buildings had empty areas, and some realized that they could offer space and even support for the emerging technology the customer groups needed. This would require quite a leap, however. It would lead them into a very different business from the one they had led to date. Providing value-added high-technology services to the industry they served is a significantly different business from that of simply "leasing space," yet the marketplace showed a clear need and preference for it.

When the owners and managers understood the significant impacts on their industry from the changing business environment, they faced the challenge of redesigning their futures to incorporate the shift from the real estate business alone to include technology services as part of their expanded offering to the marketplace. They faced many critical decisions. What would their "product" actually be in the marketplace? Would it still have a real estate component at all (such as "smart buildings")? How would they redesign their organizations to deliver this new type of product and services? Would they need new people? New policies? New work cultures? How would they get all the critical stakeholders to see what they had just discovered?

The industry association faced an equivalent shift in its own new role. This would be a dramatic era for the industry as a whole. Whereas the association had previously served mostly as a gathering for collegiality and networking, member companies now needed the association to take a more strategic role. Member companies needed it to provide resources and guidance for an industry in the midst of major transformation.

At the end of the second day into this work, the CEO who had first inquired about our knowledge of his business came up to us, quite apologetic, yet also quite enthusiastic. He said, "You know, we didn't really know about our industry anymore. Everything is different now, but I am beginning to see what our real problems are and what we could do about them. There's a lot of potential that still exists in this new world. In the future, I don't think we will look anything like we do today, but I can see what it will take to get us there."

This association had learned that it couldn't only look to an outside content expert to bring the right answer (although content expertise was also needed). Its members had discovered a process through which they could work together to understand the forces around them fairly quickly and to find their own best course of action. They now had to build this ability into their companies. In the midst of an industry restructuring, the ability to recognize new data in their business environment and respond to it quickly could make the difference between their future success or failure. They were learning to become a Dynamic Enterprise.

Definition of the Dynamic Enterprise

The Dynamic Enterprise continually transforms the multitude of changes occurring around it into coordinated strategic actions by its people to further the development of its products and services. The Dynamic Enterprise captures the momentum of change in the external environment and converts it into fuel for its own development forward.

The work the industry association did provides a good example for the requirements of the Dynamic Enterprise. The Dynamic Enterprise must scan the environment for emerging trends that could significantly affect its future. Then it must be able to make sense out of these trends, to understand their impacts, and to evaluate and prioritize them. It must be able to translate the emerging trends into a strategic direction for the enterprise.

The Dynamic Enterprise must actually go even further than the example described here. It must also be able to implement the emerging enterprise strategy, to funnel the strategy quickly and smoothly into products and services to deliver back to the marketplace.

Furthermore, the Dynamic Enterprise must be able to translate emerging change into products and services, not just once but on an ongoing basis. The Dynamic Enterprise

- Scans the external business environment for emerging trends that could significantly affect its future. It is a future-directed enterprise.
- Makes sense of emerging trends and new information. It understands the potential impact of various trends and evaluates and prioritizes them. It catches potential obstacles and confronts them early on and sights new opportunities as well. It leverages the chaos and change in the external business environment to its future advantage.
- Translates emerging trends into a clear strategic direction for the company.
- Translates emerging strategies quickly and smoothly into its products and services.
- Translates company strategies for products and services into day-to-day actions by individuals, departments, teams, or networks.
- Builds the organization, and rebuilds it as needed, to serve current business needs most efficiently.
- Enables its people to respond rapidly, proactively, and collaboratively to change.
- Builds and maintains a culture of dynamism, full of spirit and energy for changes required.
- Accomplishes all these tasks simultaneously, if needed, and on a continual basis.

What Does a Dynamic Enterprise Look Like?

How is the Dynamic Enterprise organized? It depends.

The specific form of the Dynamic Enterprise depends on the conditions each particular business faces and on when the question is asked. The Dynamic Enterprise is not a business or institution defined by a particular form; having one of the new organizational structures, such as a networked or project-based organization, that attempts to support flexibility is no guarantee of dynamism. The Dynamic Enterprise is one whose people can respond to changes in the external and internal environments and can determine the best form for their particular conditions. The Dynamic Enterprise is described by its capabilities, not by its structure.

In a time of exponential change, the best organizational form for a Dynamic Enterprise changes quickly. All aspects of the organization—from structures, processes, and policies to employee skills and the company culture—must support the organization's ability to respond judiciously, yet rapidly, to change. The methods to accomplish this are quite likely to change as the environment itself changes. For example, in 1997, as we looked at methods companies used to gather input from the external environment, pages on the World Wide Web became increasingly popular and brought new possibilities for using the Internet as a means to gather data from visitors to Web sites. While we looked at human resource (HR) practices that promoted flexibility and change responsiveness, the growing use of HR kiosks and desktop systems began to offer new possibilities for promoting employee self-sufficiency and easy access to HR data. While we looked at how changes could be communicated throughout an enterprise, use of the Intranet (companies' internal use of the Internet) became increasingly widespread. We realized that the topic of this discussion—defining the form of the organization best equipped to deal with exponential change—was itself evolving too quickly to pin down into one set of best practices.

Rather than attempting to describe the single best form, it makes more sense to define an approach that can help each enterprise develop its own best version of a Dynamic Enterprise. There are no absolute answers during significant ongoing change (at least not ones that last very long). There are only ways to find good answers for a given enterprise at a given time.

The Dynamic Enterprise is actually not a "thing" at all, not a static structure or end point that can be named and categorized. Instead, the Dynamic Enterprise goes on creating and re-creating itself. It is the description of how an enterprise *acts* to integrate rapidly the dynamism in the environment into products and services responsive to that dynamism.

What a Dynamic Enterprise Is Not

In contrast to the industry association we described, which was able to take an honest though challenging look at the implications of the data in its environment, many enterprises close themselves off to feedback and the discomfort it may cause. They represent the opposite of a Dynamic Enterprise—a closed or stagnant enterprise with no capacity to integrate and act on new data.

One government institution we recently encountered made the following claim: "First our customers said they wanted uniform quality. They wanted to know that any office could give them a similar level of service. We worked for five years and really struggled to accomplish this. We have built up a cohesive network that offers uniform quality across all locations. Now they want us to offer specialized services in a few of the locations!" Staff were shocked and offended that after they worked years to accomplish one goal, their customers would have the nerve to want something new. They felt personally insulted and were completely closed to the new information. Because they were legitimately always very busy, they ignored their customers' new requests. It is easy to imagine the impact this had and will continue to have on their customers, in effect negating the good work that had actually been done during the previous five years to improve the quality of their service.

A People-Driven Enterprise

The responsiveness, adaptability, and imagination essential for handling the dynamism of today's business environment can be fulfilled only by its most responsive, adaptive, and imaginative element: its people.

In the traditional, hierarchical "functional organization," the organization structure itself was designed to settle and focus people, to determine their actions. Organizations were structured to create high levels of clarity and predictability so that people could be most productive. In a rather predictable environment, relatively static and structured job descriptions and stable performance criteria were entirely adequate to guide people's choices. One knew one's job, could perform to specifications, and could fairly easily experience a sense of accomplishment and satisfaction about a job well done. If an unexpected problem arose, it was not at all unusual for individuals to claim they couldn't fix it because that particular issue wasn't part of their job description. Everyone *expected* them to work within the frame (and limits) of their job.

In the Dynamic Enterprise, it is the people, rather than the organization structure, that guide the strategic choices to be made. Only people can integrate the shifting and diverse input, make the necessary strategic decisions, and coordinate with other people as needed for each new situation. Preset organization forms and job descriptions are no longer sufficient to guide the array of choices to be made. People are needed because dynamism requires choice, imagination, and courage.

However, even when the reality of the enterprise is one of insta-bility and dynamism, the need for some kind of stability and pre-dictability remains a psychological requirement for competent human performance. If the organization's form and specific job descriptions can no longer settle people and help them focus their work, what can?

What People Need to Create the Dynamic Enterprise

In a dynamic environment, people need tools to help them navi-gate through the complexities of the ever-changing enterprise. They need tools for formulating information in ways that make it meaningful for guiding the enterprise on an ongoing basis, that provide a process for continuing strategic thinking. They also need ways to change the mind-set of all members of the enterprise, that encourage them to keep an eye on the changing conditions with-out getting confused and to make continual adjustments without massive disruption.

To create the Dynamic Enterprise, people need to

- See the big picture, to simplify and understand the complexity of forces affecting their enterprise, so that they can choose the best strategic direction.
- Engage all key stakeholders and build a sense of ownership and responsibility among them so that they can contribute

their best thinking to the challenges ahead and will be willing to put their plans into action when it is time to implement.
- Enable dialogue and coordinated change throughout the enterprise.

Seeing the Big Picture

At the very time companies are making numerous changes, both internally and externally, the people in the enterprise may actually not be aware of all the changes occurring or may not see them from the same perspective. They are missing the "big picture." One group may see one subset of changes, while another group is more familiar with others.

Furthermore, during unsettled times, tensions naturally run high. People often do not display their best behavior under changing conditions. Sometimes change-related conflicts are labeled as "teams that are not working well together," "turf battles," "personality wars," or "management style issues." Whenever we have worked with individuals or teams in conflict or with whole divisions and enterprises, we have typically found that work process or personality and style issues do exist. But something else is generally in operation as well, something that has a powerful impact and often prevents any one change (such as business process reengineering, team building, or leadership coaching) from having a lasting effect.

Time after time, we have found that in the midst of profound and complex changes, more than one significant aspect of the enterprise is changing at once. Often key leaders or team members don't see the whole system in the same way—each sees a different portion of the overall picture. They generally do not agree on the range of forces affecting their business or on their importance. They often do not have shared views on the key strategies the business should use to respond to these forces, what the business must become, where they currently stand, or how they will go about the change or development that is needed to survive in the changing environment. Even when different members see parts of the system from a common perspective, key elements in the system are often "invisible" to any particular group, and their disagreements often lie in just these invisible areas. Conflicts arise because not everyone is on the same page regarding the key elements of the enterprise as a whole.

We recently worked with a research division affiliated with a major university. In the group, dissension and conflict ran high. Some members attributed tensions to the leader's autocratic and highly critical leadership style, while others thought personality differences between key team members were more to blame. The division was looking for coaching for the leader and team building for the group as a whole. As we examined the overall system of the enterprise more closely, previously "invisible" areas began to emerge. For months, team members had been getting signals from others outside their group that their funding might not be renewed. Their area of research was being seen as "too soft," too socially oriented, or not generating enough profit or prestige for the university. Funding to similar areas in other universities was being cut dramatically.

This group had previously chosen to focus its attention on its internal dynamics and had avoided facing the worrisome external signs. By making all elements of the enterprise visible, including external forces and internal ones, the members of the group were soon able to recognize that they had to reconnect as a working team if they were to make a convincing case to funding sources for their continued existence. Time was short. A dose of seeing the full state of their enterprise did much more for their team functioning than simple coaching on leadership style or more generic team-building exercises could have achieved. They quickly learned where to concentrate their efforts. They began to work out their long-standing personal differences because they knew they had to and began to work more cooperatively with the leader despite the shortcomings of her leadership style.

People must agree on the key issues facing the enterprise to be able to choose from the growing supply of business and organizational interventions. We have found that many groups attempt to reorganize, introduce quality management, downsize, or offer a new training program when in fact the chosen solution would not solve the real problems and consequently would not yield the expected results.

How do members of the enterprise judge which solution is most critical for them at a particular time? How can they tell if they are ready or even capable of implementing a given intervention that is popular at the time? How do they pick the "right" change?

The pressure is on to make and implement decisions quickly. However, for the enterprise to move forward successfully and realistically, key individuals must agree on the most critical elements of their enterprise and where it needs to go. They need to be able to build a shared view of the big picture.

Engaging All Stakeholders

In this age of empowerment, flatter organizations, cross-functional work teams, and global communications, changes in an enterprise can no longer be dictated from the top with an expectation that the directives will cascade down through command-and-control functional lines of authority, free of ambiguity. If change ever did actually proceed along these lines, it is rarely succeeding in this way today.

Gifford and Elizabeth Pinchot warn that the business challenges we are facing today are so complex and shifting so rapidly that enterprises must harness all the available intelligence in the organization in order to have a competitive advantage. They provocatively point out that "the potential intelligence of any human organization is widely distributed because the brains are widely distributed—one per person" (Pinchot and Pinchot, 1994, p. xvi). They caution that using the intelligence of a few decision makers rather than all available intelligence most often leads to mediocre performance—it falls far short of "organizational brilliance" and simply will not be adequate to face the challenges of the twenty-first century.

In addition, we are living in what Charles Handy calls "a culture of consent." He observes that "intelligent people prefer to agree rather than obey" (Handy, 1990, p. 162). It is not only that stakeholders may not make their best contribution if they are not engaged in designing the changes they must implement, but that they may downright refuse to implement those changes. We have seen too many elegant organization designs and business plans end up on the shelf or in the back of a drawer.

The Dynamic Enterprise has the capability to bring all stakeholders involved into conversations about shifting conditions and challenges. This means that there must be a way to see the big picture together and ensure that it permeates the whole enterprise. Stakeholders, including the CEO and senior executives, managers, front-line workers, union representatives, and even key customers or essential suppliers, need a way to create a shared "big picture" to communicate quickly with one another, using concepts that all can understand.

A community-based example demonstrates how important it is to gain early involvement of all key stakeholder groups. Parents in a California city recently attempted to convince their school district to offer "school within a school" programs. They hoped to create smaller learning communities within the larger school environments that could still offer the range of choices that a larger program could provide. Local school officials led parents through the formal steps to gain approval for the change. Hundreds of parents were involved in the effort over the course of a year's time. Many proposals were developed and presented to the local school board, meetings were held with principals, surveys and petitions were conducted, letters were written, and large numbers of parents showed strong public support at school board meetings. By the end of the school year, the school board informed parents that over the past few years, the schools had moved to more "site-based decision making" and that teachers were now the real decision makers. However, following the traditional hierarchical decision-making process in the school district, teachers had not been involved at all up to that point. A key stakeholder group had been left out of the change process.

When teachers were finally told about the proposals, they were angry, refused to meet with parents, and gave an unbending "no" to the ideas presented to them. In a few short days, teachers killed off a year's worth of work by hundreds of people. This enterprise—if we may view the whole community of parents, students, and school district staff as an enterprise—spent a great deal of resources but could not respond effectively to change. An initial overview of the whole system, identifying *all* key decision makers and implementers, followed by early engagement of the key stakeholders, would likely have prevented months of wasted effort.

Enabling Dialogue and Coordinated Change Throughout the Enterprise

Because change rarely occurs in just one area of an enterprise, shifts in one area affect other areas quite profoundly. For example, in a health maintenance organization (HMO) struggling to control health care costs, cardiologists decided that they could cut the costs in their department by eliminating weekend stress tests for cardiac patients. This change would cut the expenses associated with weekend on-call time for cardiologists. Although this did reduce the budget for the cardiology department, it considerably increased the cost of hospital operations: under the new arrangement, a substantial number of cardiac patients had to stay in the hospital over the weekend because they could not be discharged until they took their stress tests, and they now had to wait until Monday morning. The costs incurred to keep the patients in the hospital over the weekend, including nursing care, use of monitoring equipment, and dietary and facilities costs, exceeded the amount saved by the cardiologists fivefold! Clearly, when one group institutes changes without a larger-picture view of changes set off elsewhere, the system as a whole can suffer, and apparent results can be illusory.

In another example, members of a department in a manufacturing facility began to focus on customer service, designing their own products around the "voice of the customer." The more they paid attention to their own customers, the more they began to recognize their own role as customers of their human resources staff, their accounting department, and their management. They began to demand service from each of these groups as they shifted to regarding themselves as internal customers. What began as a new perspective on customer service to the external marketplace quickly put new pressures on internal functions as well.

Time after time, we see that interventions or change programs in one department can spread quickly and destabilize the equilibrium of other departments.

Tools and Practices for Establishing the Dynamic Enterprise

If people need to see the big picture, engage all key stakeholders, and enable dialogue and coordinated change throughout their enterprise, what can help them do this in times of great change? These tasks are not so easy to do in the midst of an already busy work schedule. (One group we worked with described this as "having to change the tires while still riding the bike.") What makes it more likely that people can accomplish these tasks?

In times of complex, multidimensional, and exponentially increasing change, people need tools to help them think strategically and to coordinate the changes they themselves will need to implement. They need a way to reduce the complexity into a manageable number of categories and to understand how these categories relate to each other.

We have found that when given a unified model using commonsense language, people are able to simplify and understand the complexity around them. This capability settles people. It enables them to think clearly about difficult issues, build shared views and maps with others, and work collaboratively with them. It enables them to communicate about complex business challenges. It promotes a sense of predictability in an otherwise unpredictable environment.

In times of great change, the most helpful strategy and change tools provide

- A manageable number of basic building blocks.
- Straightforward connections between the building blocks.
- Commonsense, concrete language.
- A shared vocabulary for change.
- A map to clarify the big picture.

A Manageable Number of Basic Building Blocks

People within the enterprise need to be able to simplify the complexity of modern organizational life into a manageable number of critical elements. When members of an enterprise see the chaotic complexity of their work experience categorized into a limited number of basic elements, they find relief in the increased clarity and increased predictability of the events around them.

Straightforward Connections Between the Building Blocks

In addition, it is helpful to see how the elements relate to one another and how they constitute the enterprise as a whole through their dynamic interaction. An enterprisewide overview of all the elements and the unique relationships among them makes it easier to see how a force or change affecting one building block will affect the others as well. The enterprisewide vantage point makes it easier to predict the subsequent changes needed through the rest of the system, and these can be more easily incorporated into initial plans.

Commonsense, Concrete Language

Because members throughout the enterprise need to be able to communicate with one another and contribute their intelligence to the ongoing development of their enterprise, they need ways to describe the building blocks and relationships between them that all can understand. They need concepts and language that help them organize their thinking, that make sense, and that do not rely on jargon known only to a few.

We want to emphasize the importance of this point: using a simple conceptual framework to present the most important business and organizational issues an enterprise faces allows all stakeholders to contribute to the decisions being made and actions being taken. Understanding the strategy behind the business is not the domain of the CEO and senior executives alone. When all members of the enterprise share a language for thinking about the key business issues and feel comfortable using that language, they can join in and contribute their best ideas to critical decisions.

A Shared Vocabulary for Change

It is often claimed that native Alaskans have many different words for snow because they differentiate many different kinds and qualities of snow. We could certainly use this kind of differentiation and clarity for our vocabulary for *change*. We have very few words available to us for business or organizational change, yet our enterprises face an immense variety of changes. There are changes from the external marketplace and the culture and innumerable changes that organizations initiate from within. There are small changes affecting one team or work process, and there are more profound changes that may involve the restructuring of an entire industry. When people within the enterprise begin to discuss change, they often speak at cross-purposes because they are discussing different elements of the same change or even different levels of change affecting them simultaneously. A shared vocabulary for change helps people clarify their conceptual and strategic thinking about the changes they face and assists them in having necessary dialogues with one another.

A Map to Clarify the Big Picture

Often when we work with groups, people describe the multi-dimensional changes they are dealing with as "all over the map." In addition to a shared vocabulary for change, it helps, if the enterprise is facing changes occurring "all over the map," to have the whole map. Many people respond to the visual-spatial image of change, as well as to the words describing it. Mapping all changes that are occurring makes it clear how each separate change relates to, overlaps with, or affects another. Each work group can put its own change issues on the map and see how they relate to the bigger picture.

In addition, a map reveals not only what changes are occurring but also what plans for moving forward may be necessary. A change map shows the current pressures and the variety of changes anticipated and frames a project plan showing who is expected to do what, by when, so that the enterprise can move ahead.

Good News and Bad News

Time after time, we find ourselves saying to clients that we have good news and bad news. The bad news is that their worst fears are true. After assessing their situation, we must often conclude that it is, indeed, as difficult and challenging as they had indicated and feared. In fact, it is almost always worse. Clients may come to us with an identified breakdown in one particular area or a need for redesign or reinvention in another. However, when the whole system is understood, the need is in fact almost always greater than first presumed—more pervasive, involving a larger system in the enterprise, or requiring a more profound level of change.

Yet invariably, we also have good news: though the issues are sometimes larger than first suspected, the solutions are usually simpler and more straightforward than previously thought. Basic and clear avenues exist for dealing with complex business and organizational issues, even for a large enterprise living through a time of dynamic change.

A solution *is* possible. It is possible to hold simple conversations about complex and profound issues, with large numbers of people. It is possible to develop a shared map of the key systems of the whole enterprise. It is possible to understand the array of complex forces that are changing all at once and to reinvent the enterprise to respond to them most effectively. It is possible to have large numbers of people share key learnings, make collaborative decisions, and take the individual actions necessary to bring the Dynamic Enterprise into being. We call this process *Enterprise Development,* to which we turn in Chapter Three.

Part Two

From Chaos to Strategy

Chapter Three

An Overview of Enterprise Development

*True magic begins when individual people begin to
become aware of the threads of interconnectedness in
any one thing or activity.*
RUDITE EMIR AND BARBARA BUTTERFIELD,
"Co-Creation at Work: Connecting to Each Other
and to the Whole"

Today, all members of an enterprise must be able to understand
the multiple dimensions of change their enterprise faces and have
the ability to work together with all the people needed to reach the
required future. They need a way to sort through the chaos, to create the strategic view of the future, to understand where they are
starting, and to determine what will be required to move forward.
They must learn how to engage key members of their enterprise
to bring their full intelligence and commitment to the actual
design and implementation. As implementation progresses and
new dynamics continue to emerge along the way, members must
be continually open to evaluate their progress and build their
learning into their next actions. In short, to create a Dynamic
Enterprise, members throughout the enterprise must be expert at
leading and implementing strategic multidimensional change.

As we noted in Chapter Two, the Enterprise Development
framework is designed to support this range of capabilities—to promote widespread strategic thinking, planning, communication,
and change management throughout the enterprise.

The Enterprise Development Framework

The creation of the Dynamic Enterprise requires six developmental capabilities or core competencies from people throughout the enterprise. These competencies carry the enterprise through the comprehensive process of strategizing and changing, from beginning to end—from first glimmer of external forces shifting on the far horizon to engaging the key people in the enterprise in strategy, design, and implementation all the way through to measuring that the changes planned were actually completed. The Enterprise Development framework offers six practices or "tools" to help build each of these core competencies:

1. Seeing the whole system of the enterprise
2. Creating a shared future for the enterprise
3. Seeing the past and current enterprise honestly and accurately
4. Understanding the nature of the change
5. Mobilizing and aligning the three essential drivers for change
6. Implementing the change—turning strategy into performance

Each of the next six chapters describes one of the tools in greater detail and provides more in-depth examples from different enterprises as they worked to build (or failed to build) these competencies. This chapter provides an overview of all six competencies and shows how they link together in the Enterprise Development framework.

These six competencies are needed at all levels of the enterprise. In a time of continuous and exponential change, strategy development and change management skills have to be as competently practiced as other essential work skills. Strategy and change skills are no longer restricted to the realm of board members or senior executives or the organization development department. Because a Dynamic Enterprise needs to respond to change quickly and smoothly, not just for one change but on an ongoing basis, people throughout the enterprise must know how to do this, routinely and often. In recent years, workers have upgraded the technical skills needed for their jobs and have learned a great deal about other organizational skills, such as quality improvement, project management, financial management, and teamwork.

Figure 3.1. Template for the Enterprise Development Map.

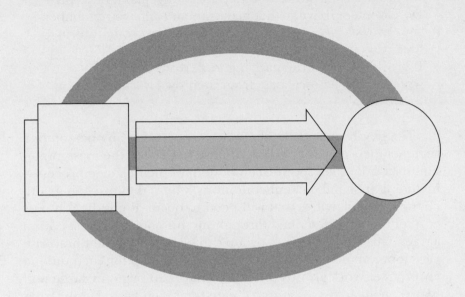

Given a dynamic work environment that will likely change more quickly with each year that passes, the skills needed to create a Dynamic Enterprise will become increasingly essential at *all* levels of work.

The Enterprise Development Map

The *Enterprise Development map* serves as an integrating, comprehensive framework for the steps necessary to build a Dynamic Enterprise. Each area of the map corresponds to one particular core competency needed. Viewing the six competencies together clarifies how each area relates to the others and how they all fit into an integrated whole. Figure 3.1 gives the basic template for the map. The following discussion will outline each of the six competencies and add the corresponding detail to the map to show how the framework is built, step by step. (The complete framework, incorporating each competency, will appear in Figure 3.10.)

The map functions as a strategy and change tool in itself, providing several benefits:

- It clarifies how each core competency links to the others.
- It graphically illustrates the essential concepts of Enterprise Development in a way that makes them easier to remember.
- It provides a clear image that can be used to communicate ideas to others.
- It provides a practical mapping tool. Work groups can write the most critical data from their own work groups on to the map.

The graphic image of the framework serves as an open outline that members of a work group can use to write in the most important data from each specific component of their change process—including past and current conditions, where they are going, and changes and activities that will need to occur along the way. For each of the steps described throughout this book, the most critical agreements in a given work group can be noted on the Enterprise Development map to provide a customized map for each unique enterprise. Work groups often use chart pad pages or large wall maps spread across a room to create their own map. These larger maps can also be condensed and reduced to provide notebook-sized handouts or can be posted on a Web site or computer network for electronic access.

Creating this map helps keep the development process visible to all members of the enterprise. It also provides a living, dynamic map that changes as the Enterprise Development process progresses. Documenting shared agreements as they are made helps build common ground for the work ahead.

Competency 1: Seeing the Whole System of the Enterprise

An enterprise is a business supported by an organization. The business delivers products and services into an external environment (consisting of a marketplace with opportunities and competition, as well as culture, economy, government regulations, social systems, resources, partners, and other forces or groups that can affect the enterprise). The function of the organization is to help the business succeed within its environment. As the environment changes, the business and the organization may both have to change.

It is important for members of the enterprise to understand the fundamental elements of the business and organization system and how these affect each other. Once these fundamental categories are clear, as any new force enters from the external environment or from an internal change, a general outline of the expected impacts can be traced around the whole enterprise system.

The enterprise is a system composed of five components that interact dynamically, as shown in Figure 3.2:

- *Structure*—the structural elements of the organization, including formal organization chart, job descriptions, physical facilities, information systems, management policies, human resource policies, and incentive systems
- *Task*—the products and services that the business offers to the marketplace

Figure 3.2. Dynamic Interaction Among the Elements of the Enterprise System.

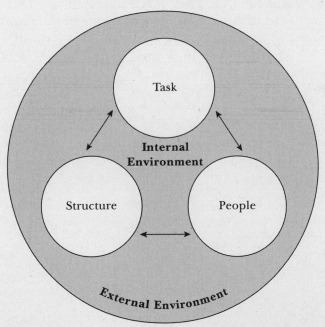

- *External Environment*—marketplace opportunities, competition, suppliers, culture, economy, regulations, resources,
  and potential venture partners
- *Internal Environment*—internal culture and organizational
  climate
- *People*—skills and talents of the people, how they get along
  and communicate with one another, and quality and effectiveness of their working relationships

We refer to these system components using the acronym *STEP*
(for *structure, task, environment,* and *people*). The *STEP Model* is a
tool that enterprises can use to clarify the full enterprise system
and to highlight where strategic interventions most need to occur
(further details are provided in Chapter Four).

Competency 2: Creating a Shared Future for the Enterprise

The enterprise system moves through time; it does not stand still.
The Dynamic Enterprise is a system driven by the opportunities of
the future. To capitalize on those future opportunities, people need
to be able to look forward. They need to anticipate (to the best of
their ability) what the future business environment will most likely
bring them and what the future enterprise system will need to
become. Figure 3.3 shows where this view of the future is represented on the map of the Enterprise Development framework.

Creating a clear and compelling shared future vision of their
enterprise gives people confidence in their ability to compete
successfully in the marketplace of the future. It appeals to their
hearts and spirits and imparts a higher purpose to the work they
do. It creates a sense of direction and focus for their business,
orients their actions, and gives them a sense of predictability
about the changes ahead.

Many people think of "vision" as the "softer" side of the enterprise: its values and principles, the hopes of the people, and the
work culture they want to create. However, within Enterprise Development, the vision of the future enterprise goes far beyond these
ideas. Vision, to be powerful and compelling, must be inclusive of
all STEP elements. For example, it must project in some detail

Figure 3.3. Future STEP.

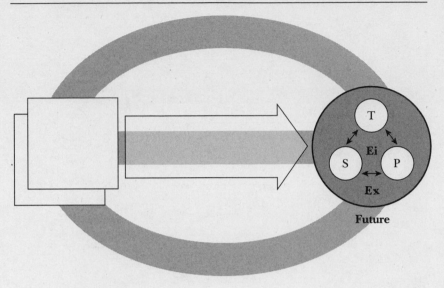

what key business endeavors are expected for the company in the future. What will its competitive advantage be? What type of organization will best support its business? What systems and structures will be required? What kinds of people will be needed, what must they know, and how will they work together? Finally, what type of internal environment, culture, and values will be desirable and necessary for success in the envisioned future?

A comprehensive vision helps leaders and stakeholders have a clear picture of both the business and the organization they must build together. (Chapter Five presents more detail about creating a shared vision of the future enterprise.)

Competency 3: Seeing the Past and Current Enterprise Honestly and Accurately

Just as individuals need a clear and shared vision of where the enterprise should go, they also need to agree on where it has come from and where it is currently positioned. If some members think the enterprise is almost where it needs to be while others believe it is hopelessly far away, agreement on a common development

Figure 3.4. Past and Current STEP.

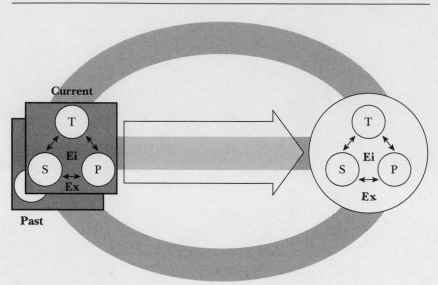

path will be difficult to achieve. It is also important that the picture of the current state of the enterprise be honest and "unflinching" so that development can begin from a realistic point.

Figure 3.4 shows where the information on the past and the current conditions can be filled in on the Enterprise Development map, and Chapter Six gives further examples and details.

Competency 4: Understanding the Nature of the Change

Once people have agreed on where they want to go and where they are starting, they need to discuss how to get from here to there. This requires further negotiation and agreement. This work involves "filling in the arrow" in the Enterprise Development map (see Figure 3.5). First, members of the enterprise identify the predominant "pushes" from current and past conditions. What are the issues that demand resolution, that motivate action? Then they explore opportunities and identify the "pulls" toward the future. What are the compelling opportunities that excite, that mobilize passion and a willingness to make sometimes dramatic change?

Figure 3.5. Strategic Development Path.

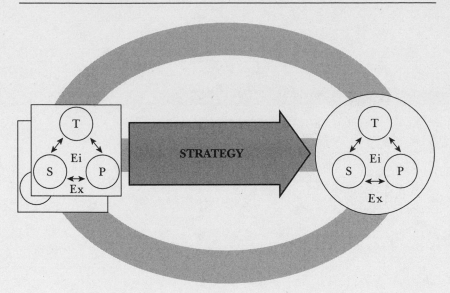

Identifying the most compelling issues in the vision is essential for success and can help people focus and channel their energy. Once both "pushes" and "pulls" are clear, people can negotiate and agree on key strategic thrusts and the specific actions and commitments necessary to connect the present enterprise to its desired future.

In addition to understanding what needs to change to get from here to there, it is also important to understand the magnitude of the change and the particular nature of the possible leap required. There are natural phases of development for both the business and the organization.

Figure 3.6 shows the outline of the business and organization life cycle phases. Chapter Seven will describe these models in more detail and illustrate how they serve as useful tools for enterprise strategy and change.

Understanding where an enterprise is positioned on the life cycle models illuminates whether an enterprise is facing a time of continuous change (within a given developmental phase) or discontinuous

Figure 3.6. Life Cycle Models.

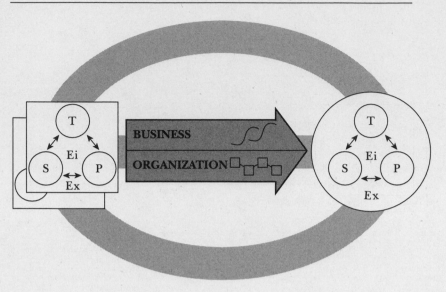

change (between phases). Understanding life cycle phases can help people determine the particular nature of the change ahead, which is often crucial information to the design of enterprise strategy and change. Different types of changes—change from one point to another on the life cycle—pose different sets of challenges and need to be managed in different ways. For example, the human life cycle illustrates this point: a two-year-old child facing a developmental challenge will need something quite different from a sixteen-year-old, a forty-five-year-old, or a seventy-five-year-old. The challenges to be faced and the transitions to be navigated are different at each stage, as are the resources and skills available to the individual facing them. In a similar way, businesses or organizations positioned at different points of their life cycle will face very different challenges, will come to these challenges equipped with different skills and resources, and would benefit from very different approaches to "change management."

Chapter Seven will illustrate how understanding the life cycle phases of both the business and the organization helps members of an enterprise predict the conditions they are most likely to encounter in a given change initiative or development effort. Anticipating what lies ahead can then help them proactively frame the next steps that may be required. When people understand life cycle dynamics and developmental forces, they can learn to predict and manage these forces and can use them as powerful guides for determining realistic next steps.

Competency 5: Mobilizing and Aligning the Three Essential Drivers for Change

As described earlier, it is people who create the Dynamic Enterprise. Three groups of people in particular are essential to drive the enterprise toward its envisioned future: leaders, stakeholders, and providers of performance support. All three groups must collaborate and be in constant communication if they are to guide the development together. *Planned development will not succeed without these drivers firmly in place.*

Figure 3.7 shows how these drivers are represented in the Enterprise Development framework, and Chapter Eight provides further information and examples.

Figure 3.7. The Three Drivers for Change.

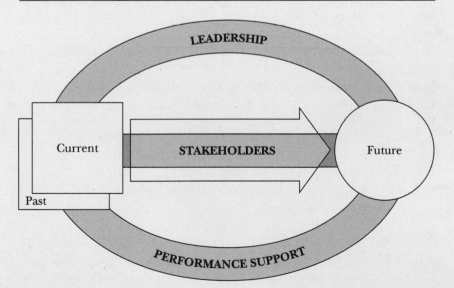

Leaders

Leaders can be informal as well as formal leaders and may include members from outside the enterprise as well. The leadership for an Enterprise Development effort must include the formal leaders of the enterprise but is not limited to this group.

To guide development effectively, the leadership role shifts substantially. Senior leadership and key managers must become committed to the development of their enterprise, not just to the performance of current business tasks. Development of the enterprise must be considered part of the work, not an extra task that occurs in the spaces between the "real work." Change and development—that *is* the real work. This concept redefines the role of leaders from leading in service of current core and administrative activities to being responsible for the ongoing development of the enterprise.

Who: The leadership of the enterprise consists of the individuals who hold the authority to make decisions about the enterprise. The leadership may include senior executives, managers, the sponsors or process owners of a change effort, and informal leaders as well.

What: Leaders must demonstrate their commitment to the ongoing development of their enterprise, not only to current performance of the core business.

How: Leaders move change forward in the following ways:

- Through holding and advocating the strategic direction. They stand for the future of the organization.
- By being able and willing to see the current organization clearly and honestly and fostering an environment where staff openly share information; they do not withhold or try to conceal the real data about the current situation.
- By reflecting their commitment to change through communication and their own actions.

Stakeholders

Stakeholders enact or inhibit the development of the organization. They must become the owners of the development process. If they do not take ownership, it doesn't happen. Stakeholders cannot be passive—there is a great deal for them to do in the development process. They act as the key designers and implementers of the changes ahead. Stakeholders are the ones living through the transitions, letting go of old practices, and learning new ways of doing the work.

Who: Anyone who has influence over the direction of the enterprise is a stakeholder, including employees, customers or clients, vendors or suppliers, regulatory agencies, founders, community members, and strategic partners.

What: Stakeholders are the real owners of a change or development process; if they don't own it, it doesn't happen.

How: Stakeholders move change forward in the following ways.

• By acting as the key designers and implementers of the development process
• By being the ones who ultimately enact the repairs, improvements, and transformations
• By actively participating, giving their time and ideas
• By working with other stakeholder groups to coordinate needed changes
• By overcoming inhibiting background conversations and negative assumptions, by committing to a future possibility

Performance Support

A great deal has been written and thought about the role of leadership in large-scale change, as well as the need for stakeholder participation, ownership, and empowerment. The idea of performance support as a distinct function is still relatively new. Just as the advent of rapidly emerging new information technologies has led to a growth of information technology specialists in many enterprises, the recognition of ongoing change and development as an integral part of the work of the organization must lead to a demand for development specialists. When development and performance in a continually adjusting future are seen as a core task of an enterprise, performance support becomes an essential function that can make the difference between success and failure.

Who: Internal or external development specialists and change team members.

What: Performance support enables the successful development of the organization, coordinates the details, and connects stakeholders with the resources they need.

How: Performance support moves change forward in the following ways.

- By facilitating the shaping or creating of business processes, organizational structures, and information systems to support the new goals
- By being responsible for overall coordination, project management, and logistics support
- By facilitating the shaping or creating of systems to support the new vision
- By facilitating engagement, collaboration, and participation
- By promoting communication and visibility of the development process
- By enhancing connections and helping build networks that further development
- By providing trustworthy emotional support to leaders and stakeholders during the transition
- By catching the inevitable breakdowns and attending to them to ensure that the development effort stays on track

Tests

Each of these three groups of drivers—leaders, stakeholders, and performance support—will be tested during the course of change. Once the requirement for change is clarified, members of the enterprise almost instantly begin to test the resolve of all those involved in the change. Testing always occurs. Human beings do not seem to be able to change, to move forward into unknown futures, without questioning and challenging each step along the way. They naturally double-check what is demanded of them (which is a useful habit for learning to function successfully in an emerging enterprise). People listen to what they are told, then test the words with their behavior. They watch for the response—not always consciously—and act on the implied message.

For example, as leaders are tested as to whether they mean what they say, their responses may suggest that there are no new actions behind their new words. Failure to act in new ways may become part of the natural course of events during everyday split-second decisions. People often do not even realize that they are acting in all the old ways. If leaders lapse into old behaviors, stakeholders are also unlikely to change their usual behaviors.

By contrast, when leaders respond successfully to tests, they reveal their personal commitment to the intended change and generate the momentum that drives the Dynamic Enterprise. Testing and the subsequent responses are the fuel for turning planned change into reality. It is important that these tests be anticipated.

The leaders, stakeholders, and performance support members will each be tested in unique ways (described further in Chapter Eight). Understanding this ahead of time can help each group prepare to meet these tests. Figure 3.8 shows how these tests are represented on the Enterprise Development map.

Figure 3.8. Tests for Each of the Three Drivers.

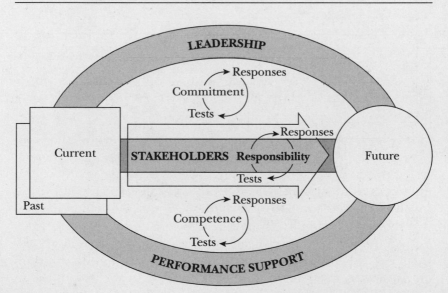

Competency 6: Implementing the Change— Turning Strategy into Performance

Once members of the enterprise have agreed on where they want to go, where they are starting from, and what will be required to get there, and once the people who are leading, enacting, and supporting the changes are working together, the strategies and plans still need to be turned into reality. The Enterprise Development Workplan (see Figure 3.9) presents a step-by-step, phased implementation process. The workplan presents an outline for planning, monitoring, and mapping dynamic and large-scale change. The purpose of the workplan is to turn understanding into planning and ultimately into performance.

The workplan formulates a series of six phases and outlines the actions in each phase that lead to sustainable performance. The phases are shown in the approximate sequence in which they take

**Figure 3.9. The Six Phases of the
Enterprise Development Workplan.**

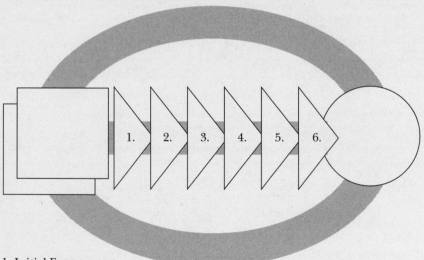

1. Initial Engagement
2. Foundations for Development
3. Vision and Strategy
4. Design
5. Change
6. Continuous Learning

place, but they can occur in parallel or in an iterative process that moves between one phase and another.

As indicated in the figure, the implementation phases are initial engagement, foundations for development, vision and strategy, design, change, and continuous learning. This succession of phases is not new in the field of organization or business development. Many books on change implementation or project management describe the activities within each phase in great detail. Chapter Nine highlights a few key challenges of implementation that stand out as particularly subtle tests.

Each of the three groups described as essential drivers for change—leadership, stakeholders, and performance support—have a unique role in implementation:

- Leadership stewards the development process and authorizes action.
- Stakeholders deliver the vitality for development and take responsibility for design and implementation.
- The performance support team enables development to occur with the fewest obstacles and promotes the competence of leaders and stakeholders to enact the change required.

These groups must all be involved in each phase of implementation, to see the changes through from conception to completion. If any of the driver groups gives up on any phase, or if the groups are not aligned with each other during a phase, the work and results of that phase are at risk. The final form of the envisioned change will be affected in very predictable ways by any implementation activity that was ignored or skipped over. Everyone is busy in a time of rapid and complex change, but there are no shortcuts. What is left out inevitably shows up in the results.

Figure 3.10 shows the complete Enterprise Development map, which incorporates all of the six core competencies described in this chapter. Enterprise Development offers a step-by-step approach to understanding the enterprise system and how it develops over time in relation to its ever-changing external environment. This understanding allows the people of the enterprise, leaders and stakeholders alike, to feel confident and empowered to guide their enterprise toward the envisioned future.

Figure 3.10. The Enterprise Development Map.

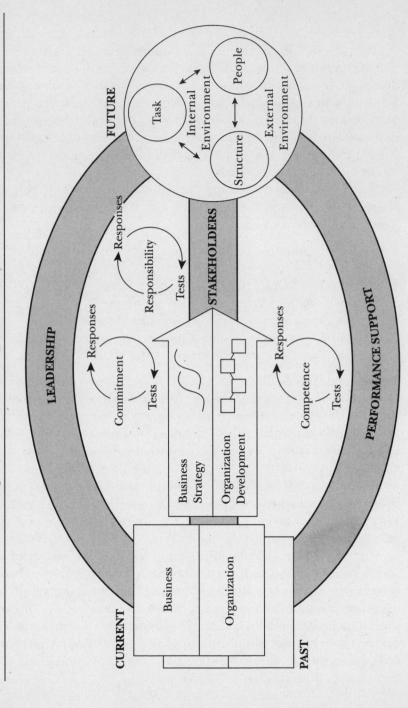

Using Enterprise Development Across a Wide Range of Changes

Some companies, agencies, or teams embrace the concepts of the Dynamic Enterprise and attempt to use the Enterprise Development framework to make their enterprise more future-oriented, responsive to change, and capable of rapid and widespread implementation. However, not all work groups are interested in taking on a full-scale development effort. Some may be interested in building one or more characteristics of the Dynamic Enterprise without instituting all capabilities at once. Some enterprises may already have strong capabilities in one area or another and can use Enterprise Development concepts to help identify the additional skills they need most.

In addition, most enterprises today are in the midst of change, and many have already conceptualized how these efforts will proceed. In these cases, the ideas for the development of a Dynamic Enterprise may be useful guidelines that can be integrated into existing and ongoing change efforts.

To date, we have seen groups use Enterprise Development ideas to guide a multitude of developments occurring in their enterprises, including creating a shared vision, developing business plans, business process redesign or reengineering efforts, quality improvement initiatives, organizational restructuring, downsizing, introduction of new technology, team building, identifying strategic learning needs, conflict resolution, diversity initiatives, culture change (most often to increase speed, flexibility, innovation and creativity, customer focus, or learning in the organization), leadership development, management development, managing change or transition, training the transition or change team, alliance building and partnering, and launching implementation (for a number of changes architected or designed but still awaiting implementation).

We have worked with groups who have applied these ideas in very diverse settings, to changes of many different sizes, scope, and significance. The Enterprise Development framework has been used with work groups that were implementing "repairs" or incremental improvements, as well as those responding to profound and discontinuous changes, such as the industry restructuring in the example about distribution centers described earlier.

Many functions within organizations are facing their own version of industry transformation. Technology or changing customer needs are creating pressures leading to the redefinition of these functions from their traditional roles in the organization. For example, many human resource departments are installing new technologies and streamlining processes to reduce their transaction-oriented roles while simultaneously developing a more strategic business role. When these changes are taken seriously, a whole new identity and core competency is added to the HR function.

Likewise, the materials management and procurement function in many companies is undergoing radical transformation, moving away from warehousing and moving goods toward becoming a group capable of partnering with suppliers to understand each other's business priorities. As suppliers and customers develop a shared business and organizational strategy, the roles that each takes on may be very different from those defined by their previous working relationship or company boundaries. For example, suppliers may take over the role of stocking the shelves for customers and maintain the function of keeping adequate supplies available at the customer's location. Or as each group understands the other's business priorities, processes, and cost constraints, teams can collaborate to redesign the overall work flow across the two (or more) companies to maximize quality while decreasing cost.

Chapter Seven provides more examples of how work groups can understand the nature of the change they are facing, see how their change compares to or relates to other changes occurring, and "place their change on the map."

Risks and Rewards of a Shared Framework

We know from our work with many types of companies and institutions that some people love models and others hate them. Enterprise Development is a model that ties together numerous concepts about strategy development and change management in a single graphic representation. Each area of the image can then be highlighted to reveal the thinking and analysis behind that particular portion of the picture. People who love models will likely enjoy the ability to condense an entire book's worth of ideas onto one page, and those who hate models have very real reasons for feeling that this is an inadequate way to describe a complex situation. Many members of groups we have worked work with ignore the graphics and simply use the ideas about the competencies needed for a Dynamic Enterprise. Others, however, have found that having a map or visual representation of changes is helpful to facilitate planning and communication among widely diverse groups of people who need to work together.

One health care group in the United States worked with the Enterprise Development framework, filling in the map of its future and current enterprise, in a day-long meeting held in late January several years ago. Suddenly, one member stood back from the large map covering the wall and remarked, "It looks like a football!" Even after Super Bowl fever had passed, the name stuck, and soon everyone could communicate with others about "the ED football" for their own team or department.

To another group from a financial services company in South Africa who had first learned this framework in the United States, the graphic looked much more like a "hamburger." After several months of work back in South Africa, not only did they have the "company hamburger," but many departments had their own "team hamburger" as well. These shared images were important, not simply because they represented an agreed-on reality and certainly not just because they hung on the wall, but because they gave people throughout the organization the ability to think and communicate with one another about the massive changes they faced. Their "hamburgers" were useful as a shared frame of reference. These change maps provided a basis for linking plans and actions for teams trying to reorient their businesses in South Africa in a time of great social and political upheaval.

In the spirit of dynamism and change, we present Enterprise Development as a working model, a living model open for continuing learning and expansion. Enterprise Development is not a model representing truth or reality but rather an integrated collection of practices we have found necessary for developing a Dynamic Enterprise. In fact, ED is an open framework; the content must be filled in by members in each enterprise. We can imagine that the forces driving enterprises ten years from now will look quite different, the starting place will be different, and the magnitude and nature of the changes will be different as well. The type of leadership required, the means to engage stakeholders, and the support needed will all vary in synchronization with the initial elements. In this way, ED is a "contentless" model. It is an open framework that points toward understanding how one force influences another and what general steps are required for change, but it does not dictate the specifics in any area.

Almost every company we have worked with has had terms relating to change or strategy that are now taboo in the organization, as well as words that are highly valued. The taboo words generally relate to past change efforts that were less than successful, that everyone wants to forget. There is generally great political danger in having been associated with these efforts, and no one wants even remotely to connect the current initiatives with those past failures. We have often had to find substitutes for the terms *strategic, change management, empowerment,* and *vision.* Likewise, each group tends to have terms that are more highly valued, that connect either to the company vision or culture or to other projects that are currently under way.

Because every work group will have its own history and its own current culture of what is most valued and most despised, it is important to take these concerns into consideration. Each group is encouraged to customize the concepts presented here in the ways that are most usable and to adjust the language to fit the local dynamics while also taking care not to lose the substance of the ideas themselves.

Chapter Four

Seeing the Whole
The Enterprise as a Dynamic System

*All organizations are perfectly designed to
get the results they get.*
ARTHUR JONES, QUOTED IN D. HANNA,
Designing Organizations for High Performance

People at work must be able to see the multiple impacts and changes occurring outside and inside their company, institution, or team. They must be able to integrate these and understand how the separate forces are connected, and they must be able to condense complex and multiple inputs into an understandable and usable form. A fundamental competency of the Dynamic Enterprise is to understand the whole system of the enterprise. Changes and upheavals no longer come one at a time, in a logical sequence, with breathing room in between. As shown by the examples in the earlier chapters, companies may confront simultaneous change: profound industrywide redefinitions in their business or service, redesign of work processes, organization restructuring, new performance review systems, new technology, new staff, new leaders, new partners or alliances, and perhaps new company cultures. At the same time, shifts in the marketplace and in customer demands may require the constant updating of products or services.

People working in such dynamic environments need methods for organizing their thinking and for viewing the whole system of forces and impacts. When people get overwhelmed by too much data, they are tempted to leave out parts of the picture, to limit the scope of the information. A clear way to organize complex inputs can enable them to set priorities, make decisions, and take action based on an integrated picture rather than on a partial view.

The ability to see the whole is also important when planning for a change in one particular area or system of the enterprise (such as the introduction of new technology, organization redesign, or leadership development). Each change is generally linked to numerous other changes, often in seemingly unrelated areas. All must change together for smooth implementation to occur. For example, successful technology installation may be linked to incentive systems that indirectly encourage people to use the new systems; successful organization redesign may be linked to company culture, norms, and expectations that encourage people to act in new roles; leadership development may be linked to strategic changes in the external business environment that demand new leadership skills. Up-front analysis and systems thinking help clarify these linkages and save a great deal of time and resources in subsequent implementation.

The STEP Model for Enterprise Systems Thinking

There are many models of systems thinking that organizations use to help clarify and synthesize complex inputs. McKinsey's 7-S model (Pascale, 1990), Peter Senge's model of reinforcing and inhibiting loops presented in *The Fifth Discipline* (1990), and the computer-based model I Think (Peterson and Richmond, 1993) are several such frameworks. Through our work as practitioners, we have shaped an enterprise systems model, STEP, that enables users to organize and condense the data most relevant to their companies or projects and to determine the most immediate implications from the data. The synthesized data are typically also produced as a graphic image, or map, of the user's system and contain the key points that the users need to communicate to others. The STEP Model is based on the theory and practice of systems thinking and has been further shaped by groups who have used it over the course of the past fifteen years. We present STEP as a model of enterprise systems thinking that has emerged from this collaborative shaping process, as a tool to help groups simplify the chaos around them into clear, meaningful, and strategic information.

Business and Organization

An enterprise is a business supported by an organization. This distinction is embarrassingly simple yet rarely made, even though it has important implications for the success of the enterprise.

The function of the *business* is to provide products or services to its marketplace. The task of the *organization* is to provide structure, form, and resources that enable the business to meet its objectives. When the business and the organization are not aligned, the enterprise generally finds itself in trouble.

The distinction between business and organization is a very simple concept. Even though it seems so obvious, confusion between these two areas often leads to costly and time-consuming interventions aimed at the wrong area. People often use the terms *business* and *organization* interchangeably, and this nondiscriminating use muddles thinking, planning, and outcomes. We frequently find businesses trying to implement an organizational solution when a new *business* strategy is clearly required. If the product no longer fits its marketplace, no amount of organizational fixes (downsizing, cost cutting, restructuring the organization chart, or team building) will help the business thrive. Likewise, if an enterprise has just the right product or service for a receptive marketplace, and yet the organization is poorly designed to deliver the needed performance, no amount of customer surveying or strategic business planning will help the *organization* deliver the appropriate capabilities to the business it must serve. It is important to distinguish up front whether an emerging need is primarily in the business or organizational area.

In practice, we generally begin with questions about the business: *What is going on with the business? What is happening in the marketplace and external environment? What are the key issues the business is facing? How are the functions being accomplished?* We then move to questions about the organization and its alignment with the defined business: *Are the organizational arrangements appropriate for the current and future requirements of the business?*

At their most basic level, these questions generate conversations that provide insight about how the business is *functioning* in its marketplace and whether the *form* of the organization supports the business function. Form follows function. Before issues of function are addressed, discussions of form can be misleading.

The enterprise is the sum of the business dynamics and the organizational dynamics. The blending of a business and organization perspective into one integrated picture distinguishes Enterprise Development from the separate fields of strategic business planning or organization development.

Overview of STEP

As indicated in Chapter Three, the enterprise is a system made up of five components that interact dynamically: structure, task, internal environment, external environment, and people (see Figure 4.1). We use the acronym *STEP* to make these components—structure, task, environment, people—easier to remember. To gain a clear understanding of an enterprise, it is important to understand these components both individually and in relation to one another.

An enterprise exists within a given *external environment* of multiple forces: customers; competition; cultural, economic, and social trends; regulations; resources; and new opportunities.

In the *business* of an enterprise, the task is to create and deliver products or services within the demands, constraints, and opportunities present in the external environment. The *task* component includes work processes and standards, job characteristics, and goals. The enterprise task has to interact effectively with its environment. Its ability to deliver products or services to the external environment determines whether it thrives or fails. When the interaction between the environment and the task breaks down, the breakdown is typically recognized as a business problem.

The *organization* supports the business through the systematic arrangements and administration of its resources. Each enterprise develops certain *structures* to help the business accomplish its tasks through *people*. Structures include elements such as policies and procedures, communication mechanisms, and reporting relationships. The people component includes the needs, expectations, and talents of the personnel of the enterprise, as well as its general

Figure 4.1. Enterprise STEP Model.

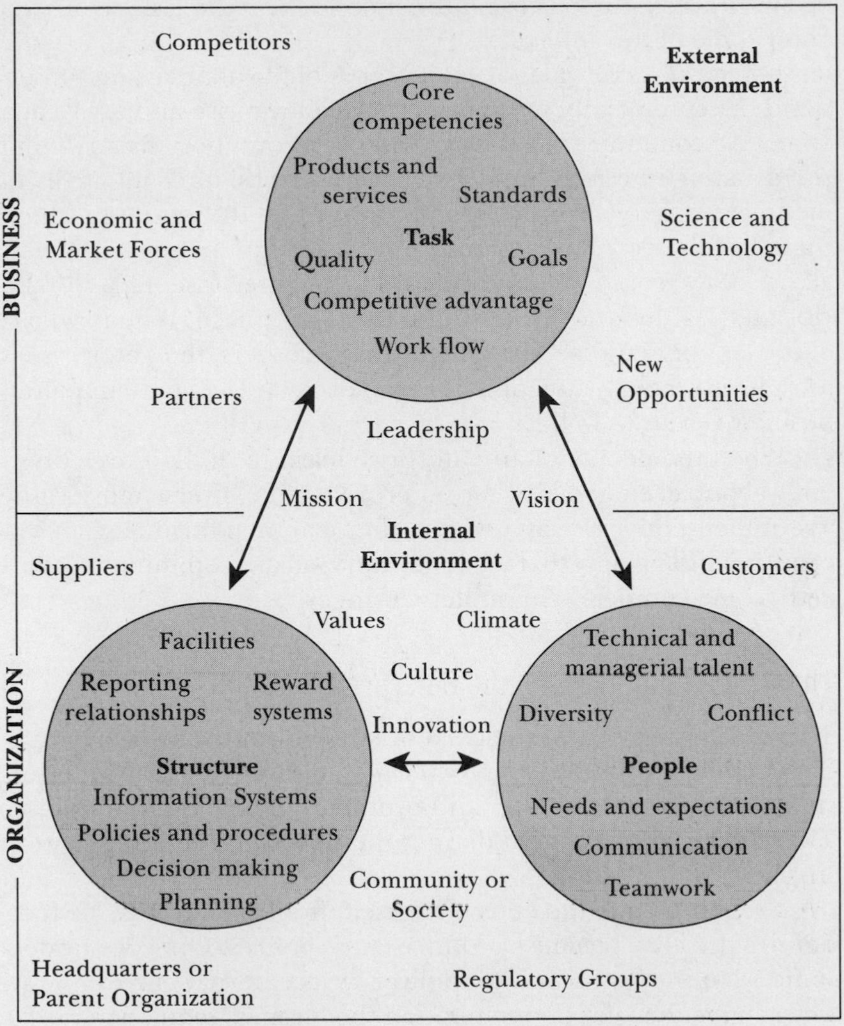

demographics. The degree to which the structure guides people to accomplish their tasks successfully determines the strength and viability of the organization.

The configuration and the dynamic interactions between the task, structure, and people of the enterprise in turn create their own unique *internal environment,* which includes the culture, identity, and morale or climate of the enterprise. The internal environment becomes the setting or context in which the work of the enterprise occurs, thus exerting its own influence back on the task, structure, and people of the enterprise.

Using the STEP categories, it is possible to analyze and understand the complex forces at work in the enterprise and arrive at a coherent, commonsense description of its condition. By analyzing the dynamic interplay among structures, tasks, internal environment, external environment, and people and the extent to which these factors are aligned, significant insight can be gained. When all five of the components are aligned, the enterprise is likely to be vibrant, healthy, and successful in its marketplace. When *any one* of the components is not aligned with the others, the enterprise is most likely to be dysfunctional in some way and will have impaired business results as well.

When the people of an enterprise learn to think more coherently about all elements of the enterprise and converse more easily about their enterprise as a system, they can then formulate a powerful common reality that all understand, all are committed to, and all become competent at implementing.

The STEP Components of the Enterprise

To build an overview of the current enterprise system, we typically begin by examining the *external environment*. We want to understand the forces that affect and ultimately shape the enterprise. The external environment defines the performance necessary for success.

Next we turn to the enterprise itself, first looking at *task,* which defines the core business products and services. Once we understand what the business must deliver to its external environment, we examine the kind of organization the business requires: its *structure, people,* and *internal environment.*

External Environment

The external environment exerts tremendous formative pressures on an enterprise from conditions outside its own boundaries (such as customers, competitors, changing markets, emerging technology, regulatory groups, opportunities, and threats). A critical measure of the success and viability of a business is its ability to adapt to the ever-changing nature of the external environment. One of the greatest challenges—particularly for historically successful companies—lies in avoiding the natural tendency to continue responding automatically to changing environmental conditions with methods proved effective in the past. Methods that worked in the past were based on the past environment. Shifting environments demand new methods—and often new attitudes, skills, and resources.

These are some of the questions we typically ask when assessing the external and internal environment:

- Who are your customers or clients, and what is the nature of your relationship with them? Are customer or client needs and preferences clear?
- Who are your suppliers, and what is the nature of your relationship with them?
- How does changing technology affect your enterprise?
- How do government regulations affect your enterprise?
- What economic, political, environmental, and social trends are having a significant impact on your enterprise?
- What new opportunities exist in your environment?
- What new threats exist in your environment?
- What is the state of your industry, and how are you positioned within it?

Task

Task is the component of the enterprise system that contains the central or predominant work activities: what the enterprise actually does. Successful completion of its work tasks enables the enterprise to manufacture products or deliver services that let it compete in the marketplace. Products and services are delivered using some systematic method or technological process to achieve a desired goal. How well the people responsible for the enterprise's product and services understand the goals and methods for accomplishing their task and how explicitly those goals and methods are expressed can be decisive factors in terms of product quality, cost, safety, customer satisfaction, and ultimate success or failure.

Here are some of the questions we typically ask when assessing an enterprise's task:

- What business are you in?
- What is your competitive advantage?
- What is your long-term business strategy?
- What is your short-term business strategy?
- What are the core work processes? How effective are they?
- How effective are your overall current operations?
- Are goals clearly stated, agreed on by the individuals who must achieve them, and consistent with your company's business strategy?
- What constitutes good performance and high quality, and how do people know when these have been achieved?

Structure

Structure is defined as the arrangements and systems that support and coordinate the core work process. Examples of structural elements include the organizational structure, management systems and reporting relationships, job descriptions, team structures, policies and procedures, planning processes, decision-making systems, reward systems and other human resource systems, communication systems, financial systems, technology and information systems, meeting systems, and physical structures such as facilities.

Organization structure arranges people and tasks in ways that allow the accomplishment of the mission of the enterprise. Managers or members of self-managed work teams are usually given authority to assign roles, establish responsibilities, and determine structure. They decide on the arrangements, rules, processes, policies, and procedures that will lead to the greatest effectiveness for the organization to accomplish its stated mission, given a particular *environment,* particular requirements of the *task,* and the needs and capabilities of the *people.* Structures are enduring agreements inside the organization to maximize operating efficiency. Though there is no single "right" structure for any organizational situation, structures that are more effective or less effective can be identified, given a certain environment, task, and people. Structures can be open and flexible or vague and ill-defined; they can be clear and specific or closed, even rigid. As will be shown in greater detail later on, in some situations the enterprise is better served by open structures, and in others it is better served by higher levels of definition and discipline.

These are some of the questions we typically ask when assessing an enterprise's structure:

- How is the enterprise organized?
- How well does the structure suit the tasks of your department or the overall enterprise?
- How well do management methods and systems enable the effective performance of the business tasks?
- Which structures and systems are most helpful, and which ones interfere with effective functioning?
- How are decisions made and by whom?
- How do people communicate with one another? What is the direction and quality of the information flow?
- What rewards exist, and for which behaviors? Are these rewards valued?
- How are resources such as time, money, and information allocated and managed?

People

People are the employees or members of the enterprise. They are the lifeblood of the enterprise. Whether or not people are aligned with the purposes and tasks of the enterprise has a significant impact on its success. When people feel good about their company or institution, they are more likely to be concerned for their customers or clients; when they are satisfied, they are more likely to be concerned about the quality of their work. Not only are people resources to the enterprise, but the enterprise is also a resource to its people. From work, people gain a sense of meaning, self-esteem, belonging, and security.

To understand the people dimension of an enterprise, we look at the demographics and diversity in the organization and how people work together to accomplish the tasks. We examine the dominant styles of communication; the nature of the working relationships; the degree of collaboration, commitment, motivation, and conflict; and the way conflicts are handled when they arise. Perhaps most important, we try to make an assessment of the talent and skills in the organization and how well these match the demands of the task, as well as the way the work is structured.

These are some of the questions we typically ask when assessing an enterprise's people:

- What kinds of talent are present in your enterprise? What is the level of that talent?
- What knowledge and skills are required for your company's task?
- What are the strengths and weaknesses of the workforce?
- How well do people understand the enterprise strategy and goals? Do they understand how their own role links into the strategy and goals?
- How well do individuals and groups get along?
- How well do people communicate and collaborate to meet the enterprise goals?
- How do people manage conflict?
- How motivated and satisfied are the people?
- How well are people's needs met by the tasks they perform?

Internal Environment

The internal environment is the collection of forces influencing the enterprise from within. The internal environment provides a sense of identity for the enterprise. Key determinants contributing to identity include leadership style and direction, vision, core values, and guiding principles. The internal environment is also sometimes described as the *culture* of the enterprise, which includes such factors as climate and morale; levels of trust, openness, and honesty; levels of anxiety, conflict, negativity, and blame; speed or pace of work and change; degree of flexibility and readiness for change; degree of innovation and creativity; levels of diversity; levels of empowerment; and feelings of ownership and responsibility.

Some of the questions we typically ask when assessing an enterprise's internal environment are these:

- How responsive or open is your enterprise to environmental influence?
- What is the purpose of your enterprise?
- What does your enterprise stand for? What are its values and guiding principles?

- What is the predominant leadership style in your enterprise, and how appropriate is it?
- How are creativity and innovation supported?
- What are the significant myths, rituals, and symbols of your enterprise? Is there an enterprise "story" that many employees would recognize?
- How is everyday life experienced in your enterprise?
- In what ways is working at your enterprise different from working elsewhere?

The internal environment actually spans both the business and the organization. The values in the internal environment can drive the unique ways in which the business delivers products or services to its marketplace. For example, businesses offering similar products in the same market might be designed very differently, depending on whether they were positioned to deliver market share, maximum profit, highest current return to shareholders, highest product quality, environmental sustainability, or community development.

Likewise, once the business objective is clear, the function of the business in turn demands a particular type of internal environment to make the business successful. A business designed to maximize profit would necessarily require a very different overall internal environment from one designed to maximize environmental sustainability.

Scope of the Enterprise System

STEP is a tool that can be effectively used at all levels of the enterprise. The STEP Model can be applied to any size system or group where work is being done. When used to clarify dynamics of smaller groups within a larger enterprise, boundaries must be redefined to reflect the environment and the work group or system being diagnosed. For example, if we were to perform a STEP assessment on a department rather than the overall enterprise, the external environment would include the parent organization itself and other departments and units. The internal environment would include the mission of the department and not only that of the larger enterprise. Products and resources would be limited to those produced and consumed by the department. The tasks, people, and structures described would all be those of the department.

Observations on Using STEP

STEP is very basic. Its view of systems dynamics is not unusually complex or unique. After all, it differentiates only five key building blocks of the system. Yet we have found that these five components of the enterprise system are almost never understood clearly, and the process of working with the stakeholders of an enterprise to analyze all five elements in depth has *always* led to surprising results.

When using the STEP Model for enterprise diagnosis, we engage in an interesting informal survey. When we are called in to consult on an issue in any area of the enterprise—business or organizational—we typically ask our clients to describe the challenges they face using their own words and their own concepts. This gives us the opportunity to see how differently a large number of stakeholders in many diverse enterprises describe their business or organizational issues when given the open-ended opportunity to express a personal view of the enterprise. In fifteen years of using this model, we have almost never had clients spontaneously describe all five components of the system. In fact, the average is two or three. We have seen group members sketch detailed organizational charts and reporting relationships in the organizational structure and expound on new reorganizations on the horizon—and yet remain oblivious to the viability of their products in the marketplace or competitors arriving from directions they had never anticipated. We have seen groups enmeshed in interpersonal struggles who knew every nuance of informal alliances and politics—which teams worked together well and which did not, who had adequate skills and who did not—and yet these same groups had little interest in how management structures or technology influenced people's behavior.

One of the paradoxes—which actually makes good sense, upon reflection—is that the most productive data were generally in areas the groups knew the least about. The enterprises had already incorporated the intelligence from the areas of highest interest and yet were still quite undeveloped and naive in the areas of least concern. Therefore, the sources of the most challenging and often the most urgent dilemmas were accumulating in the areas that had received the least attention to date. Even a brief assessment using the STEP Model makes these discrepancies quickly apparent.

The biggest danger in using STEP is that the categories are viewed as separate items rather than as components that interact dynamically to comprise an enterprise system. STEP viewed as a list of isolated components stays flat and lifeless. A STEP analysis is more than simply asking questions about each component and then collating the answers. Occasionally this exercise could uncover helpful information, but not often. STEP becomes a powerful tool only when each individual component is understood in relation to the others and to the system as a whole. For example, an organization structure or leadership style that may work well for one enterprise could be disastrous for another that faces different threats and opportunities in its external environment and confronts a different business challenge.

Often in examining the five STEP components, one particular area stands out as a primary leverage point, demanding attention. The remaining STEP components may look quite different when viewed in light of this determining factor or effect. Each component of STEP both influences and is influenced by the complete enterprise system.

Using STEP for Enterprise Realignment

The STEP Model has been particularly useful when enterprises are in need of realignment and adaptation to new circumstances.

• STEP provides focus. In midst of multiple shifting inputs, STEP can provide members of a work group with categories to organize their thinking and to clarify their priorities. This is particularly helpful in cases where different members see different parts of the puzzle. In a great many instances, one person or group is focused on one component, such as people or structure, while another is focused on changes in the external environment. They often talk past each other when trying to get the other to understand their own perspective. Using STEP enables people to put all perspectives on the map, to create a unified picture out of all the input, and then to differentiate the implications and priorities.

- STEP provides a framework to understand the impact from changes in one area of the enterprise and how these may ripple throughout the other components of the system.
- Similarly, STEP can provide a reminder for the changes throughout the system that ought to occur when a planned, targeted change is introduced in one area. For example, a new training effort may require new incentive systems or new technology to deliver the intended results.
- Symptoms of difficulties do not always show up where the source of those difficulties actually lies. STEP can help clarify the relationship between the components of the system, to help track the source (or sources) of an identified problem.

The examples that follow will illustrate how business problems can arise from organizational difficulties or interpersonal issues can arise from conflicting business strategies. Treating the most glaring symptom directly often will not fix the problem. In these cases, STEP can help identify the *right change* that is needed. This STEP application can be extremely useful in preventing time and money from being wasted implementing a change that will not address the real issues.

Applications: STEP Stories

Simply reading the basic descriptions of the STEP components can make them appear fairly boring, mechanical, and uninspiring. However, when the details of an actual enterprise are plugged into the categories, the STEP assessment takes on a much more dramatic and colorful life. All of the enterprises we have encountered have had serious challenges to face. With the help of the STEP Model, we have been able to bring the contributing factors to those challenges to light by using the stakeholders' own observations and words.

The stories presented here demonstrate how particular groups have used the STEP categories to clarify and often reframe the issues they identified as most urgent. These groups often started with a focus on one component, but soon the emphasis shifted to another. In the end, each example incorporated all of the elements of STEP and in this way produced a *new enterprise solution* in which all the components of the enterprise were aligned.

External Environment

In a dynamic and changing environment, the relationship of an enterprise with its external environment is critical to the Dynamic Enterprise. Paradoxically, the external environment is generally the least familiar component of the enterprise system to many people at work. Understanding what is going on in the outside business environment, in the society or culture, and in the parent company or departments outside one's own is generally considered the CEO's or top management's territory. Even senior managers are often much more internally focused, more knowledgeable about the specifics and everyday workings of the functions reporting to them or about the boss immediately above them than about the shifts and changes in the external environment (including competitor or industry trends). Many of the most powerful interventions for the creation of the Dynamic Enterprise involve relating the business or organizational elements to the shifting external environment.

A software company used STEP to focus on critical changes in the external environment and to track how these new conditions would reverberate through the system. Each critical driving force in the external environment would require changes in the task, structure, people, and internal environment of the enterprise. These changes were fairly obvious once the company systematically considered the implications of the changing environment. (Examples of how a company can further differentiate the intensity, magnitude, or type of particular changes required by its changing external environment are presented in Chapter Seven.)

This technology company had grown by 40 to 50 percent in each of the past three years and was expecting to grow at a similar rate in the current year. However, as two members of the senior team gathered data from sales managers throughout the company, they realized that their company was likely to "hit a wall" in the upcoming year—it could not continue to grow at the same rate with its current product and current mode of business.

To maintain the recent rate of growth, the company would have to move into a "new market space." In the past, it had grown by selling smaller software applications to individual departments within customer companies. Now more advanced technology was available, and the company's customers faced new business pressures of their own. Given these two shifts in the external environment, customers now wanted more comprehensive and integrated "business solutions," customized to their particular industry, available globally.

In the past, the company had succeeded by having the best features in its software product. It had risen to the top of its field on the basis of superior technological expertise. Customers would buy its product, combine it with their own hardware and industry knowledge, integrate it with their current systems, and put the application to use.

Now, however, customers were saying, "Here is my business problem. I need a business solution." They did not want to buy the software and hardware separately and did not want to have to figure out themselves how to integrate the new materials with their current systems. They wanted to present their business problem to vendors and have the vendors in the marketplace work together and come back with a solution. A customer would then interview several networks of providers and choose the integrated solution that would work best to solve its particular problem. This was quite obviously a very different business!

This fundamental change in customers' needs and demands led to a series of other changes throughout the other STEP components of the enterprise system. Because customers wanted customized and comprehensive solutions, the software product was now only one component of a larger product that customers wanted to buy. Now the company would have to pair up with other companies who would provide the hardware, the industry expertise, the industry application, and the system integration. The race was on in the industry to consolidate networks and partners.

In addition, because the customer was buying a larger product, "an integrated, comprehensive business solution," the contact person in the customer company was changing as well. The customer who would buy this new product was quite likely at the higher levels of the company, and the purchase would require COO or CEO approval. This new customer was likely more business-driven and less concerned with the details of the technology. Given the size of the customer companies, this new customer wanted to buy a package for the global business as well. The new product package would not only have to work in a small department within a business in one country but would also have to be applicable at the enterprise level across many countries. The company was, suddenly and to its surprise, selling a new product to a new customer.

STEP allowed a group of senior managers to focus their thinking and plan their next actions in the course of a two-day retreat. They drew a large wall map, based on all inputs, and identified the themes in the *external environment* that would be critical driving forces behind the success of their business in the next year. They then stood back, took a deep breath, and began to consider the implications of having a new customer who wanted a new (larger and more complex) product.

When they examined the implications for their *task,* they realized that their business was changing in significant ways. Their core technology was basically the same, but the way they had to package their product and take it to market had to be entirely different. Their new product would be a more complex, higher-value product and would have to function globally. They would also need to team up with other suppliers and to sell to a business-oriented customer at a higher level in the customer company.

STEP helped them quickly see that their current *structures* were not designed for lower-volume, high-value products; for global products; for industry customization; or for complex partnerships with other firms. Most current systems and incentives were based on quantity measurements. They would also need to reorganize to support global product development, technical support, and sales and to target separate industries—a capability they didn't yet have. Finally, partnering was currently regarded, both formally and informally, as a sign of weakness. They did not have policies or procedures in place to form successful partner relationships, and in fact their current incentive systems encouraged their people to avoid partnering.

Likewise, their *people* would need new skills. Currently, they were well equipped with technology-centered skills but lacked many of the others needed to succeed in the new business they were designing.

They also realized that some areas of the company, such as sales, were already trying to respond to the new marketplace, while other key divisions, such as product development and marketing, were still working from the old paradigm, focusing on features and technology. People in different divisions were already getting into conflicts over their different, but not yet clearly articulated, business priorities.

Finally, they realized that their *internal environment* would have to change dramatically as well. They currently had a culture of energetic and talented individual contributors. They had always viewed companies who needed to join with others to make sales as second-rate, as unable to "complete a product" on their own. Individual heroes gained the formal rewards, as well as the respect and the promotions. Because of this individualistic stance, the managers had also never been strong on internal communication and integration. The marketplace shifts were suddenly requiring that they make quantum leaps forward in the areas of integration and collaboration across company lines.

By the end of the two-day retreat, these managers had identified critical changes in their external environment and several key changes this shift would necessitate throughout their company. They were already clear about their longer-term direction and many of the next steps they needed to take as soon as possible. They quickly made decisions on internal partner arrangements, determining who would communicate with each of their colleagues and leaders who needed to see the same picture they were seeing.

Figure 4.2 shows how they outlined their data on a STEP map.

The managers realized that it would take at least a year to complete all the changes they outlined: organizational restructuring, building partner relationships, focusing on targeted industries, policy realignments, skills development, and culture change. They also knew they had to begin the transition as soon as possible. They had to get the key people on board to help them further clarify the picture they had painted and move it forward. They resolved to take their findings to members of their executive team, product development, product support, marketing, finance, sales, human resources, potential partners, and key customer groups, to continue to develop the strategy and work out the details for implementation.

Team Building Through a Shared View of the External Environment

When enterprises do not deal with the changes in the external environment, the business often begins to experience problems but may not be clear about the source of the problems. For businesses or institutions that do not track these changes systematically, people are generally vaguely aware of the issues but often cannot articulate them clearly, and the issues may surface as tensions among individuals or work groups. The example just given revealed that some departments became aware of the changes their business was facing before others did. Without a clear understanding that they were seeing new trends first (because they were the ones closest to the customers, where these particular changes were originating), they did not understand their need to communicate change to others. This communication was also not considered a legitimate part of their role—their peers and colleagues would not have been particularly welcoming of new input. Given

Figure 4.2. Sample STEP Map.

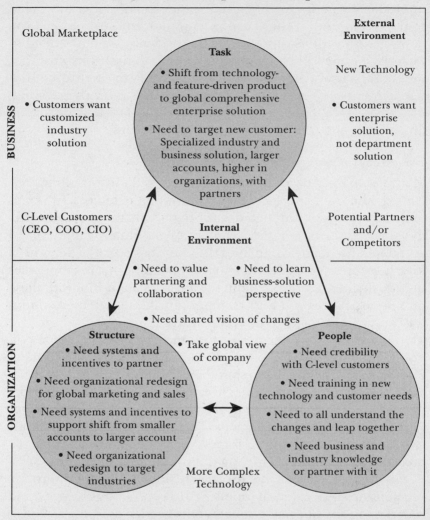

their differing views on external business demands, various teams that needed to work together were in conflict (such as sales and product development, or sales and customer support). This same phenomenon happens not only between teams but within teams and departments as well.

In general, we have found that a clear and shared understanding of the external environment and the implications for the rest of the enterprise is an important part of team building and interteam collaboration. Teams must understand why they need to be a team (and if there is not an important business reason, maybe they don't need to be a team) and also why they need to work with others. What makes it essential to their business that they act as a team? Why is it essential that they partner with other departments or teams? When purpose and urgency are clear, other, more people-centered team-building work will proceed much faster and produce more significant results.

Using STEP to Realign External Relationships

Many companies have recently concentrated most of their cost-cutting, improvement, and change efforts on the internal workings of their enterprises (through downsizings, reorganizations, or quality initiatives). Yet when the numbers are accurately gathered and accounted for, many companies discover that 50 to 75 percent of their expenses are related to external spending—with companies outside their enterprise! Building strategic relationships with these outside companies is at least as important as internal interventions for companies striving to be competitive.

This realization is causing profound transformations in corporate functions such as procurement or materials management. Companies are beginning to shift their traditional purchasing practices to leverage a more strategic view of their customer and supply network. The role of the procurement department no longer focuses only on purchasing goods. The new role shifts dramatically to include understanding customers' priorities, assessing "total life cycle cost of supplies," clarifying the supply and distribution strategy to meet customers' needs, structuring and maintaining the relationships with external suppliers that support this strategy, and redesigning any internal arrangements needed as well.

Implementing this strategic approach to supply chain management (or supply network management) typically includes building alliances with key suppliers to cut costs, decrease supply cycle time, increase innovation, and deliver higher quality. This work often delivers a 10 to 15 percent drop in annual external spending (and sometimes as high as 30 percent) while securing higher-quality goods and services in the areas most important to customers.

Customers and suppliers in a network can consider themselves an "enterprise" and work together to gain a shared perspective of their system. This perspective often enables them to "find solutions in the system" that would have been hard for any single company, or even any pair of companies, to see alone. In one of the simplest examples of this principle at work, one oil company working in a remote location discovered while working with a supplier that this supplier also delivered to the oil company's closest local competitor. The two oil companies discovered that if they could team up to work with this supplier, the increased volume and predictability in this remote site helped their supplier cut costs and coordinate quicker deliveries to each of them. Lower supply costs then translated into lower costs to the oil companies for more frequent and reliable service.

New relationships with companies in the external environment make new demands on the internal organization as well. New systems and structures (such as measurements, information and communication systems, or reward systems) are often needed to support the new activities. In addition, people who have worked in traditional roles in order processing, warehousing, or distribution frequently need a whole new set of skills—in total cost assessment, creating strategy, and structuring and nurturing strategic relationships. Other skills, such as negotiation, alliance building, or partnering, may be needed to work collaboratively with others outside the formal boundaries of the enterprise. Building this strategic supply chain network begins with a task and external environment relationship but ultimately must spread to all the other STEP components to be fully successful.

Task

The business *task* is generally the element of the enterprise system that is the first to respond to shifts in the marketplace and in the external environment in which the business operates.

Businesses use innumerable ways to question and redefine their core tasks to make sure they align with the needs of the external environment and the enterprise as a whole. The changes come in almost every size and shape, from minor repairs and improvements to major transformations that affect the very identity of the enterprise and how it defines its strategic core competencies. Task interventions are those designed to improve the quality of the product or service delivered or the way it is produced. Typical examples in many of today's companies include strategic business planning, business process redesign, quality improvement programs, and new product or service launches.

STEP adds three key ingredients to many of these change efforts that enterprises may already have under way:

- STEP relates the task of the business to its external environment and helps clarify whether the two are aligned.
- STEP emphasizes that all components of the enterprise system need to be understood before beginning a task intervention.
- STEP helps clarify when issues that first show up in other parts of the enterprise are actually related to needed changes in task.

The business must deliver products and services to its marketplace within the demands, constraints, and opportunities offered by the external environment. We are surprised at how often task interventions are initiated without a full understanding of the scope of the environmental conditions. Relating the intended task-driven solution to needs and opportunities in the external environment often gives the stakeholders of the enterprise a basic tool to understand whether their business as defined can succeed in its given environment. William Bridges (1988), in his writings and workshops on managing transition, often asks, "Is the Band-Aid big enough?"

Aligning Task and External Environment

The example of the distribution centers in Chapter Two illustrates that task interventions must be aligned with conditions in the external environment. The centers housed manufacturers representatives, where buyers from retail companies could visit and order merchandise for their stores. Many centers originally chose a task intervention to deal with tenants who were leaving their buildings, which seemed to be a logical enough approach when only task data were taken into consideration. If tenants were leaving the buildings, it seemed obvious that interventions designed to get them to stay (such as tenant relations committees, building improvements, and better communication systems) would help reverse the trend. However, the analysis of the full picture of the system showed that the driving force behind tenants' leaving lay in the external environment, where new technology was leading to a restructuring of distribution chains.

Tenants themselves did not always see these trends either and so could not have expressed them in exit interviews. The tenants simply knew their own businesses were in decline and that they could no longer afford to rent space in the centers. A study of the larger picture showed that the customers of the centers—manufacturers representatives who were middlemen in the retail distribution system—were being replaced by direct connections between large manufacturers and large retail conglomerates. The centers were in trouble because their customers' industry was in decline. Simply cleaning up the operations of their current business to serve their current customers better was not going to be a "big enough Band-Aid."

Once the centers understood the external environment clearly and saw the implications for the task of their business, they were free to imagine different ways they could serve the emerging external environment. They needed to realign the core task of their business with the marketplace. They had to redefine their business to offer services that would add value in the new marketplace (such as technology, consulting skills, or industry expertise). They had to redefine the qualities that would make them attractive as a meeting ground in an era when physical meeting places were no longer absolutely required.

Aligning Task Interventions with the Whole Enterprise System

When change efforts are unidimensional, they are much more prone to fail before they are fully implemented and integrated into the enterprise. We have seen innumerable change efforts abandoned around seven to nine months after they were launched. These failing change efforts were often undermined by elements of the system that had been left unexamined and therefore remained unchanged, exerting a strong pull to bring the old system back into equilibrium.

A manufacturing plant launched a $60 million redesign of multiple business systems. The core manufacturing processes were supposed to remain the same, but the "background business systems" (such as procurement, human resource information systems, capital asset management, budgeting, general ledger, and other core financial systems) were all being redesigned. This complex change effort had originally grown out of a need to replace outdated information systems, but as is often the case, no one wanted to automate equally outdated, dysfunctional business processes.

A major redesign effort was launched in conjunction with the information systems overhaul. Redesign teams of eight to fifteen individuals worked with each major business process and with parallel teams from the information systems departments. This effort was planned to be a three-year project to redesign how the business would operate and involved over one hundred workers considered to be the company's best and brightest. The ultimate goal was to standardize and streamline business processes throughout the company. Business units that had each had their own individualized systems in place would shift to new systems that were shared companywide.

We began working with this group one year into their three-year change process. When we began to use Enterprise Development as a guideline to examine their overall change process, team after team reported that they expected failure from the redesign overall. This was news worth listening to! STEP framed their thinking and allowed team members to verbalize concerns they had had for many months.

When the whole STEP map was filled in, the change teams agreed that it made sense at the task level to update the business processes and it made sense from the structure level to introduce new information systems to enable this work. However, the people and the internal environment would oppose these changes each step of the way. Team members didn't believe the company's people and culture would accept the new business processes. They fully expected their new designs to be rejected (and didn't believe their leaders had the commitment to push back against this rejection). If they looked ahead two more years, they didn't expect many of the systems they were designing to be implemented.

This was a company that had always rewarded individual decisions on the part of the business units and the individual contributions of the leaders within those units. It was also a company in which the separate business units competed for corporate resources and did not trust one another or the centralized corporate staff to run the company effectively. Owing to their history and their corporate culture, they had no concept of "shared business processes and information systems" for the common good of the larger company. Each business unit was busy making the case for why its unit needed exceptions to the systems proposed and why it couldn't accept the streamlining because it needed additional resources. The units didn't accept the basic premise that this kind of redesign was needed. Powerful leaders in the business units undermined the redesign teams each step of the way, and team members doubted they could keep to their time frames or their budgets.

We see companies approach change this way quite often: task interventions are launched with little concern as to how they fit with the rest of the norms, skills, and culture of the enterprise. The technical changes required are completely clear to the change initiators, and they assume that key stakeholders will understand them as well and "go along." In these cases, STEP can provide a tool that helps clarify whether particular task interventions can succeed with the existing people, structure, and internal environment or whether these areas will need to change along with the targeted area.

When Problems Arising in Other STEP Components Need Task Intervention

STEP can clarify task interventions when members of the enterprise are in conflict and it is not yet clear that task is the core issue. People or teams in conflict in the workplace often assume that their conflicts are interpersonal and may not be aware of the business issues fueling the fire. In fact, conflict is often one of the first signs of much larger changes brewing within the enterprise or industry.

The senior leaders of a large health care institution asked us to facilitate a conflict resolution effort among members of its top management team, comprised of leaders from both the medical and administrative staff. Conflict on the team was extensive and deep-rooted and was beginning to disrupt the smooth functioning of the medical center. Team members attributed their difficulties to differences in personality and management style between several team members and one other member. However, when we looked at all the STEP components to understand the full context of this issue, it became apparent that the issue was much larger than simple personality conflicts.

The conflict went far beyond the senior team (as is not unusual, as conflicts at this level are generally reflected throughout the rest of the enterprise). Much of the hospital and medical center had effectively chosen sides, dividing into separate camps along neat, disciplinary boundaries: the physicians and medical staff against the administrative staff. The situation was tempting for them to dismiss as a continuation of old turf battles between professional groups that had often been in conflict in the past. However, the senior leadership team persisted in working to understand all STEP components related to their struggle and discovered that much more important issues were leading to their conflict than personalities alone.

As the team members examined their external environment, they recognized that health care institutions were under the same pressures bearing down on other industries: to cut costs while increasing quality and accessibility to services or care. The member of the leadership team who was the most disliked for her "abrasive management style" was the member who was most vocal about business demands.

The administrative staff agreed with this leader, who saw a need for introducing business concepts into the practice of medicine. They believed that the medical staff needed to upgrade their financial skills and to take on clear accountability for budgeting. They also thought services should be designed around the "voice of the customer." This would include operational changes such as extending clinic hours, providing minimal waiting time for scheduling routine appointments, coordinating care across different departments, and increasing the information available to customers (about medical procedures, access to care, and preventive health practices).

The medical staff, for its part, strongly disliked the term *customer* because it seemed to make their clinical profession sound like a business at a time when they distrusted the cost cutting this implied. Most members had chosen their profession out of a sense of caring for people, and their day-to-day practice focused on finding the best treatment for each individual patient. Customers, budgets, and business concepts sounded less ethical to them, and they were afraid this would compromise individual patient care. In addition, many medical professionals feared that the pressures to shift to standardized treatment protocols (to the most cost-effective means of treatment in particular) threatened to replace their independent clinical judgment.

As the leadership team examined the enterprise using the STEP Model, members began to realize that the struggles they had acted out in such personal terms were being enacted in many hospitals and clinics around the country. They realized that their "personality conflicts" were a sign of their opposing visions of health care, which mirrored the divided views in the rest of the nation. This discovery paradoxically provided some encouragement and relief: they were not the only ones struggling with these issues. Throughout the country, politicians, employer groups, patients, and health care professionals were debating the complex issues of how to build a health care system that could meet the needs of divergent groups. The medical staff could see that their own administrative team members were not crazy, unethical, or irresponsible but were responding to trends in the larger health care industry.

Group members also realized they could not wait for an entire nation to resolve its political views of health care. They had a hospital and medical clinic to run. They realized that they must develop a vision of health care that they could all agree to. Could "patients" be considered "customers," and if so, what effect would that have on their day-to-day practice? Could they realistically provide higher-quality health care at lower cost?

Because these tensions had involved staff throughout the medical center, the senior management group ultimately involved all stakeholders in the institution in developing a shared view of health care (realigning the task with the emerging external environment). The managers realized that the financial pressures on health care were not going to go away and that cutting costs would make health care accessible to more people. They began to see how this could be done in line with the values that were important to them. Over several months, they created a vision of "high-quality, affordable, customer-driven health care" that all stakeholders could understand and support. Their conflict had actually led them to discover and create a powerful new vision for their medical center.

The changes in the definition of their central business task then had enormous implications for how their enterprise was organized. "Customer-driven health care" meant they had to consider care from the patient perspective rather than the provider perspective. Work groups throughout the medical center began to examine their structures in multiple ways—from asking whether they could continue to close their offices during lunch hour to breaking down their separate, hierarchical department structures into cross-functional teams designed to meet customer needs quickly and inexpensively. For example, anxious parents who brought in a child for severe asthma should not get shuffled from one department to another for the child to get treatment. Children brought into any department—emergency, urgent care, allergy, pediatrics, or medicine—should receive prompt and consistent care. To deliver such service, each of these departments needed to define this care in collaboration with the others and agree on how to deliver it most appropriately.

Finally, staff throughout the hospital and medical center needed to find a way to heal the rifts in their internal environment. An institution composed of two hostile, warring camps would not likely succeed in reaching its vision. The staff had learned a great deal about how to turn conflict into issues to be worked out and had gained a new appreciation for how conflict could yield valuable data that helped them understand important business issues. They realized that they had to build a work culture of collaboration, respect, and increased communication if they ever hoped to complete a successful transition from a traditional, provider-driven medical establishment to a customer-driven health care enterprise of the twenty-first century.

Structure

Changes in the core tasks of many businesses, paired with simultaneous changes in technology, are having a massive impact on the structures of today's enterprises. As they face more complex tasks and a greater likelihood of change in the definition of these tasks, many large enterprises are restructuring their organizational charts, moving from steep hierarchies to flatter, leaner, and more flexible organizational structures. Others are changing to team, networked, or project structures and are partnering with groups both inside and outside their traditional enterprise boundaries. Many are implementing new information technologies, which further increase the communication and networking possibilities both inside and outside the enterprise. Market, customer, and management information that used to be reserved for only the most senior staff is now widely available throughout the enterprise. New management systems, policies, roles, and job descriptions frequently reflect these changes as decision-making responsibility is moved to the front lines, closest to the customer. Even the physical facilities where people work are open for redesign, reflecting the changes in flatter, networked, or flexible organizations. Where people work, how they work together, when they work, and even if they work in facilities at all (versus telecommuting from home) are all organization structures that are open for decision.

STEP has been useful to work groups to help clarify when the structure needs to change in response to interventions in other parts of the enterprise system. It also helps clarify what other parts of the enterprise may need to change when a structure intervention is planned. The overall objective is that structure be integrated as one part of an enterprisewide solution.

The following example illustrates how putting the appropriate structures in place can be essential to the success of task-oriented initiatives. The business task may be well suited to the needs of the external environment, but a bottleneck in the organization can impede the enterprise's ability to produce or deliver it.

One high-tech company that wanted to grow its global operations realized it was in fact "international" rather than "global." The company already sold products in different countries but did not have consistent worldwide business systems. For example, its organizational structure and HR policies were designed for earlier times in the company's history when each office sold products within its own local territory. Now, however, the marketplace had shifted. Customers—who were becoming global themselves—wanted the same product in all of their locations. A customer buying for a company based in New York might buy for the London office as well, or vice versa. However, because sales offices based in different countries would qualify for separate commissions, teams from multiple locations would often pursue the same global client. The London office might try to give a better deal to the client than the New York office, so that its own team would get the commission, but then the New York office would offer an even bigger discount. The international sales managers quickly realized that they needed to design a new organization structure and incentive plan to support the growth of global operations to global customers in order to stop undercutting their own business.

Sometimes the organizational solution to structure issues can be straightforward and much simpler than the business task issue itself but can hold back business progress when left undiagnosed.

We worked with a multidisciplinary team of engineers charged with designing a satellite much lighter than any the company had produced before. After two years of work, the satellite was still too heavy, and time was running out for funding. Team members faced a very complex technical task. If the project was to succeed, team members needed to create a design never before imagined, to leap to a "breakthrough solution."

In the course of our work with this group, team members confronted many complex and challenging technical design issues about the satellite itself, as well as issues around working together across their range of specialties. We asked them what they found to be the most difficult aspect of this project and were surprised to hear one member respond, "My boss!" Several others echoed this sentiment. Given the technical difficulty of their project, we had expected a technical impediment and pushed further for a response. It turned out that the group was quite serious.

Even though these design team members were encouraged by their project leader to engage in "blue-sky thinking," each team member still formally reported to the manager in his or her traditional functional department. Most of these managers held much more conservative views, and they rarely communicated with the project leader. Performance appraisals (tied to team members' compensation and bonuses) were completed primarily by the functional manager and were based on the company's traditional, risk-averse work processes and values ("Show your work," "Be able to prove, step by step, how you get there from here," "Don't take risks with the company's reputation—don't bet the store").

Because the management structure and incentive systems didn't support innovation, design team members didn't feel secure enough to take risks just because their current project leader verbally encouraged them to do so. They feared that any attempts at uncharacteristic "leaps to the impossible" would injure their longer-term working relationships with their functional bosses, their chances for promotion, and their reputations throughout the rest of the company. All the breakthrough thinking and team skills in the world were not going to help this group. They needed to know that their management system supported risk taking before they would consider trying out new behavior.

Many business issues can be resolved only with structure interventions along with business interventions (interventions aimed at the task–external environment interface). When the current organization structure (or even parts of the structure, such as the appraisal process just described) is designed for the current business, the business may not be able to change without a corresponding change in the structure.

The satellite design team also illustrates a fairly common structure difficulty in larger, traditional companies that need to launch innovative projects. New projects are often attempted within the confines of the existing structures and systems that were designed for more traditional work groups (see Chapter Seven for more discussion about the fit between business and organizational systems). Innovative or start-up projects within a larger enterprise can often be overwhelmed by an organization structure designed for a more developed, mature business.

The next example illustrates how all STEP components were needed to turn around one division of 250 people, but the key lever for change was the structure. The concept of "lever" was helpful to this group because the people involved could see where they most urgently needed to direct their time and attention. They had to redesign the whole system of their enterprise to make the business functional, but the reorganization in structure was the primary catalyst to enable the other areas to change.

The new leader of facilities development asked us to conduct an enterprisewide assessment to determine the range of needs in this division. She had recently been brought in to turn around this division, which was regarded as dysfunctional by much of the larger enterprise. When she first moved into the position, she received ten to twenty complaints each day from high-level leaders in other areas of the business. Her division of 250 people was responsible for building and maintaining the buildings for its growing parent company, but growth was being stifled by this division's inability to build or renovate facilities quickly enough. In some offices, work was taking place in hallways, closets, or any space where someone could find a desk to share. Not surprisingly, tempers flared.

As this leader assessed changes in the external environment to determine customer needs and assessed the internal business operations and organization, she learned that the division was currently delivering $50 million per year of completed building projects, while the parent company had an annual demand of $300 million—and the demand was growing! She also realized that the division couldn't deliver on its task because it didn't have the organization structure in place to support this amount of work. In a retreat with her top team, managers recognized that while the division might be able to improve its productivity, they could not likely improve it from $50 million of construction to $300 million annually. Their people could work harder and smarter, but not that much harder and smarter.

The leader assembled all of the key stakeholders and members in her division and presented them with a radical design challenge: they were all fired. Their current organization was out of business because it could not accomplish the task required. It was gone, and with it, all their jobs were gone. They did still have work, however, and their current work was to use all their skills to design a system that could deliver the needed productivity within six months' time. If they could accomplish this task successfully, they would all have jobs again, although undoubtedly in new roles and positions.

Starting from the required task at hand, the members of this enterprise collectively and collaboratively worked in teams to design new work processes and a new organization structure that could deliver these processes. They tore apart the hierarchical functional organization and rebuilt it into team-oriented project units. They rewrote job descriptions to fit the new organization and then applied for jobs in the new organization. (They even hired a résumé writer to help anyone who needed coaching on applying for a new job.) They tried to match people with the new skills needed, and many moved to a new level in the organization, different from their previous position in the hierarchy.

By the six-month deadline, the new organization was up and running effectively. The division was producing at the rate required to meet existing demand and support continued growth. Productivity had increased by 600 percent!

When others in the parent company asked members of this group how they had accomplished this task so thoroughly in such a short time, they mentioned that several things had been important to them: they themselves had understood the need for the changes, they had collectively participated in designing the changes, and they supported the process fully. They understood the key drivers in the external environment (the expansion needs of the parent company), and they believed in the new task (the need to build needed facilities as quickly as possible). They were then given the support and freedom to design the organizational structure that could accomplish the task. Because of this work together, they were willing to let go of their past ways of working, their past roles, as well as their former culture. Their participation in designing a new organizational structure led them to create an energetic, collaborative, and fast-paced new culture for their internal work environment.

A few years later, one of the leaders from this division reminisced about the project. He said, "When we first started, I thought this was the most outrageous and silliest thing I had ever been a part of. But you know what? It worked—and keeps on working even today. Not only did we change the things we needed to change back then, but we also learned how to change— and have already done it a few more times with equal results." The signs of a Dynamic Enterprise!

People

People are quite amazing. They love to create drama and intrigue. When we observe many of the interactions that occur within an enterprise, we sometimes wonder how productive work is ever accomplished. Yet it does get accomplished, and often quite beautifully and creatively, but in midst of this creation, people carry on the same dramas at work that they do in the rest of their lives. We have never worked with an enterprise where dramas did not occur. After all, most of the people in an enterprise spend more time at work than they do anywhere else.

Because enterprises accomplish their work through people, the dynamics of their interpersonal relationships and group interactions will affect any change effort, improvement program, or enterprisewide development. We typically watch for four categories of issues with people that affect the success of the enterprise. Let us examine them one at a time.

Enterprise Change Requires People to Change

In the simplest and most straightforward situation, as the external environment, task, or structure of the enterprise changes, people must learn to work in newly defined roles, with new responsibilities and accountabilities. They may need new skills or technical knowledge to do this successfully. They may also need to work together in very different ways as they encounter different demands for leadership, management, teamwork, collaboration, and communication. The software company moving to build comprehensive global business solutions was a good example. A new business environment and task clearly required new skills and new ways of working from people in the enterprise.

People Issues as Symptoms of Enterprise System Misalignment

Sometimes tensions emerge in people's working relationships, but these tensions reflect people's emotional responses to an enterprise that is not aligned. Although the "symptoms" may show up first in the people area, the primary underlying concerns are actually business or structural, not interpersonal.

When an organizational structure is not adequate for accomplishing a task, people will not be able to work effectively. Similarly, when the task is not suited for a newly changed marketplace, people cannot succeed. Sometimes it is the people area or the internal environment that does not fit the task at hand, and the people will feel conflicting pulls and pressures. The tensions created by an enterprise that is not aligned begin to affect people's morale and feelings. Soon conflict typically emerges. However, as shown in several of the examples earlier in this chapter, intervention in the people area alone will not fix the problem. The enterprise system itself needs to be realigned so that tensions among people can be resolved.

In most cases, people feel the effects of the misalignment at varying times and will voice the pressures of these witnessed failures. However, they are often not conscious of the underlying causes; they just know that "something isn't working."

A problem in the enterprise system usually shows up in someone's territory and is often considered that person's or team's fault. It is rarely identified as a systems issue that grew out of decisions made by a large number of people over a long period of time. A particularly tricky aspect of a system's problem is the fact that it doesn't lie within a single person's or department's domain. To fix a system's problem, a large number of people in different departments and at various levels throughout an enterprise must recognize the need for a shift in the entire enterprise system (all the elements of STEP), and the solution must be enacted across the larger group. The people issues will not go away until this shift occurs.

Our earlier example of the health care leadership team (see pp. 79–82) illustrates how conflict can show up most urgently in the interpersonal working relationships among the people of an enterprise but actually be a symptom of a far different dilemma. The external environment in the health care industry was beginning to change, and different leaders had different views about how this should affect the core business or task of their enterprise. Because the people in this group were not focused on the external environment and had not yet begun to articulate the changes they were living through, they tended to stay internally focused and paid more attention to the personalities of the leaders.

People had sided with each other to protect and guard the old culture against the "newcomers trying to change things," and they questioned whether drastic change was needed. They fought this struggle in the interpersonal realm, paying much more attention to people's personality characteristics and management style (whether the new leaders were respectful or rude) or to who was aligned with whom, rather than recognizing the fundamental shifts facing their industry. Intervention in the people area had made no impression on their tensions; retreats and team-building workshops had not significantly minimized their conflicts. Given that the tensions were about much more than leadership style or respect, people would not shift their positions.

When the leaders in this group recognized that different personalities had chosen different visions for the institution—the ones who loved challenge, adventure, and new technology were out to change the face of health care, and the ones who loved the richness and history of all they had built to date and who had seen frivolous trends come and go wanted to keep their systems as they were. They all came to see that their conflicts were personality-based but that the different personalities were connected to different ideas that were critical to defining the future of their institution.

In addition, because their decision was at such a fundamental strategic level of defining health care, each vision represented an entirely different enterprise. The institution would look and operate very differently, depending on which model of health care they chose to follow. The day-to-day tasks, management structures, use of technology, working relationships between people, culture needed for success, and many other elements of the enterprise would all be different. Each time leaders or managers would reach a tactical decision point, they would choose different sides.

By fighting the battle in the field of personalities, they had established "definition by conflict"—whoever won the war would get to decide the future of the enterprise. When instead they agreed to create a shared vision of health care together, to listen to all sides, and to build a collaborative strategy about where to go, they found the first decrease in the tension in their working relationships. As they developed the vision for their enterprise together, they found that they in fact still needed team building. However, now the team-building exercise began to yield results.

People-Centered Dysfunction

Certain working relationships can be dysfunctional without larger systemwide issues' being involved. We frequently see this phenomenon when key individuals in the enterprise have personal problems, such as alcohol or drug abuse or a personality issue that affects their work. The problem exists independent of successes or failures in the enterprise system and generally exists in the individual's personal life as well. When these situations are not dealt with (through management intervention, coaching, referral to an employee assistance program, or other means), the group can take on the dysfunction of the individual and magnify it. Issues that begin as individual issues can become part of a group's norm or working culture if they are not addressed.

We are regularly asked to assist work groups in which a leader or team member is highly talented and has some almost irreplaceable technical skill but also has a fatal flaw that impairs working relationships. The individual is technically brilliant but interpersonally inept. For example, one particular leader was known throughout Silicon Valley to be so hostile and abrasive to subordinates that many talented engineers refused to work for him. In his company, three hundred people reported to him, but he currently had almost one hundred openings that were very difficult to fill. He had the possibility to be one of the most productive leaders in the area but could not fulfill the potential.

The Dynamic Enterprise must have the ability to deal with its most difficult people issues when they arise because these problems ultimately spread to the other elements of the enterprise if they are left unresolved. Dysfunctional interpersonal working relationships or team dynamics will influence the quality of the work, the morale of the department or company, and ultimately the product delivered to customers. Because the enterprise is a system, a dysfunction in any one area will eventually influence all the others.

A History of Dysfunction

Some groups become dysfunctional because the rest of the enterprise has been out of alignment for so long that the dysfunction takes on a life of its own. It may then be impossible to work on realigning the enterprise because it has been so dysfunctional that members cannot work together. Healing may need to take place in people's working relationships before the enterprise can be realigned (or redesigned) to ensure that the interpersonal issues are fully resolved.

> We were called in to work with the quality council for a 1,500-person branch of a large company to help resolve tensions between various council members. For two years, members had argued about different views about the role of the quality department within the branch. One group thought the quality control department should audit 100 percent of priority operations, as other branches did, while others preferred the current approach of auditing a small percentage

of the operations but providing more in-depth consulting services about how to resolve quality issues.

A key point of the controversy was who had the authority to decide what the quality department should do. The people in the primary operations group saw themselves as the customer and the quality department as their service provider. They thought that if they wanted 100 percent of their operations checked, the quality department should provide that service. Conversely, the people in the quality department saw themselves as experts and thought they were better qualified to determine the best use of their staff. The two groups on the council had never reached a shared agreement on the fundamental role of the department.

We began to work with the quality council to create a new vision of the role of quality in the enterprise, assuming that it would not look like *either* of the current perspectives. The existing system had quality defined and measured by a central committee, with reports given to the people in operations. Council members realized that the new definition of the role of quality would likely lead to entirely different tasks for the quality council and most likely to a new structure for the function, one that was not likely to be based in a separate, central department. People would move into new roles and would be building a new culture of quality throughout the enterprise of their local branch. This perception generated a certain excitement about this work: the council members felt they were on track.

However, they had lived with their unresolved conflict for so long that they had built up great animosity. They had undermined each other, had backroom conversations about others on the council, had tried to get one another kicked off the council, and had even tried to get one another fired altogether. This activity occurred in a culture that had a very active grapevine, where anything said to anyone else always got back to the person it was said about. Secret conversations were virtually impossible—everyone knew what had been said and who had said it.

Whenever we would walk into the room to work on creating a shared vision for quality in the enterprise, many members of the group would remain silent, often glaring at others in the group or undercutting others' comments with sarcastic remarks. It was clear that this group was in no condition to create a visionary quality council. It could not work on content issues while maintaining such a dysfunctional process.

This example and other instances have shown us that work groups can go through phases when their members can no longer perform their task because the people issues have become too great an obstacle. A group may spend time in meetings and appear to be working, but no real work gets done. At such a point, the group must stop, address the people issues, and get them resolved so that productive task work can resume. Designing and implementing an appropriate and direct people intervention generally takes a fraction of the time already being spent in wasted meetings and planning.

The quality council members ultimately had to recognize that they were sabotaging each other's work and that it had become a hurtful process for all of them. STEP then served as a neutral framework to help them look forward, to see what they could become, to discuss the new working relationships they would need (people) to introduce the new vision for the quality function in their institution (task).

They agreed that they couldn't continue in their old patterns. They had to build a culture of open communication among themselves, one of trust and respect, if they wanted their quality program to succeed. They agreed to work on the issues with a person with whom they disagreed rather than going off to tell someone—who already agreed with their own position—how wrong someone else was. They recognized that their previous distrust had kept them from reaching agreements on key quality issues over the past two years. Once they began to heal their interpersonal working relationships and build an initial basis of trust, they actually began to redesign the quality program together.

STEP as a Tool for Developmental Conflict Resolution

In cases where conflict among members of an enterprise is related to misalignment in the larger system, STEP can be a helpful tool for conflict resolution. Many battles being fought between people look very different when the entire enterprise is analyzed in some detail and the data are displayed on a map on the wall. More often than not, each side sees that the others had a valid (though perhaps limited) perspective. The ultimate result may not be simply one view or another but all views, plus a little more besides. People learn they were seeing different elements of the system that often were part of an even larger whole. This experience is reminiscent of the well-known Sufi story in which five blind men were each feeling a part of an elephant—trunk, leg, back, tail, and ear. Each swore that an elephant was a completely different animal from the one the others were describing, and each was in fact right on the basis of the information at hand. STEP enables group members to "see the elephant" as a whole. Particularly lately, the "elephant" is generally bigger and more challenging than most people first predict.

Thanks to the shared perspective created by a systems view, many conflicts are more easily resolved. People generally accept the urgency of getting to work to see what they must do next. In our recent experience, a side effect of looking at the whole system of the enterprise in the context of its external environment is that members in conflict frequently discover not only that each side of the argument was important but also that while they were squabbling, a smaller, quicker competitor began moving in to take over their marketplace.

Internal Environment

The internal environment of the enterprise is affected by its task, structure, and people and in turn exerts an influence on them as well. Some work group environments are dynamic, exciting, and characterized by a clear sense of purpose. Others are more hostile and blaming; morale is low, and people spend more energy in complaining or finger-pointing than in accomplishing the work task. As is clear from earlier examples, internal environments often reflect alignment and clarity in the rest of the enterprise system. When the enterprise system is finely tuned—when the business is aligned with the external environment and the organization supports the business—the internal environment will generally be experienced as more positive. A dynamic and aligned internal environment in turn seems to generate its own energy and improve the quality of the work being done in the enterprise.

Conversely, when business and organization are not aligned to deliver to the external environment, the resultant internal environment can make going to work a miserable experience. A member of one technology firm told of "driving to work at about seven miles an hour" because he did not really want to arrive. Another member of an information systems department described his own awkward situation: he was supposed to work with an internal client team in a building separate from the one in which he worked. The members of his client team complained so much each time he went to see them that he said he could not walk past a desk without having to deal with "negativity." He needed a half hour just to get to the office where he was headed. His solution was to stop going to see the client! Obviously, examples such as these create tremendous amounts of waste in the business by draining work time, attention, and resources from core work tasks. Such working conditions also lead to burnout and lawsuits and cause people to wonder why they go to work. Some people leave these environments; others "quit and stay."

We have found that STEP is a useful tool for building more positive internal environments that are aligned with the entire enterprise system. STEP can be used to help understand the kind of internal environment best suited for a given enterprise at a given time, as well as to help turn around negative, dysfunctional internal environments. As the examples in the people areas showed, the best solution for building a positive internal environment, one aligned with the business and organization, may not be possible simply by focusing on the internal environment alone. It can be much easier to resolve issues in the internal environment once a full view of the whole enterprise system is seen.

We were asked to work with a cross-functional team composed of members from two separate divisions in a company. The previous division leaders were now the joint leaders of the new project, but this arrangement was not working well. Team members from the separate divisions were in constant disagreement, and morale was terrible. The group members spent so much time complaining and fighting each other's decisions that they were virtually paralyzed. Outwardly, they looked as if they were accomplishing a great deal of work as they made many plans and charts, but when it came time to make decisions, they blocked each other's ideas. For all their hard work and time spent, they had made no real progress. Team members were frustrated and discouraged.

Once again, they initially thought of their issues as interpersonal and asked for help with their team dynamics. The leaders of the two divisions were diametric opposites in their personality styles. However, as we explored the wider perspective of the enterprise system, it seemed that each leader's personality was a reflection of the views of that division. Conflict after conflict seemed to boil down to a very similar pattern of disagreements. They did not really have hundreds of disagreements—they had one basic disagreement in hundreds of different forms.

One division was more entrepreneurial and wanted to create its new product as "world-class, knock-your-socks-off, best at any cost." Its members believed that if they created the best, they would create their own market and get their money back. The other division was much more fiscally conservative. The company was experiencing financial pressures, and the perspective in this division had always been "create a world-class product, but keep it within budget." "World-class" and "world-class *within budget*" turned out to be completely different fundamental business philosophies. Any time a decision would need to be made, from choosing the architect on a new building to hiring new employees, each division lobbied for a different choice. The two did not find common ground or compromise because each division thought it was acting in the enterprise's best interests. From each division's vantage point, it would have been unethical to compromise.

This disagreement was difficult to resolve because there was a structural dysfunction as well—lack of clarity about who had the authority to decide the ultimate nature of the new product. One leader had been told that he was the primary leader, the customer, and that the other division was there to support him. He believed that he had the authority to define the vision for the new product. The other leader had been told that the two divisions were equal partners in this joint effort. When they took the issue to a higher level of management, a decision about the nature of the product was refused. The message instead was, "Work it out." However, the upper level of management had introduced structural confusion into the project by giving out two separate messages about *how* the divisions would work it out: one message said one division should listen to the other, and the other message said the divisions should decide by consensus.

This fundamental disagreement about the nature of the task, paired with the structural confusion about who had the authority to end the dispute, created a very negative internal environment throughout the new team. People's daily work lives were full of conflict, contention, competitive feelings, and anger toward "the other side." Each group saw the other as malicious, even dangerous to the parent company. Overall morale sank lower each day, and many members of each division chose to leave the company entirely. For those who stayed, the primary work task each day was the ongoing battle with the other side.

This example shows how the dysfunction in the task and structure areas severely affected the internal environment. The internal environment then became the most noticeable aspect of the enterprise. Members of the two divisions could rarely talk with us without focusing on the nature of the internal environment. They did see some business disagreements, but they did not see the pattern underlying the hundreds of separate disagreements. They tended to dwell on each separate disagreement as if surprised that, once again, the opposing side had picked a different choice from the one they knew was correct.

People most naturally want to fix the situation where it hurts. Yet in this case, retreats, team-building sessions, and culture change efforts per se could not ameliorate the painful (and wasteful) internal environment. Seeing the whole enterprise system allowed the leaders and members in these divisions to understand at last the underlying causes for their daily distress. Fundamental business decisions had to be made and decision-making authority had to be clarified before this group could begin to improve its internal environment.

In another case, an individual manager used her enterprise system's understanding to work her way out of a blaming and hostile internal environment and effect a department turnaround. Being able to relate her own actions to both the internal environment and the key business issues in her department enabled her to view her behavior as part of a larger picture. The objectivity this encouraged allowed her some distance from her own actions and enabled her to make choices about her actions within this system.

This woman, a senior manager in the corporate marketing department of a large technology firm, was first referred to us for executive coaching because her internal customers, the marketing staff in the field, felt that she was "not a team player." Her role was to develop marketing materials for staff in the field, but the field staff complained that she didn't involve them in collaborative decisions, didn't deliver the materials they needed most, and increasingly displayed a negative attitude, at times losing her temper.

During the initial phase of her coaching, we tried to get a clear view of the enterprise system in which she operated by gathering data from her and from others in the field. It became clear that the atmosphere in the entire marketing department was contentious. No one else was a team player either! No one had clear ideas about what the rules were, particularly around resource allocation. The marketing staff in the field who had complained about this manager were actually competing with each other for resources, and each felt shortchanged. For example, the U.S. domestic group was by far the largest group, and its members felt they deserved the most marketing support. The smaller international groups felt that they needed to grow because they were smaller—and therefore *they* deserved the most support. People in each group complained about not getting what they wanted from this manager, but they were complaining for opposite reasons.

The manager was caught in the middle of internal competition and had not responded to it very well. The culture was one of internal rivalry, in which all groups felt cheated and angry and blamed it on her. The manager felt that there was no way for her to win as a member of the central corporate marketing group. She felt unfairly placed in the role of "bad guy," and she became angry as well. She bought into the common culture of resentment and blame.

As a result of the coaching work, this manager discovered that she was actually quite talented at seeing the overall enterprise picture and at explaining it to others. She learned that rather than joining in the current culture of being angry about an unfair situation, she could simply help the group work out its issues. She could help others see the culture they were creating and recognize that no one could win in the current struggle if they all kept fighting against one another. She could act as a catalyst in creating a new culture. She began to see choices for herself: she could become a "woman of vision." By viewing her current dilemma in the context of the larger picture, she could help lead her enterprise to clarify its marketing strategy up front (so that everyone could stop fighting over resources) and help build a more positive internal environment.

The manager decided to model positive initiative and problem solving. She brought key members together from corporate and field marketing departments to set clear policies about resources that all could agree to. (They had to decide—together as a combined team—how they would divide their resources between domestic and international offices. She set the standard that they could not continue to fight about this issue forever but must create a solution together.) She also helped design a retreat to bring key team members together who needed to work together more collaboratively. This work began a growing commitment to developing shared marketing strategies and collaborative decision making, rather than infighting. The diverse field marketing departments began to see themselves as members of one larger group, with their futures intertwined, not just as separate internal groups competing for resources.

The eventual change in the internal environment grew out of one woman's willingness to confront her own personality and emotions and to

take responsibility for them. As she "stepped outside" the department culture
of blame and tried to understand the enterprise system, she could see the
business issues contributing to the divisive environment and identify the key
levers needed for change. To improve the internal environment, her department had to work on both task and internal environment simultaneously:
members had to develop a shared marketing strategy that clarified resource
allocation, and they had to begin to see themselves as a unified department
with common goals, committed to working as a group of collaborative teams.

When the whole enterprise system is seen clearly, sometimes
the key lever to creating a Dynamic Enterprise lies more in one
component or another. One area can provide the central focus,
the organizing principle that moves the enterprise forward,
although that element alone can never be the only element of the
system to change. Ultimately, all STEP components of the system
must be aligned.

While many of its competitors were focusing on business
process reengineering and structural reorganizations, one technology company we recently worked with focused its attention on
its internal environment as the key lever for business success. The
company's managers believed that redesigning work processes and
restructuring the organization could keep them in the game but
could not give them a competitive advantage. They needed something extra if they were to stay ahead of the competitors constantly
at their heels.

The leaders of the human resources (HR) division of a large technology
company wanted to develop a three-year strategic plan for their human
resource function. For this process, they brought together company managers
and stakeholders from their HR departments from around the globe. They
began the work by establishing an overall enterprisewide view of their company. They described their company as being one of the first to "catch a big
wave." They had "ridden the last wave all the way to the beach." They were
now on the beach, looking out at the waves, wondering whether they would
be bright enough and lucky enough to catch the next big one. HR felt it had a
key responsibility in enabling the company to find that wave and that longer-
term company survival depended on it.

As they examined their external environment, they discovered the pressures of increased need for quality in a time of decreasing costs and increasing technological complexity, along with increasing customer demands for choice—quite common in their technology industry. However, the most pressing influence on their company was the rapid acceleration of product life cycles. They thought the speed with which they could "spot a wave" and get the next product to market was the most critical factor in their company's success. They identified speed as the single most critical determinant in their company's competitive advantage. Given this understanding, a key task for HR within the larger enterprise must be to help create a "culture of speed."

The members of the HR group made the commitment to help build the internal environment of the company around speed as a core driver. They wanted to become known as the company that could produce quickly and "change on a dime." They wanted everyone in the enterprise to feel pride in this ability and excitement about it.

To accomplish this goal, they would have to redesign many of their existing structures, to infuse the concept of speed into all elements of their organization. For example, they needed to have some common global policies, systems, and organization charts so that members could transfer from one working environment to another anywhere in the company and still hit the ground running. They needed to commit to technology platforms that had flexibility built in. They needed to cross-train their people so that employees could be shifted quickly to projects where their skills were most needed. They needed to provide incentives to people at all levels to take the necessary and calculated risks that change would entail, and they needed to ensure that their leadership development programs and promotion opportunities rewarded those who mastered the art of quick change and successful delivery. HR could be the driving force in the enterprise to build an internal environment where people expected and welcomed change.

The members of this group saw HR's role in shaping the company's culture as a serious responsibility. They believed that their success or failure could make or break the company in its current moment of standing on the beach, between waves.

These team members saw that they had to shape the company internal environment, but they knew that they could not do this with culture change efforts alone. They planned to shape the internal environment on all fronts: through communicating the business rationale for a culture of speed; through reshaping job descriptions; through structures, systems, and technology; and through the ways in which they recruited and developed their people. They had to shape the internal environment through interventions in all elements of the enterprise.

Chapter Five

Creating a Shared Vision of the Future Enterprise

Three stonecutters were asked what they were doing.
The first replied: "I am making a living." The second
kept on hammering while he said: "I am doing the best
job of stonecutting in the entire county." The third one
looked up with a visionary gleam in his eyes and said:
"I am building a cathedral."
PETER DRUCKER, *The Practice of Management*

In some enterprises, *vision* is a forbidden word. Many leaders hate the term because they see vision as "soft," "fuzzy," "full of fluff," or one of a class of "feel good" slogans that have no relevance to the operational issues of running a business. We have found that this view predominates when leaders consider vision synonymous with the values inherent in the business. Whereas many leaders are strongly values-oriented and take a stand for the principles that guide the way they operate, others are much more focused on business or organizational details. We often see the latter group of leaders, and team members as well, becoming impatient or irritated with the work of creating a shared vision. They cannot see the return on investment from time and resources spent. What does a vision have to do with running a business? What does vision have to do with becoming a Dynamic Enterprise?

Like *change, vision* is a word that means different things in different enterprises. We have seen vision statements such as "We will be better than the best" that are meant to inspire the workforce to reach for the highest quality possible. However, because there is no specificity—better in what ways? in which areas? to which customers?—people can interpret this to mean whatever they want. Such a "vision" has the potential to confuse and create conflict as much as to inspire. Ultimately, many people become cynical about the vision, and that may be worse than no vision at all.

Other visions focus on the values of the company, in ways that are genuine and give guidance in this area. However, people are often left wanting something more. Vision statements such as "We value our people" or "We will build an environment of trust and respect" do provide clarity about the internal environment but do not tell people what will they *do* in the future. A vision based only on values doesn't tell what the enterprise hopes to accomplish or where it is going and how it plans to get there.

Given the cost pressures typical of the mid-1990s, we have seen many companies try to streamline their change process. They left out the visioning phase in the hope that they could simply "get to work on the change." After all, didn't everyone know what to do? However, farther into the work (sometimes months later), they often discovered the effects of conflicting or unclear objectives that were never clarified up front.

The company described in Chapter Four, in which one division wanted "world-class" while another wanted "world-class within budget," had to go back and clarify its vision before these divisions could work together to build one product. Until then, teams fought for months and valuable staff left the company over the disagreements that arose at every decision point. They paid a high price for skipping the time required to make sure that they were all on the same page before they jumped into the work.

Similarly, one financial services company instituting a large business process redesign found its teams working at cross-purposes nine months into the project because each had created its own set of priorities. The company was redesigning several new business systems while the information systems (IS) department was buying or building new technology to support them. There were eleven redesign teams, each made up of employees from the business functions and from the IS department. Each team assumed that all other teams naturally saw the priorities exactly as it did—but that of course wasn't the case. Some teams designed their systems for highest quality and reliability, while others worked strictly to cut costs. Some teams tried to create the simplest systems they could create in the fastest time frame—to get the new technology up and running as soon as possible. Still other teams consciously took a slower route, working carefully with users to plan and install technology that would see the company farther into the future. Teams working with the various priorities (highest quality, lowest cost, fastest time to implementation, longest life span) came up with very different solutions. Because all the redesigned business processes ultimately had to work together for the same set of users, the emerging set of business systems was becoming a chaotic jumble of mismatched technologies and processes. The lack of a unifying underlying purpose made it impossible for teams to proceed successfully.

People confronting powerful changes in their work can also long for a vision, for reasons far beyond their rational need for coordination and integration. Planning and implementing change can be very difficult, challenging, anxiety-provoking. People may feel insecure about their jobs or the jobs of close friends and colleagues. They may be designing a future that changes familiar (and cherished) roles in significant ways. They want to know they are doing this for a worthwhile reason.

At a university working to streamline its administrative business processes, members from multiple project teams expressed a wish for an "overarching reason" for their work. This need was difficult for them to voice in a time when the focus was on efficiency and cost cutting, but several teams expressed it clearly nonetheless: they wanted a reason for their work, "beyond cutting costs." Members most often voiced this wish in tentative, almost apologetic, quiet voices—as if they were the only ones wanting this (and as if they really shouldn't need it at all). But many did want it. They wanted to know, "Cost cutting for what purpose?"

Team members wanted to find something in their change effort that they could believe in, that they would be excited to spend their work lives producing. If they cut expenses, what did this provide for the university? Where would the money go? Would the money be used to improve the quality of education and research? Would it keep tuition costs lower for the university, enabling students from more diverse backgrounds to attend? Or would it provide funding for new programs or be used to help the university explore the impact of new technologies on future teaching? What kind of university were they creating for the twenty-first century—with lower costs, what could it do? (They had lots of hopes!) Team members wanted to understand and visualize the future university they were helping to create. They longed to place their current work within the larger context of a visionary purpose, a purpose more compelling than saving money for an unknown reason.

A Shared Vision: What Does It Give to an Enterprise?

A vision that adds value to the enterprise gives clarity and coordination to the work in the enterprise and provides inspiration as well. It encourages people to see ideas and possibilities for the future that they might not see otherwise, and it promotes enough alignment among stakeholders to increase the probability that ideas can be effectively implemented.

A powerful vision is an image of what stakeholders want their future enterprise to be. It is more than values or a description of the internal environment. It embodies predictions of what the company will look like in the future, what markets it will pursue, what types of products and services it will have, what size it will be, which values it will represent, and what image and reputation it will have. A vision serves to define what is possible for the enterprise.

A compelling vision gives the people of the enterprise pride. Though based on sound business logic, a vision appeals to people's hearts and spirits and gives them a higher purpose and meaning for the work they do. Powerful visions do not have to be crystal clear—rather, they offer a general framework that people can work toward, adjust to, and use to guide their development. Visions capitalize on the organization's native strengths and unique identity to infuse people's work with meaning and direction.

A good vision

- Creates a sense of alignment, coordination, and clarity.
- Gives a sense of security, stability, and clear destiny (even in a time of turmoil) because it clarifies what the organization is becoming.
- Orients and provides a sense of purpose and meaning.
- Captures people's hearts, minds, and spirits.
- Ennobles, empowers, and excites.
- Creates a sense of belonging and togetherness.

- Engenders courage.
- Inspires proactive work.

Direction and Alignment

Dynamic Enterprises typically have a workforce that shares a clear view of what employees are trying to accomplish, a picture they have created together and one that is congruent with their expectations and experiences at work. Performance is enhanced when people's own values, principles, and personal aspirations are aligned with those of the enterprise and its envisioned future.

Without a shared understanding of where they are headed, people often find themselves working at cross-purposes—out of synchronization with the larger efforts of the organization or with other people or teams in the company. Many of the STEP stories in Chapter Four illustrated that unguided or poorly integrated objectives produce high levels of frustration and burnout and result in an enormous drain of energy from the system. A clear vision allows people to focus productive energy on shared business objectives, with everyone pulling together in the same direction.

Empowerment

Many work groups tell us they dislike the term *empowerment* because it has been overused or used too often to refer to a power transfer that never occurred. Many are cynical about whether real empowerment will occur or think that the term is often trivialized. Yet empowerment is an important concept for the Dynamic Enterprise. If members of a work group understand clearly where their group is headed, they will be much more likely to succeed in taking the individual actions and decisions required to get there.

A useful enterprise vision "empowers" the people of the organization to create their future. It establishes criteria for decision making that allow people to take control of and responsibility for the factors that affect their current and future work situations. The ability to influence decisions generates a sense of self-determination and participation, and people no longer feel like victims helplessly reacting to outside forces.

A strong vision moves people to do the things that must be done to accomplish it. Provided with clear direction, people can function proactively and anticipate the needs of the organization. People filled with a sense of purpose and an understanding of what they are looking for will unleash their innovative spirit and take advantage of opportunities that might otherwise have been missed.

A Sense of Community

When visionaries live out their visions, they do so by building a constituency, or community, around those visions. When they express their visions, they do so to a group of people who understand because they have come to believe in the visions through the acts and deeds of their leaders. Words and actions are congruent. When Martin Luther King Jr. said, "I have a dream," he did so after years of activities that symbolized that dream. And he spoke to a group of people who had joined with him in his ideals through their own acts. They were a community, fulfilling their need for belonging with a sense of meaning and purpose.

Thus the most important purpose of an organization's vision is to bring people together, to enable them to pursue a shared mission energetically, and to join them together in a community with a strong sense of belonging.

Using STEP to Create a Shared, Compelling Vision

The STEP Model described in Chapter Four provides a framework for creating a vision of the future enterprise. The following example shows how the members of one work group from South Africa used STEP to create a powerful vision for their company in a way that both focused their task work and provided meaning that energized their team. They first examined and clarified each STEP component: external environment, task, structure, people, and internal environment. However, when team members reached the people discussion, they realized they had left out vital information in their earlier descriptions. After adding their new insights, they began a second iteration of STEP. Their second round of STEP thinking led them to develop a vision that none of them had expected.

Similar to many large companies, this South African financial services company was facing many new competitive pressures and needed to learn how to respond to them more rapidly. A small group of the top-performing managers came to the United States to learn more about how to implement learning organizations. They had studied Peter Senge's principles of learning organizations and visited with us to study how they might implement these principles, how they could instill skills for rapid learning throughout a large multinational corporation. Although creating a learning organization is primarily an internal organizational improvement, we began by using the STEP tools to gain an understanding of their entire system, to place their specific goal in the context of their larger enterprise picture.

The members of this work group entered with an established vision of their company. Their current vision was to be "the largest company of their type" in the geographic area where they functioned. When team members described this vision, they spoke about it in neutral voices, with little emotion. It was not an energizing vision, and they seemed to care very little about it. They didn't reject it; they just didn't seem overly excited about making it happen. The vision was simply a given, a standard business concept they did not think much about.

As we worked through the STEP Model, we began to look at future STEP configurations to understand where the company needed to go in the future. We worked in an iterative fashion, back and forth between the categories before a more compelling view of the future began to emerge.

First, we began to examine the external environment. Participants explained that many smaller providers were entering their marketplace in southern Africa and were beginning to steal market share from their larger, more traditional company. For years, their company had built its reputation on offering reliable and stable products to their customers. Now newer, smaller companies were offering new products and services, and customers liked the expanded range of choice.

As we sketched future STEP with this group, the picture emerged of an enterprise that would respond more quickly and flexibly to the needs and opportunities in the external environment. Its future task was to expand the levels of service offered for its traditional products while increasing the development of new products. The participants noted new organizational structures and roles that would be required, new skills people would need, and necessary changes in the work culture.

Rapid responsiveness to the changes in the marketplace was clearly critical to this business success. The group members felt strongly that their primary lever for change lay in their people's abilities to learn and adapt more quickly. They wanted to "empower" those who worked closest to the customers to initiate change, to have increased responsibility for decision making and for new product development. One member said that people needed to be willing to take risks, to be strong, to act from "the top of Maslow's hierarchy of needs" (to be self-actualized). These managers wanted their people to have the formal roles, skills, and inner attitude to be responsive to the competitive threats and new opportunities in their changing external environment.

A turning point in the work of this group occurred as we worked on the people and internal environment categories. A few members of the group began to sound hesitant. We explored their reservations, and critical new data emerged. These team members looked at the picture of their emerging future vision and reacted as many groups do when contrasting the future with the current situation (additional examples are given in Chapter Six). Seeing future needs made it clear how distant they *currently* were from the ideal. For a moment, the participants seemed to feel almost hopeless, questioning whether they could stretch so far. Their people were far from acting "empowered" and "self-actualized"—in fact, their people were currently anxious and distracted. Even if they brought back the best tools they could find, they doubted that their people would jump at the challenge of risk taking (empowered or not) needed to create learning organizations.

Rather than ignoring this moment of discomfort, we examined it more closely—to see if it signaled information the group needed to pay attention to. (We always pay close attention to the reasons people think their rationally planned change initiatives are likely to fail—this often provides the richest and most important data.) The dialogue turned to people in the current conditions: Why were their people anxious, and why were they unlikely to take up the challenge to create a learning organization?

Team members realized that their people concerns were linked to essential elements in the external environment that had been left off the map. A successful vision cannot grow out of a partial picture of the conditions faced—all the important data have to be on the map to create a strong and workable vision.

Team members explained that their people were anxious because their country was in the midst of a social revolution. (This work took place before the dismantling of apartheid and the first democratic elections in South Africa, at a time when the ultimate outcome and consequences for South African society were not at all clear.) If the country could accomplish its transformation from white minority rule to black majority rule peacefully, the future for their business would look very different than if revolutionary violence spread throughout the country. Participants realized that their employees could not realistically concentrate on competitive pressures while they were worried about their physical safety, economic well-being, and the future of their country.

As members of one of the largest firms in the country, they began to see how intricately interwoven their business was with the society in which they lived. If their country did well, their business could do well. If their country fell apart, no amount of learning organization or visioning skills could help them. Their immediate external environment was facing critical times in the years ahead. Group members' first reaction was to feel somewhat defeated. Whatever business skills and tools they learned on their journey to America might not be helpful to them at all back home.

At this point, we began to explore a new question: If the external environment was the true critical success factor, the key lever to their business (and personal) success, then what could they do to influence this? At first glance, they thought there was very little they could do—they were a business, not a government or social agency. However, as they examined the possibilities, they realized that given their size and function, they invested a great deal of money in the country and did have a significant effect on their external environment. Also, in their role as managers of a large company, they had considerable political influence as well.

Working through the STEP map helped these managers confront a very fundamental choice they faced. They could ignore elements of the external environment that they had identified as most critical (the sociopolitical developments) and conduct "business as usual," acting as if they were separate from the environment. Or they could acknowledge the enormity of the situation and jump into the external environment in some way to further the development of both their company and their country. Given this choice, they decided to find ways to assist their country in its struggle to transform itself. This decision led them to create a new vision for their company: rather than striving to become one of biggest companies in its field, it would become "the company dedicated to the renewal of South Africa as an African nation."

This new vision carried much more power and meaning for what team members could accomplish through their work. They carried their new vision back home and convinced others in the company to work with them on it. This vision directed their approach to becoming a learning organization: they could define the critical skills they most needed to learn. The vision also infused each STEP component of the future enterprise they would work to create with significant meaning: the very products that they would offer to be successful in the newly emerging environment, the shift from traditional to redesigned organizational structures (as they considered the redesign needed to transition from a "European-style corporation" to an "African corporation"), the diversity of the people working in their company, and ways to address the concerns that all their people had about the uncertainties in the future. They found that once back in South Africa, a vision that acknowledged the crisis in the external environment and gave people a way to contribute in their own way to its resolution assuaged people's anxieties. The future enterprise they envisioned would allow them to help build their country as they built their business.

Four Definitions of Vision

Although it is clear that a shared vision can help people bring their full range of energy and talent into their work and can help them align their individual efforts with the goals of the enterprise, in reality, people rarely agree on what they mean by *vision*. Once an enterprise decides to create a shared vision, people are often confused because the term itself means different things in different settings. When vision is being discussed, and particularly when vision activities are being planned, it is important to know that everyone involved has the same kind of vision in mind.

We have seen the term *vision* used in four ways. We think it is important to determine which definition of vision we are using in our work. If our own definition differs from the definition in use in the enterprise where we are working, we adjust the language so that it works in the prevailing culture. Being clear about our own definitions helps us recognize when to change terms so that they are not confusing to members of an enterprise. We enlist members' help to find the words from the language of their own work culture that best describe the concepts under discussion.

Vision as Values

First, vision often means the values on which the enterprise is based. In this context, vision is part of the internal environment of an enterprise. Companies sometimes refer to their "vision and values statement" and differentiate this from a mission statement or charter, which sets forth the business objectives of the company. Typical visions in this category might include: "We will be a company where all employees have an opportunity to contribute, learn, grow, and advance," "We want our people to feel respect, pride, and a sense of ownership," "We are dedicated to the highest-quality work in everything we do," and "Our people are our strongest asset."

Task Vision

Another common type of vision statement is similar to a mission statement or clarification of the strategic business objective of the enterprise. In STEP terminology, this strategic business vision could be called a *task vision*. Typical task visions include "We will be the predominant distributor of Product XYZ in the western United States" and "We will provide customer-driven health care at affordable cost." This vision tells what the enterprise will do without clarifying how or when it will do it. A good task vision generally clarifies the market or customer to be served, the product or service to be delivered, and often particular features about the product or service or its expected level of quality.

Enterprise Vision

A third type of vision, and one that we frequently use in Enterprise Development, is vision as the ideal whole enterprise of the future, or *future STEP*. This vision includes all the elements of the enterprise system—the task vision plus a bit more information. The full enterprise vision includes the task or key business identity, the way the business will be organized (structure and people), and a description of the ideal internal environment needed to support these, including the values that will drive the enterprise. Visions in this category include "We will support our people to collaborate and innovate to provide the highest-quality XYZ in the marketplace" and "We are all leaders, who can change whatever is needed to deliver the highest-quality XYZ to our customers."

Enterprise Development Vision

Some companies go even further and produce an even more comprehensive vision. An *Enterprise Development vision* (or *change vision*) begins with the basic enterprise vision by clarifying the ideal future enterprise. However, this more inclusive vision adds information about current conditions and the change process planned. This fourth type of vision gives members of an enterprise not just a shared vision about the future they want to create together but also a vision of the change process involved—*how* they will create this enterprise, what will be required, how they will be involved. It could be called the "vision for reaching the enterprise vision."

This fourth type of vision is particularly useful when large groups of people are brought in to help create the vision or in the enrollment process for a new vision. The advantage of the more comprehensive Enterprise Development vision is that it incorporates and responds to questions people tend to ask whenever they are presented with a basic vision. The theory behind this expanded vision goes something like this: as long as you will be asked to give this information anyway, you might as well anticipate the questions ahead of time and be ready with the answers.

Whenever individuals or groups are brought into the visioning process, they see the outline emerging for the desired future enterprise and begin to formulate questions such as these:

- But what about . . . (and they name aspects of the *current* enterprise that are most difficult)?
- How long will it take to get there?
- What resources will we have?
- Who is going to work on this?
- Do (leaders X, Y, and Z) support this?
- How are we going to get (key stakeholders A, B, and C) on board?
- Will we run a pilot first, or do we all start on this now?
- What are our next steps?
- What is my own role in this?

Because these questions seem to be a natural by-product of the visioning process, an effective vision proactively includes them along with the vision description itself. The Enterprise Development map (see Chapter Three) provides prompts for each of these questions by making sure to cover not only the enterprise future but the other elements of Enterprise Development as well: past and current conditions; plans for change; kinds of change that will be required; leaders of the change; stakeholders and how they will be involved; change support that will be provided; and an overview of the phases of implementation.

Receiving information about all areas of inquiry tends to reassure stakeholders not only that the future is being well thought out but also that current conditions are understood, the development process has been sketched out, leaders understand and are committed to the overall change process, basic change support is in place, and there is an initial plan to proceed. People know more about what the vision will mean to them and about what changes to expect ahead.

Levels of Change: How Far Is the Stretch?

When working with groups creating a shared vision, we have discovered that one of the most significant areas of confusion is that group members may be "all over the map" about the degree of change they propose for the future enterprise. Some discuss small changes and quick fixes, while others contemplate multiyear shifts in identity. All of the changes may be important to incorporate into the vision, but the risk is that they may become an unmanageable jumble of unrelated items.

We have found it helpful to distinguish three different levels of change to be built into the vision of the future enterprise: repair, continuous improvement, and transformation or breakthrough (see Figure 5.1). Visions for repair and continuous improvement address incremental changes in the existing enterprise to become an ideal version of what it could be. Repairs are needed when performance falls below expected standards, whereas continuous improvement efforts raise incrementally the standards. A transformation or breakthrough vision, by contrast, typically suggests a radically different definition of what the enterprise could become. This vision embodies discontinuous change— a revolution.

Figure 5.1. The Necessity for Change on Three Levels: Repairs, Continuous Improvement, and Transformation (Breakthrough).

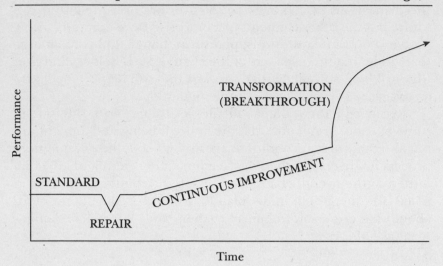

Repairs

Most members in any enterprise have knowledge of critical areas that just don't function as they should. Many people in the enterprise are usually familiar with breakdowns that occur either in work processes or in working relationships but have never been resolved effectively. Sometimes the troubled area is relatively minor, but the breakdown can create big headaches if customers or employees care deeply about that particular area. Whenever an enterprise begins to create a vision, these well-known breakdowns *always* surface as members hope that this time the needed repairs may actually be made.

Although the repair of breakdowns may seem minor compared to the grander scope of continuous improvement or transformation, a larger-scale change effort will rarely succeed if the repairs are not attended to. The breakdowns may be small in scope, but they often stand out in the day-to-day work life of the members of the enterprise. It is almost impossible for members to pursue more fundamental and far-reaching changes with any honesty or credibility when the day-to-day events are glaringly dysfunctional.

For members of an enterprise to move forward toward designing the larger vision of the future enterprise, they need to understand and face their current breakdowns and commit to the difficult and sometimes awkward steps of beginning the needed repairs.

Here are some typical examples of breakdowns that need repair:

- Key relationships that do not work well
- Crises and conflicts
- Lack of clear goals
- Processes that do not work well
- Lack of proper systems and procedures
- Lack of clear roles
- Inadequate technology for the task
- Departmental "turf" battles
- Lack of communication, trust, respect
- Apathy
- A negative culture of anger and blame
- Wrong staff size or skills
- Pain, burnout, and stress
- Leadership or personnel problems
- Loss, confusion, and resentment following a major change that are not being addressed because of fear or lack of skill

Continuous Improvement

Continuous improvement is based not on process breakdowns but on the agreement to institute improvements on an incremental and cross-functional basis. The focal elements of this level of vision are often oriented toward systemic and broad-based improvements in quality or effectiveness and are not isolated in one area, as a specific repair may be. This level of vision includes goals for the intended cumulative effects of numerous incremental improvements to be implemented over a longer period of time. For example, quality enhancement, more effective flow of work processes within and across departments, waste reduction, creation of better systems of collaboration and collective learning throughout the enterprise, or ongoing leadership and management development are all efforts designed to lead to higher performance over time.

Transformation or Breakthrough

Given tumultuous conditions in the external business environment, the changing pressures from many different sources at once, many enterprises are finding that even the best of repairs and continuous improvements will not be enough to meet their goals in the future. For example, imagine that in today's technological environment, a typewriter company trained all its staff in customer service and set up twenty-four-hour toll-free telephone numbers for improved customer service. These improvements would be of little value if customers really wanted a different product altogether, such as a handheld personal communicator that sent e-mail and faxes, available in a range of trendy colors. Something other than improvement in the existing business would then be needed.

As Figure 5.1 indicates, transformational changes go far beyond simply repairing or improving something in the existing system or in the way products and services are delivered. They deliver *breakthrough* performance by transforming elements of the enterprise to operate in entirely new ways. Transformational changes are the most risky of all but can also make the most significant impact, as they often involve reengineering the way core business processes are performed or even redefining the fundamental identity of the products or services to be delivered. Indeed, some breakthrough visions transform the basic identity of the enterprise itself.

If we accept that we are living in times of exponential change, in the midst of a cultural and technological revolution, new products and services must emerge to meet new market demands. If we also accept that one of the key factors in this current external transformation is a shifting of our traditional boundaries, as well as increased interest and capability created by broad-based networks and alliances, the identities of many businesses and industries are likely to be shaped by these external forces. Many products and services must be rethought entirely.

Many industries that have previously been confined within clear boundaries, separate from other industries, businesses, or social institutions, must now reconfigure themselves in new ways. For example, video, telephone, and computer technologies are in the process of merging into one integrated technology, which is in turn merging with the entertainment and education industries to produce products for electronic "edutainment." It is not yet clear what this and other new alliances and associations will look like.

Many industries are experiencing more than a shift in partnering and alliance building: they are reexamining their core identity. Consider health care as an illustrative example. What will health care look like in a superconnected information age, when customers can link through their own computers into larger health care databanks, when health care professionals can connect to expert systems to guide their work, and when video connects specialists to local family practitioners in communities that could not otherwise afford specialists on their own? What happens as customers come to expect the twenty-four-hour access or levels of service that other industries offer? In the years ahead, emerging communication technology will open new possibilities for our definition of health care as an industry.

In their book *Competing for the Future,* Gary Hamel and C. K. Prahalad (1994) describe the creation of a transformational vision exceptionally well. They encourage leaders of an enterprise to go beyond improvement and reengineering of their existing enterprises to develop new products or services that will transform the future of their industries. These authors are quite critical of cost-cutting measures alone, which may help the enterprise survive in the short run but do not guarantee a long-term future, particularly in a highly dynamic environment. An enterprise needs to ask, What new products will generate excitement and create their own market? What is the copy machine, Sony Walkman, or fax machine of the future? They caution that improving existing businesses alone is not enough. They urge leaders to go beyond reengineering and redesign to create the innovative new products and services that will give birth to the new enterprise of the future.

Another kind of breakthrough vision is one that describes the essential business product or service as remaining the same but creates a revolutionized organization for delivering that product or service in entirely new ways. How can the existing products or services be produced or delivered in ways never before imagined? What new systems or new alliances will help this transformation occur successfully?

Integrating All Three Levels of Change into the Vision

All three levels of change are necessary for the success of the future enterprise and must be developed simultaneously, in parallel. Repairs must be faced honestly and included in the vision of the future enterprise. Improvements must also be included because even in an enterprise committed to developing a breakthrough vision, the existing business still does exist. In fact, the existing business most often supports the new breakthrough business in its early development until the new business is developed enough to survive on its own. This existing business must therefore still be continually improved if it is to thrive and be able to support the new business.

The existing transformational external environment of the 1990s, where old walls are coming down and traditional ways of doing business are changing in almost every industry, provides a strong pull for breakthrough or transformation visions. An enterprise that focuses only on repairs, improvements, reengineering, restructuring, and even realigning its existing approaches runs the risk of losing out to competitors who redefine the very boundaries and definitions of their industry.

The work of each of the three levels of change informs what needs to be done in the others. If a deeper level of change or a farther-reaching change is needed, it will become apparent through this work. For example, if repairs are taken seriously, they will generally lead to a desire for a more widespread system of continuous improvement, to prevent further breakdowns before they occur. Likewise, if in-depth continuous improvement work is done, it will usually lead to the recognition of the need for transformation, if this degree of change is realistically needed to deliver the desired improvements. When enterprises study customer needs and wishes and benchmark other companies, transformations that are on the horizon almost always become visible. When there is a willingness to build each of these three levels of change into the vision, enterprises naturally move toward the appropriate levels of visioning and can focus in the areas most essential to the enterprise at the time. Further details and examples of how each level of change relates to different kinds of change strategies are given in Chapter Seven. The following example illustrates how teams can work simultaneously on three levels of change—repairs, continuous improvements, and breakthrough changes—to realize a shared vision.

Recall from Chapter Four the health care facility that adopted the vision of "customer-driven health care." When the managers of this facility began to implement this vision throughout their larger institution, they realized that various departments were working on different levels of change. Some work teams and departments had begun to work on relatively minor changes, while others initiated plans for changes that could redefine the core identity of the enterprise. Teams first began to work at cross-purposes, not understanding why others were looking at the vision differently than they had. Once they could clarify that they needed to work at all three levels and could differentiate who worked in which areas, teams could easily accept each other's work.

Teams working on repairs interpreted customer-driven health care to mean cleaning up the breakdowns they all knew existed, including some that had been identified as many as thirteen years earlier, but had never yet been effectively changed. Minor changes suggested by these team members included proposals for posting clear signs and maps at all entrances and throughout all buildings so that customers would not get lost. Other repairs recommended ways to reduce long waiting times for scheduling appointments.

One breakdown example was so dramatic and well known that it became the symbol for repairs that needed to occur before more transformational visions would have any credibility. The dermatology department was located in a two-story building surrounded by trees. Twice each year, tree trimmers hired by the engineering department came to cut the trees. These trees were so close to the buildings that the trimmers worked directly outside the windows of the dermatology examining rooms. Dermatology patients, who were often undressed, complained of being uncomfortable having workers directly outside the windows of their rooms. Every time this occurred, the nurses called engineering to complain. If they were warned that the tree trimmers were coming, they could easily draw the shades ahead of time and prevent their patients' discomfort. But year after year, the tree trimmers showed up at the windows unannounced.

Although this was a minor matter, it was important in the minds of the workforce. Many people in departments far outside dermatology knew about it, and it stood as a powerful symbol for how "we can never get anything changed around here." *Whenever repairs are needed—especially ones symbolic of the enterprise's ineffectiveness or inability to change—and whenever breakdowns occur that undermine the vision, they must be remedied immediately.* These occurrences are great candidates for "quick wins," opportunities to show that constructive change is indeed taking place. These changes are not usually top priorities in themselves, but they often signal to people throughout the enterprise that larger changes are possible.

While quick-win and fix-it teams began to attend to breakdowns, other teams began to draft new quality standards and processes from a customer perspective. They worked to propose ways to make existing services better, more accessible, or more affordable. Though they had always had a system for gathering patient complaints, they began to gather data proactively in order to understand patient priorities. They also began orienting staff through-out the medical center to think from the perspective of the customers. One clinic realized that it needed expanded hours, and the admitting department recognized that it should be entirely restructured. Under the present admitting system, family members of patients being admitted to the hospital had to go to five different locations to complete the necessary paperwork. The guidelines of customer-driven health care clearly implied that this process should be simpli-fied—patients or family members should be able to complete their paperwork in the areas where patients were being admitted.

Overall, customer-driven repairs and improvements led this facility to examine its current practices throughout the hospital and medical center. Staff everywhere looked for opportunities to restructure the way work was accomplished, to meet the customers' needs rather than only their own.

In contrast to repairs and improvements, the breakthrough changes proposed actually redefined the very services offered by taking advantage of changes in technology and in the changing external environment. The mem-bers of one team suggested a radical redesign of the way they delivered health care services. All of their suggested repairs and improvements had centered around how to help their current facilities optimize health care from the cus-tomer's perspective. But these plans did not question whether their *facility itself* was the best way to deliver health care services from a customer-driven perspective. This was a much larger question.

Group members began to look at a deeper (and longer-term) interpreta-tion of customer-driven health care. They questioned what their current and future customers wanted from health care and then proposed a new "inside out" approach to understanding what they could offer. They encouraged the redesign team to pursue "breakthrough thinking," to break out of the boxes of *what* services constituted health care (because this might be different from the customers' perspective), *where* health care would be offered, *who* would offer it, *when* it would be offered, and *how* it would be offered. They put the customer at the center of a circle (see Figure 5.2) and drew other concentric circles around it. They then asked themselves, "Where is the customer? Is the customer in the facility?" No, the customer is at home. Then they asked, "Who is in the home with the customer?" They settled on family, friends, and a personal computer. Then they began to examine health care from the perspective of what they could offer to the customer, at home, along with family, friends, and computer.

They next asked where the customer went most often outside of home and what health care services might look like there. They continued with various rings of the circle representing their customer's world. On the very outer ring of the circle, representing the area the patient went *least often,* was their facility!

This model of health care opened up team members' thinking about what transformational customer-driven health care might look like. They began to propose programs to help customers link to the medical center through their computers and offering health programs to teenagers in the schools and malls, rather than in the medical center itself.

Figure 5.2. Transformation Vision of Health Care.

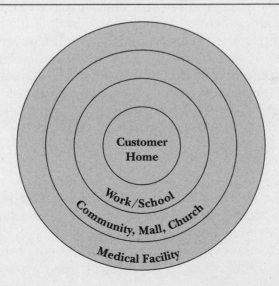

Distinguishing among the three different levels of the central vision (repairs, improvements, and transformation) allowed people to know who was working on which areas. They did not have to debate the merits of posting signs versus offering services in schools or workplaces. They knew that they were dealing with distinctly different kinds of changes, changes that would also require different levels of funding and different time frames to implement. This differentiation also allowed team members to understand their own interests and skills. Some were much better at creating immediate changes that would enable their current business to be the best it could be. Others' interests and talents were more in examining the longer-term challenges facing health care, and they preferred to think about the bigger-picture, futuristic issues inherent in the transformation vision.

Creating a Shared Vision of the Future Enterprise

Designing the vision of the future enterprise requires five basic steps.

1. Clarify the External Environment

The first step is to understand the external environment in which the enterprise must succeed. (Chapter Three gives details about the kinds of data to consider when clarifying the external environment.) What challenges are anticipated in the future environment? A powerful vision is inspirational, but it is always grounded in reality—it is a response to the anticipated external factors that influence success. What do these influences demand? What responses do they pull for? What is the external environment calling for from the enterprise?

2. Clarify the Internal Environment

Before beginning to define the ideal future enterprise, one must understand the values that lie at the heart of the enterprise. These values are part of the internal environment. The interplay or tension between the demands and opportunities of the external environment and the core values held most dear in the internal environment gives rise to the energetic core of the vision of the future enterprise.

The core values of the enterprise put meaningful limits on the wide range of possible choices about what kind of enterprise to become. For example, as we saw earlier, a business that wants to create a "world-class product" will design a different company from one that wants to create a "world-class product *within budget.*" A manufacturing company aimed primarily at maximizing short-term shareholder profit would likely build a very different enterprise from one that makes the same product but is aimed at developing long-term alliances with its suppliers, its employees, and its community. Companies may choose to emphasize delivering the highest quality in their field, achieving a given percentage of market share, or building products in ways that are socially responsible and ecologically sustainable. The choices are innumerable, and each choice implies a different enterprise configuration to meet its objectives. Before designing the enterprise, and sometimes even before designing the products or services that will be delivered, the members of the enterprise must clarify the kind of company they want to establish. They must agree on the values and guiding principles that will underlie the design process for what lies ahead.

These values are at the heart of the enterprise vision. They give meaning to the work that people do. When their own personal values are in line with the values of their enterprise, people can further their own personal development through the work they do, which adds significantly to their levels of motivation, commitment, and productivity.

3. Clarify Future STEP—the Enterprise of the Future

Once the external pressures and the internal values are clear, it is easier to design the enterprise that can best integrate the two. Dorothy Largay, a well-known expert in leadership development, draws two intersecting lines to describe the birth of an enterprise: "Enterprise occurs where the passions of the people intersect the needs of the marketplace."

Given the demands from the external environment and the passionately held values in the internal environment, what should the enterprise look like? Here are some fundamental questions to help formulate future STEP:

- What should the *task* of the business be? What products and services is the market calling for—what do customers or potential customers need—that this enterprise can best provide? What business processes are needed?
- What organization *structure* and *systems* can enable this business to deliver these products and services most effectively? What policies and procedures would best support this business? What information and communication systems are needed? What kinds of incentives would motivate people to build this future enterprise?
- What kinds of *people* are needed to create this future? What skills and talents do they need? How must they work together?
- What kind of internal environment is needed to create this future enterprise?

4. Synthesize and Condense Ideas from Future STEP to Form the Core of the Vision

The ideas in future STEP constitute valuable information, but they run the risk of sounding more like a "to do" list than a vision. Details alone do not make a vision. Once the most essential elements have been described in each area, it is important to stand back, take a look at the whole, and then envision an integrated and larger view of the future enterprise. (This is how the South African company described earlier in this chapter arrived at its vision as "the company dedicated to the renewal of South Africa as an African nation.")

What is the meaning of the whole? Sometimes a poet or an artist emerges from the group who can find the words or symbols that help synthesize the details into an inspirational vision. Sometimes we ask work groups, "If this were a book, what would its title be?" The core of the vision is a richly condensed, nonlinear, non-rational image or description that captures the spirit and potential of the future enterprise.

5. Add Details to Support the Core Vision

The core of the vision may be described in the "vision statement," but ordinarily, a great deal of detail lies behind the statement itself. The core vision statement is often a catchy, inspirational phrase or image that people can easily recall, that symbolizes the future enterprise people are hoping to build together. The larger vision then encapsulates the rest of the thinking and planning about the future enterprise and what it can (or must) become. As described in our discussion of the four definitions of vision, people embarking on a course of complex change need a great deal of information about the future they are heading toward and how they will get there. They need inspiration *and* information.

The Form of the Vision

Every company we have worked with has personalized its vision. There is no set format. Because the vision serves to motivate and guide actions, its form should be one that can best accomplish this in a given enterprise.

Some enterprises write their visions on one page, some write them out in large volumes, some draw them, and some dramatize them through theater or celebrations. Some enterprises refuse to put a vision in writing because they want to keep the process of visioning alive. In a Dynamic Enterprise, the vision is never complete—it evolves as the people and environments around it continue to change.

Who Develops the Vision?

There is also no single or best process for creating a vision and enrolling all stakeholders who need to be involved in implementing it. Many variables are involved, including these:

- How different is the vision for the future from the current enterprise?
- What has to change in the enterprise to reach the vision?
- How large are the obstacles in the way?

- Which leaders are committed and which are not?
- How ready are stakeholders for the change required?
- How large is the enterprise to be changed, and is it in one location or many?
- What funding is available for change?
- What communication channels are (or could be) available?
- Is the change urgent? What is the time frame?
- What are the change skills of key people involved?

It would be appealing to outline a single sequence of steps for vision design and implementation, but in reality, each effort we have seen has worked best when it was customized for the particular vision, the enterprise, and its current leaders and stakeholders. Ultimately, the leaders have to be committed to the vision and have to internalize it, as they play a crucial role bringing the vision to life and making it a reality. (See Chapter Eight for more details on the significant role of leadership commitment during vision implementation.) However, leaders do not have to be the first to see the vision; they only have to be open to evaluate thinking done by visionaries elsewhere in their enterprise.

Where Vision Begins

The creation of a vision can begin at almost any level within the enterprise. We have seen visions begin with a leader or leadership team and cascade down through the organization, begin in the middle and spread outward, or begin on the front lines from a grassroots effort. We worked with one group of middle managers in an oil company for one and a half years before the president of the company called us in, saying he kept seeing intriguing ideas from this group. Members had been "pushing up" their ideas, and he wanted to learn more about what they were doing. He soon joined with this group, made the vision his own, and began leading the change effort to achieve it.

We have also seen visions begin with the efforts of individuals, teams, or hundreds of people. One turnaround leader working in a utility company realized that her division was completely unprepared for the pressures of deregulation. As she examined the division's methods of operating, she found wasteful and inefficient processes as well as people in roles that added little value to the business and who had little interest in change. She realized that she had to move this division, a typical "bureaucratic utility company of the 1950s," into a new role as an "energy services company of the twenty-first century." She needed time to understand for herself the scope of the changes her people would need to make, to see the whole system of the enterprise they would need to build, and to think through her own initial game plan for how to proceed. Then she brought the management team that reported to her into the planning process, and together they explored how to build a new vision with all stakeholders concerned.

Large Group Visioning

Many enterprises choose to develop their vision in large group settings, with all the key stakeholders, to ensure that the "whole system" is represented in the initial planning. Vision meetings may include employees from all functions and business units and from all levels of the organization hierarchy. Key suppliers and customers can be included as well. Large group visioning and planning events—such as Axelrod's Conference Model(Axelrod, 1992), Dannemiller Tyson's Whole-Scale Change (Dannemiller and Jacobs, 1992), Jacobs's Real-Time Strategic Change (Jacobs, 1994), Owen's Open Space Technology (Owen, 1992), and Weisbord and Janoff's Future Search (Weisbord and Janoff, 1995)—attempt to bring the full range of knowledge in the enterprise into the visioning and planning process as quickly as possible.

Large group efforts can accelerate the visioning process by reaching large numbers of people at once. Information from all corners of the enterprise comes into vision creation and goes back out to each area more quickly. The vision doesn't have to move sequentially throughout the enterprise or cascade from one level to another. Large group visioning also accelerates later implementation. Because each key stakeholder group has been represented from the beginning, the future vision and enterprise designs that emerge are much more likely to be understood and accepted.

Participation in the Visioning Process

For a vision to be successful, people must support it and appreciate its meaning for them personally. Results are best achieved through active participation in vision creation. Participation is the most powerful tool we possess for building commitment to the vision. For this reason, we encourage the involvement of as many people as possible in the visioning process, in ways that enable the generation or reinterpretation of the vision at each level or among the various departments or units. A vision not owned is no vision at all.

The visioning *process* is every bit as important as the final product. To manage this process successfully, the leaders of the enterprise must model the envisioned behavior. As it becomes clear that particular values will be important to the enterprise, these attributes should be incorporated into the visioning process itself as early as possible. We have seen too many groups build values into their vision (such as collaboration, teamwork, respect, diversity, flexibility, or quick responsiveness) and then fail to honor them in their own process of vision creation. Stakeholders always notice the discrepancy and become cynical about the vision from its inception. They get the message. "You're telling us how to act, but you're not going to do it yourselves."

Designers of the visioning process must be aware of the ways in which their values influence the activities they design. The values should be put into practice as soon as they are known.

A vision is a beginning. Visions that exist on paper only are worse than no vision at all because people become cynical and disillusioned and are then more likely to distrust any effort at change or improvement. A vision is made to be implemented. The process of Enterprise Development begins with a vision but goes on to deliver the means for actually reaching it. The creation of the vision is followed by design, implementation, and redesign phases as the enterprise works to achieve its vision (we will return to this in Chapter Nine).

Once the vision is developed, and during each of the later phases, it is critical for leaders and change or performance support staff to move beyond talking about the vision and begin living it. Chapters Eight and Nine will describe the crucial roles of leaders and performance support in developing and maintaining focus on the vision, on keeping the vision alive and making sure it becomes reality.

Chapter Six

Understanding the Past, the Present, and the Change Required

A threat that everyone perceives but no one talks about creates more anxiety than a threat that has been clearly identified.
GARY HAMEL AND C. K. PRAHALAD, *"Strategic Intent"*

Vision alone is never enough. One reason why so many people are cynical about the value of building a shared vision is that current conditions are often ignored. Once members of an enterprise have reached shared agreement about the external environment and where the enterprise is going (including needed repairs, improvements, and transformation), they must clarify where they currently are. Building shared agreement about where the enterprise is currently and the process required to move from here to there is just as important as creating a shared vision.

Although the vision may be inspirational and guide people toward the future, a shared understanding of the realistic starting point is equally important for the vision to be implemented. We have frequently run into leadership and project teams where some members looked at the vision they had created and reacted, "No problem! We are almost there already!" At the same time, others on the team felt almost hopelessly distant from achieving the goal. They were not sure they would ever be able to change enough to reach it in time. One work group member compared his team to travelers who together had decided they were going to a lake in Vermont. However, some of them thought they were starting from New York, some from Kansas, and some from Hawaii. Others even thought they were in Singapore and had a very long trip ahead! Every time they tried to decide what needed to be done to begin, they obviously had very different opinions. Such situations underscore that both points of the change process, the desired future and the starting point, must be clearly "nailed down" in order to design the change required.

Figure 6.1 shows how the current and future enterprise are represented in the Enterprise Development framework. This figure also illustrates how a future-driven change effort begins with the vision and then clarifies the current conditions.

The number of times we have seen projects initiated before both points are clearly staked out is very high. Conflict or "fuzzy" agreements on either side of the continuum are likely to show up in implementation difficulties, disrupted change activities, or results that fail to deliver what stakeholders expect.

The following example shows that neglecting to gain shared agreement about current conditions can undermine a proposed change initiative. One particularly risky aspect of this effect is that difficulties inherent in the change process since the beginning may not show up until the implementation phase.

This example also shows that building shared agreements about the current conditions is essential to understanding the realistic starting point. When different groups see the starting point at

Figure 6.1. The Move from Current Conditions to Future Vision.

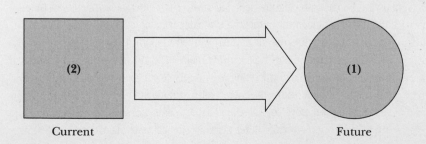

Current   Future

different places, more can often be learned by all about the real current conditions. When the starting point is not clearly agreed to, it is often a sign that valuable information has been missed, that neither side has an accurate view of the current conditions, and that the selected change process is based on incomplete or inaccurate data about what is most needed.

A division of a manufacturing firm was working to institute internal "service contracts," written agreements detailing the services that departments would provide to each other. This was a large-scale intervention designed to improve "internal customer service," and all departments in the division were required to complete the contracts with "neighboring" departments (departments that supplied resources or services to them and to whom they supplied resources or services).

The senior leadership team that launched this initiative expected each department to go to neighboring departments and research those departments' priorities. They would then negotiate the services the first department would provide and document their agreements in a written contract.

However, many groups resisted formalizing written agreements. Some departments simply refused—and complained bitterly about the requirement. Other groups undermined the process by simply calling departments in other locations to ask what they had written in *their* agreements (rather than going to their internal customers to negotiate actual needs as they were expected to). When asked, all departments agreed wholeheartedly with the company vision, and all agreed that customer service—both internal and external—was an important ingredient for their future enterprise. They simply didn't agree on the *current* conditions. Many didn't see internal customer service as a problem, so they couldn't buy into the proposed solution.

In this division, almost half of the departments claimed that their customers had "always been happy," that "the system had worked for years, so why mess with it?" They saw the written contracts as cold and mechanical, a useless bureaucratic requirement. Meanwhile, the other departments saw the situation quite differently. In their view, the departments supporting them were letting them down, and they desperately wanted supporting departments to work differently with them. They *wanted* their supporting departments to ask them what they needed. Completing written service contracts together would provide just the opportunity they were waiting for to begin these discussions.

Once it was discovered that several departments had sidestepped the service contract intervention, it was necessary to backtrack. The idea of written contracts was abandoned, and a performance support team was put in place to make sure that the needed change process itself wasn't abandoned. Leaders were still committed to improving internal customer service—but they recognized the need for a new approach to this change.

The leaders and new performance support team in the division worked with department managers to clarify both the vision and the starting point and to devise a new solution that all managers could support. As it turned out, the problem was soon recognized to be larger than first defined, and the intervention required was more than simply completing service contracts with one or more neighboring departments.

Managers began to realize that they currently did not understand the overall flow of their work, from resourcing materials to providing the end product to external customers. No one understood the whole process in a way that allowed them to see where their own department's work fit in. They not only had to learn what the neighboring departments needed, but they actually had to understand the whole flow of work in which they took part.

Managers began to develop an entirely different perspective on collaboration and internal customer service and why it was needed. They began to understand that they had failed each other in the past because no one had understood the overall picture. As they came to agree on their vision, what it truly required of them, and where they were actually starting, they could more readily agree on the solution. They designed cross-functional "process teams" and committed to collaborate in more informal communications on an as-needed basis. Although these managers never did complete written service contracts for their departments, they took the actions the agreements were meant to encourage: they developed a cross-functional understanding of their product and service lines and began to work collaboratively across department boundaries to meet the priority needs of customers.

Vision and Current Conditions: An Iterative Process

The processes of defining the future and the current enterprise are often linked. The example of the South African corporation described in Chapter Five illustrates that the process is often iterative, moving back and forth between recognizing what is required for the future and what exists at present. Clarity about what is needed in the future often triggers insights into what is required of the current enterprise, just as focus on the present often adds new levels of insight for the vision. It was only when company

leaders recognized how far their people were from feeling as decisive and empowered as the vision required them to be that they
could reflect on their current conditions. Their most powerful
insights came when they could articulate the toughest challenges
in the current conditions and reworked this insight into a new
vision for the company.

Similarly, the people of the facilities development division
(described in Chapter Four) had to understand more specifically
what they needed to build for their parent company, leading them
to recognize that they were currently able to produce only a fraction
of what was needed. They had to produce a vision and figure out
that it was impossible for them to reach it, given their current conditions. They "couldn't get there from here." This disturbing realization fueled their resolve to restructure their division completely.

Engulfed by Current Realities

We have noticed an interesting phenomenon: when leaders or
other members of an enterprise begin to describe the future of the
enterprise, nine times out of ten, people will react by raising issues
related to current conditions. Once a strong vision has been developed that sounds positive or inspiring, this optimistic view of future
potential triggers its polar opposite—pessimism based on current
realities. One client remarked that whenever he described his view
of what the enterprise could become, people "took his golden and
shiny vision and immediately covered it with mud, slime, and
garbage."

This reaction actually does make sense. When people first hear
the vision for the future enterprise, they feel hopeful and excited—
for about twenty-five seconds—and then they compare this vision
to current reality. They typically react with extremely clear statements about the current condition of the enterprise, particularly
about its current state of breakdown and disarray.

When anticipated, this phase is actually important and helpful
because people are often much more insightful about the current
enterprise during the visioning process than when they are asked
to describe the current state directly. While involved in visioning,
people bring up colorful stories about current breakdowns, qual-

ity problems, inadequacies in the existing structure, and shortfalls in the management system—all of which help clarify the current condition of the enterprise. If the people working on a vision or a change effort expect this phenomenon, leaders and other members of the enterprise can be coached to act nondefensively and use this time to capture rich and valuable information about current conditions.

Clarifying the current enterprise in a systematic way is very important at this stage, for several reasons: once people have moved past their optimism about the vision and are in the phase of complaining about the present, it is important to listen to their complaints, to take the feedback seriously, and to let people know that their input is not being minimized. They then begin to understand that their views of the current situation are being incorporated into the picture of the future enterprise. In our experience, allowing this process to take place reassures participants and helps build credibility for the development ahead. People can place their concerns on the Enterprise Development map, in the categories for current or past STEP, and can see that their input is being captured. They can see that it forms a crucial component of the change process ahead by marking the starting point. Their input is recognized, validated, and indispensable. Knowing that their issues have been attended to and will be incorporated in the vision process allows people at least temporarily to let go of their current complaints. Placing their complaints within the framework of current STEP can free them up to continue with the process of envisioning the future.

A professional services firm was working on developing a new vision to overcome business difficulties and a negative culture that had developed during a transitional time in the company. The company was experiencing declining profits for the first time in its history, and the leaders felt they needed to initiate a significant change process. Morale in the company was terrible—everyone blamed everyone else for lost clients and projects. Leaders recognized that their enterprise needed substantial repairs, process improvements, and even transformations in some areas. They ultimately wanted their people to improve the quality of the existing products, cut costs, and participate in the creation of the next generation of products and services. They knew they needed to dismantle the rigid bureaucratic organizational structure that had succeeded for so long, moving it toward a more open, flexible, and empowered organization. They also wanted to turn around the negative culture and low morale.

The leaders chose three performance support team members to help them with their change process (performance support is discussed further in Chapter Eight). This initial change team sought to enlist others in the visioning process, to have key members from all stakeholder groups involved in each step of vision creation. One of the steps in the process was to call a meeting with interested mid-level managers to see who would like to volunteer for the vision team. With much excitement and optimism, performance support team members began to present a description of the process that lay ahead. They thought this process would lead the company toward solutions it desperately needed and were looking for volunteers to join in the effort.

Their enthusiasm, however, was greeted with great hostility. The middle managers reacted to this news the same way they had reacted to everything else recently—with anger and resentment. They did not trust their top administrators and did not believe that management was serious about wanting to change anything at all. They considered the planned change effort as just a show, to make it look *as if* the leaders were taking action.

Performance support team members instinctively knew that they had to listen to these managers. They had to be willing to give up their initial agenda for the meeting and admit that the managers were not yet ready to help with the visioning process. They listened to managers' issues and began to record them on chart pads, helping managers frame their issues as legitimate business and organizational concerns. By the end of the meeting, all the walls were covered with large sheets of paper that listed managers' complaints against the administrators. One member remarked, "It was a flood!"

The performance support team concluded the meeting by thanking the managers for their help. One member later described how he had been tempted to rebuke this group for whining and complaining when presented with a chance for things to get better. However, he soon recognized that the reaction he was witnessing was a crucial and unavoidable element of Enterprise Development work. Though none of the managers had explicitly volunteered to participate in the change process, by venting their frustrations they had all actually contributed to its first step. The performance support team saw the managers' complaints as realistic feedback about the current state of the enterprise and knew how to use it.

The performance support team placed managers' concerns on a large wall map, using STEP to show how each issue related to the external environment, task, structure, people, or internal environment (as described in Chapter Four). The managers had in fact identified vital, important issues. Performance support members promised the managers they would deliver a process to "work the chart pads" and in fact did just that. They began a series of half-day meetings to bring the senior leaders together with this group of middle managers to work the identified issues. Between sixty and ninety members generally attended these meetings, and they continued until the issues had been substantially resolved, one by one.

The meetings between the managers and top administrators were not the "vision meetings" the performance support team or leaders had first designed. However, performance support members in this example were willing to meet the stakeholders where they were and do what was necessary to enable that group to work toward a new vision. In the process, they gathered very rich and valuable information that became an essential part of their development process.

"Double Vision"

The natural human tendency to recall the negative also acts as a safeguard. There are times when the current crisis in a business is so serious that it is not the right time to look only at the future possibilities. If the immediate crisis is not taken care of, there may be no future to plan. Conversely, looking toward the future often helps solve the current crisis. The research and development department described in Chapter Two is a clear example of a time when an enterprise has to pay attention to the current crisis. As members of that department began to imagine their future, they realized that their current funding sources were likely to disappear. They could not spend time envisioning a positive future without facing the crisis that they might not have a future as a department at all. To secure new funding, they would have to convince their parent organization that they had a strong and viable future. They needed "double vision," to attend to the current crisis while creating the potential for a successful future. They had to build shared agreement about the future and current enterprise concurrently.

The need for double vision, to see both the future and the current starting point in the same picture, is often essential to understanding what is needed to reach the vision. The following example illustrates how the view of the current conditions provides the foundation for realistic planning.

The human resource department of a large government institution was examining what the HR function should look like to support extensive change initiatives going on in the larger institution. Managers designed a function in which line HR staff would act as strategic business partners to the business units they each served and would offer skills to support the extensive changes occurring within each business unit. They knew that this was what their business unit customers needed from them, and from benchmark studies they knew that many other HR departments were beginning to take on this new role as well.

However, when they looked at how to provide this type of service, they realized that it was quite a design challenge to get there from where they were. They were currently regarded as the "change police." One HR director said that the managers in her unit would probably pay her to stay away when they were working on change. They saw HR as change inhibitors, as people who "told you why the change you wanted was illegal or impossible." For the HR staff, acknowledging their current "terrible reputation" was, paradoxically, a relief. They all agreed it was accurate, and having it out in the open allowed them to consider what it would genuinely take to change it. Proposing to be a strategic business partner to a group that saw them as traffic cops "just waiting to write up a moving violation" was not a scenario likely to succeed. Studying the full picture, from starting point to vision, could allow them to plan realistically what it would take to succeed.

An Honest and Unflinching View of the Current Conditions

Just as it is helpful for the vision to be moving and inspiring, to have "pull" to it, it is essential that the understanding about the current conditions be honest and unflinching. The view of current reality must capture the needed repairs and breakdowns that are common knowledge and show how these will be addressed. Seeing the worst breakdowns shown openly on the map of changes to be made often energizes a group and provides a "push" for moving ahead.

The managers in the professional services group who covered the walls with complaints about current functioning had a great investment in seeing all the breakdowns and difficulties acknowledged. Owning up to these issues helped mobilize their energy as part of the change process. We find that "resistance" often arises when the real issues have not all been put on the table. Resistance stems from concerns related to unacknowledged issues. Although every single detail can never be acknowledged and dealt with (and doesn't need to be), there are most often three or four key issues that concern a large number of stakeholders. When the most critical, primary concerns about current conditions are being addressed, "push"—motivation and effort to help move the enterprise beyond current functioning—is being mobilized.

> One medical supplies company had worked on a vision for several months. However, when people left the vision meetings, nothing happened. Managers were not taking the actions they had committed to in the meetings to enact the vision. Though this can occur for any number of reasons (given that all six competencies, not just vision, are needed in the Dynamic Enterprise), in this case a key obstacle turned out to be that managers did not have faith that their current leader could implement the vision.
>
> For the past several years, there had been many conflicts between this leader and members of the board, as well as with other senior managers in the firm. Many managers and staff had found that he did not support them in changes needed in the past year, did not follow through on commitments he made, and did not take the strategic actions required to move the company forward. He tended to have a few special working relationships with his closest colleagues but rarely created effective working teams. His leadership style would often pit people against each other, at a time when the new vision required a high level of alliance building both inside and outside the company. When comparing the future vision with the behaviors and actions of the current leader, key managers and staff did not have confidence that anything would change.
>
> Ultimately, for this vision to move forward, the board of directors had to face the discrepancy between the requirements for the new vision and the current leader's style and behavior.

As current conditions are clarified, the STEP Model described in Chapter Four can be a useful tool to make sure all the elements of the system have been added to the picture. Since many groups will focus on one area and exclude others, STEP can serve as a template to ensure that all key areas are included in the analysis. The larger framework of the Enterprise Development model then provides a way to see the vision, or future STEP, and current STEP all on the same page, as shown in Figure 6.2.

Figure 6.2. Current and Future STEP.

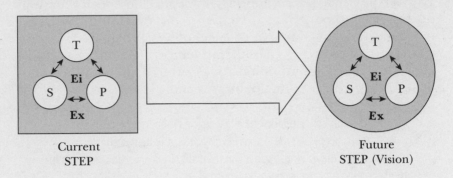

Current
STEP

Future
STEP (Vision)

Adding the Past to the Map

There are times when work groups may need to look at their past as well as their current situation, to be able to move toward the future. Often, given the urgency for change, not all groups take the time to examine their past, and in many cases their work seems to progress quite well. However, other groups find that they can actually move faster by adding the past into the picture. Acknowledging where they have come from enables some to let go of the past and be more open to change. Others find that examining the past reveals how the group has already changed and faced challenges before and can inspire more confidence to move forward. Finally, it can be a way to bring a diverse group together, to understand how they arrived at their present starting point.

Acknowledging the past often furthers people's ability to leave the past behind. William Bridges, who teaches and writes extensively about managing transition, is a strong advocate of the importance of managing "endings" for helping people deal with significant transitions. Bridges (1981) differentiates the concepts of change and transition. He defines change as the actual events that occur and transition as people's emotional response to the events. For example, a reorganization plan—a change—may begin on July 1, but people's responses—the transition—may begin months before and continue for months afterward. Bridges believes that transition "begins with the endings." Moving forward often means that people must leave behind very significant parts of their lives: old roles, old friends, old identities. They may need to mourn these very real losses before they are ready to look ahead.

We have sometimes seen examples of work groups that needed to take the time to let go of the past. Particularly in a time when some industries are moving from a very stable history to an era of change and flexibility, team members who have worked together for years in the same department need to be able to review their history together, to anchor it in their memories, to treasure it, to learn from it. Having gone through this exercise, many people become willing to move on to a new form of enterprise that may be quite unlike the community they had built and lived in for years.

> In one warehouse operation, many workers with twenty or more years of experience in the same jobs were forced to face the fact that their old roles were disappearing as their company moved to just-in-time delivery processes. Their new roles would be entirely different. Many workers resisted the new approach, as it seemed to imply that their old way was wrong. The department manager looked back in time with employees so they could understand that their old ways of working had been entirely appropriate for that time, and he helped the team celebrate their past success. Change did not mean that they had been wrong, and it did not mean that they had to leave fond memories behind. However, the world was changing around them, and they had to change along with it. Taking the time for understanding and letting go of the past helped prevent later problems during implementation, as employees were more open to understanding why and how the new business environment required them to change.

An important part of the past that is helpful for a Dynamic Enterprise to understand is its past ability to respond to change. For example, if past efforts to respond to the environment with change initiatives have been unsuccessful, these failures must be examined before launching new initiatives. It is tempting for new leaders (or new consultants) to think that whatever killed past change efforts could never happen to them, but it is often wise to make sure. It is important to understand the patterns to the failures and to use this knowledge in the planning process. What went wrong before, and what must be different this time?

Understanding and acknowledging past failures is also important for gaining authorization to initiate changes and for enrolling key stakeholders. If past efforts have failed, people *ought* to be concerned about investing time and resources again. They need to have clear information about the difference. In Chapter Four, we mentioned a manufacturing company that had initiated a $60 million change effort to redesign major business processes and install new technology to support them. The company had a history of *four* major failures at large-scale change in the past. Key stakeholder groups questioned, very reasonably, why the project sponsors of this effort thought this time would be any different from past efforts.

To reassure their skeptical stakeholders, leaders and performance support team members began to study the failed efforts from the past, to see where each one faltered, and to plan how this effort would be different. For this company, it was very important to make the past a visible part of the Enterprise Development change map. Seeing that their change leaders were aware of the past and were learning from it gave stakeholders more confidence that they could indeed move from the current conditions to the envisioned future.

Sometimes looking at the past helps groups face new changes because they realize that they have been successful at change before. One team realized that it had had several new leaders, new reporting relationships, new projects, new evaluation systems, and many new team members. Team members realized that over the course of seven years, they had changed almost everything about the way they worked. Their new vision would require them to change many of these areas again, simultaneously. It helped them recognize that they were not newcomers to change, they were "seasoned pros." Adding the past to their Enterprise Development map helped them feel more confident and ready for change. They described their internal environment as "change-competent."

Clarifying the Change Required

Once members of the enterprise have a shared view of the pressures from the external environment, a vision of the kind of enter-

Figure 6.3. Change Required.

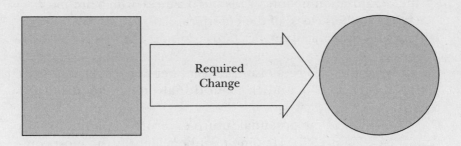

prise they want to create together, and a clear view of their current and past conditions, they are ready to fill in the specifics for "getting from here to there." They can compare the future needs to the current capabilities and clearly define the change required (see Figure 6.3).

We have found several practices to be useful in helping members of the enterprise "fill in the arrow" by identifying the most important changes to move their enterprise from where it is to its desired future. The STEP Model presented in Chapter Four adds further detail to clarifying the most strategic "pushes" from the current conditions and "pulls" toward the future.

Pushes and Pulls

True enterprise change will make people's day-to-day work lives quite different. Many will have mixed feelings about whether they want to change. Even for those who are excited about the future that lies ahead, the sense of loss is still real. It is thus important to give people compelling ways to capture and focus their ideas about *why* they want to change.

Identifying the "pushes" helps members of the enterprise see the compelling factors that demand change (see Figure 6.4). Once current conditions have been clarified, questions such as the following may be asked:

- What issues demand resolution?
- What issues are too painful to leave as they are?
- Of the range of breakdowns identified or of the areas where the organization no longer fits the business, which are most crucial to the success of the enterprise?
- What motivates action?

Identifying the concrete examples that beg for resolution helps generate the clarity and the emotional energy required for change.

The vision of the potential future enterprise also has its own "pull" (see Figure 6.5). Helping members identify the most compelling issues in the vision that are essential for success can also help them focus and channel their energy for change:

- What elements of the vision are most exciting to the people in the enterprise?
- Which are most essential to future success?
- Which offer people the most in their own professional or personal development?
- Do any elements of the vision offer a particularly powerful, positive challenge for which this group of people is uniquely qualified?

At this stage, a philosopher, an artist, or a poet may emerge in the group who creates a particularly moving image of what the

Figure 6.4. "Push" from Current Conditions.

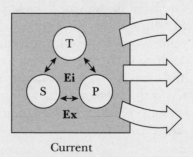

Current

Figure 6.5. "Pull" Toward the Future.

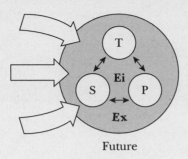

Future

future can become. This kind of image can help create the more visceral, personal human response that is needed to pull people into new actions and practices.

Key Strategic Thrusts

Once members of the enterprise have freely identified the pushes and pulls most important to them, in whichever categories those emerge, it is then helpful to check them against the STEP categories. It can be instructive to see which categories are most important to the people in any particular group. For example, did the group focus more on people issues, on redefining the business, on

Figure 6.6. Strategic Push.

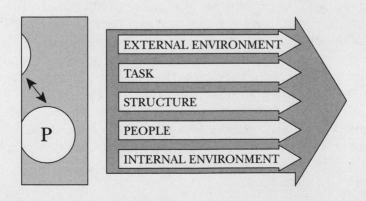

Figure 6.7. Strategic Pull.

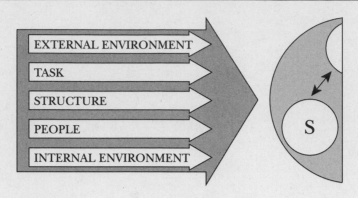

restructuring the existing systems or policies, or on other elements? However, because the development path must include the view of the whole enterprise system, it is important to go back to the list of pushes and pulls and fill in any missing categories in the system of task, structure, people, and internal and external environments.

As many examples in Chapter Four illustrated, an intervention centered on one STEP component or another needs to consider the changes required in all components of the enterprise system. Change is more likely to be successful when it includes coordinated change throughout the system. Figures 6.6 and 6.7 show a model for how all STEP components of the pushes and pulls can be represented in the Enterprise Development map.

When the task of filling in all the categories of STEP is undertaken *before* the pushes and pulls have been identified, the exercise tends to be too linear and analytical. It produces good ideas but often does not generate the emotional energy needed for change. Once the members of a group have been able to express their reasons for change in words and imagery they find moving, they are generally more open to go back to fill in the details that may have been left out initially. Ultimately, the development path must include the way in which each element of the enterprise system will need to change in order to reach the vision (see Figure 6.8).

Figure 6.8. Strategic Thrusts on the Enterprise Development Map.

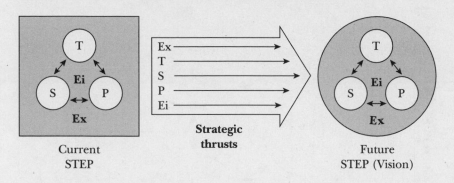

Current
STEP

Strategic thrusts

Future
STEP (Vision)

The following example shows how the high-tech firm described in Chapter Four might draw its Enterprise Development map showing the five *strategic thrusts* for the change required (one for each of the STEP components of the enterprise system; see Figure 6.8). This company's marketplace had begun to shift dramatically over the past year. Although the company had succeeded in the past based on its superior technology, its customers were beginning to request "business solutions," customized to their own industry. The products they would need to see in the future would be sold at higher levels in the company, to meet business needs company-wide. Furthermore, because its product alone could not provide a full business solution, the company would need to partner with multiple other companies to offer this alternative.

The sample Enterprise Development map in Figure 6.9, showing current STEP, future STEP, and the relevant strategic thrusts for this company, is intended to condense and highlight the most essential changes identified for each STEP category. Although examining the STEP maps of other teams or work groups is seldom very exciting for people outside the group, the experience can be quite dramatic and productive for group insiders. Individuals who have never seen such a broad range of information about their organization integrated into one picture can find it inspiring to see how everything fits together and to see what is required for the future.

Figure 6.9. Sample Map: Strategic Thrusts Required to Move from Current STEP to Future STEP.

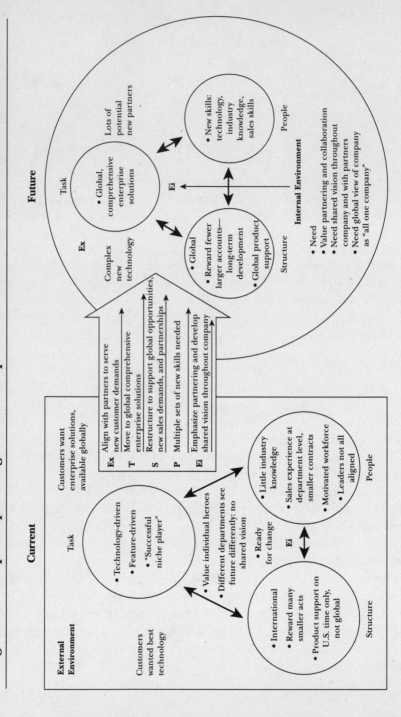

Chapter Seven

Understanding the Nature of Change
Business and Organizational Life Cycles

*We are not entering a "new" world. Rather, we are
entering a "new" world, an "old" world, and a world
still in transition. These worlds live side by side in
our hybrid society.*
WILLIAM BERGQUIST, *The Postmodern Organization:
Mastering the Art of Irreversible Change*

Once the members of the enterprise have effectively defined where
they are going, where they have been, and where they are currently, the obvious next step is to analyze the gap between these
states to learn what the enterprise needs to do to get from the present to the future. Many groups begin this task immediately and
move directly into implementing the strategies they identify as
described in Chapter Six. However, before beginning implementation, it can be helpful first to understand two developmental
models that provide more in-depth information about the changes
ahead. These developmental models—of business and organizational life cycles—help define the types of change likely to be
encountered in the transformation ahead. The models help cate-
gorize various types of gaps and are based on the assumption that
not all change is the same. Understanding the type of gap the
enterprise is trying to bridge is essential before jumping in to do
the work.

Large systems are not easy to change. They have a certain inertia, as well as a tendency to move in particular directions more easily than others. Businesses and organizations change and evolve naturally all the time as they move through predictable phases of growth and maturation. Their development (whether managed or not) is guided by basic principles that are not difficult to comprehend. If we understand the underlying forces that guide development and learn to predict them, we can use this knowledge to clarify what change is most needed or is most likely to work at a given time. We can also use this knowledge to join the natural developmental dynamics and strengthen a planned change effort rather than oppose the forces by swimming upstream. (And if we choose to swim upstream anyway, we might as well be aware of what kind of stream it is and what we are likely to encounter.) This approach is reminiscent of the martial art of aikido, in which the practitioner joins and then shapes the momentum of an oncoming force to shift it into a new direction.

Business Life Cycles

The graphic image used to illustrate business life cycles has proved to be one of the quickest and most powerful tools for Enterprise Development thinking. A simple but important life cycle assessment can help work groups understand, often very quickly, what issues are most critical to their particular venture. It focuses them on the most vital areas and helps prioritize where to place their valuable time and resources. Rather than looking at how best to accomplish change, the business life cycle model focuses attention on determining the *right* change.

Many business leaders, academics, and management consultants are now writing about and working with some version of business life cycle curves, including Davis and Davidson in their book *2020 Vision* (1991); Imparato and Harari in *Jumping the Curve* (1994); Nadler, Shaw, Walton, and Associates in *Discontinuous Change* (1995); Moore in *Crossing the Chasm* (1991) and *Inside the Tornado* (1995); Morrison in *The Second Curve* (1996); and even Intel CEO Andy Grove in *Only the Paranoid Survive* (1996). This upsurge of interest in business life cycles makes sense at a time when many transformational forces are affecting businesses so strongly and so often. Many enterprises suddenly face tremendous challenges related to the life cycle of their business and need to make sense of the changes they face.

The S-Curves

The business life cycle is typically represented by an S-shaped curve (see Figure 7.1). This simple curve sums up a natural phenomenon and is a useful way to illustrate the dynamics of business development: A business begins with slow or even negative growth in its start-up phase, moves into a phase of accelerated growth if the business succeeds, then levels off to slow growth as the business matures, reaches a plateau of no growth, and finally moves into decline and potential demise.

Discontinuous Development

As discussed in Chapter Five, an enterprise may experience times in its life cycle when it is revolutionized by forces in the external environment. These forces apparently lie outside the range of natural life cycle developments of the existing enterprise—the product did not saturate its marketplace, but the market moved on to a new product. Sometimes an entire industry confronts new ways of doing business that makes decline of the existing enterprises practically inevitable. Consider the period in history when blacksmiths, masters at making horseshoes, saw the first automobiles roll around the town square. How many blacksmiths in those days could foresee how these strange horseless carriages would revolutionize their industry and create a whole new way of life?

Discontinuous change in the external environment often forces a choice in the enterprise between accepting the impending

Figure 7.1. The Business Life Cycle.

decline or making a strategic leap to an entirely new way of doing business (see Figure 7.2). A small number of blacksmiths stayed in the traditional business (as horses continued to exist and still needed shoes), many went out of business, and others became axle makers for the new automobile industry, transforming their knowledge and skills to fit the emerging new technology.

A Time of Dual Strategies

Notice that the two curves in Figure 7.2 overlap. It is important to recognize that in a transformational time, two sets of enterprise strategies may coexist, and enterprises may be at different phases of development at the same time. The older, traditional business and the newer, transformational business coexist. They typically need different organizational structures, different people, and entirely different internal environments.

Working the Curves

Business life cycle analysis can be quick and simple to use (particularly for groups that have already worked out current and future STEP as described in Chapters Three, Four, and Five). We have found that drawing the two overlapping S-curves on a chart pad and asking people to place their business on the curves is as effective as more extensive assessments. People in work groups know what they are facing. They often simply need a forum and a structured question to frame their ideas. Profound and sometimes dis-

Figure 7.2. Overlapping Business Life Cycles.

turbing insights have come from these discussions, often in as little as one hour. (Taking the actions indicated can of course take much longer!)

The simple S-curves graph generally lets members of a group perform an impromptu business analysis to understand the conditions their business is facing. (The "business" for smaller work groups can be department goals, project deliverables, a function's key tasks, or a network's core objectives.) The members of each group can, for example, quickly and intuitively assess whether they are working in a start-up business that needs to move to accelerated growth or in a phase of rapid growth that is likely to continue. Is their business growing but beginning to show signs of slowing growth ahead? Have they already hit the plateau? Are they moving into decline?

Making the Leap

Because so many enterprises today are simultaneously facing fundamental changes in their existing industries while also needing to formulate new kinds of businesses, many are at the point of "making the leap between the curves." They need to create a future in which their business might look very different from the way it does today. The view of the two curves often helps businesses negotiate the challenges of transformation.

> The employees in the information systems department of a large company described their department as being in a "free fall." They placed themselves "in the white space between the two curves." They had already left behind their old way of designing information systems for the teams and departments they supported but had not yet defined their new way of working. They had jumped, without knowing where they would land. Most of their work no longer involved designing mainframe solutions for their clients as it had in the past; it had shifted to providing newer, client-server technology customized for each client work group. As they made this transition, many department teams were working with their internal customers to design information systems that would be incompatible with other systems they knew their colleagues were designing. Each new customer request swayed members of the department to act in a new direction. They had no clear parameters of what they would provide.

The S-curves helped these department employees articulate what they had vaguely been aware of before but had never seen completely clearly: they were essentially in a new business, and they desperately needed a clear, shared description of how this business would work. They needed to agree on what they would offer to customer groups and what they wouldn't, as well as what they would design in-house and what they would outsource. They also needed a specific guiding information architecture that would ensure that they were all designing systems in sync with each other. These agreements would in turn lead to new roles for most of them and ultimately to massive changes in the way they were organized to support this new emerging business (in their organization structure, in skills needed, in the number of people needed, and in the department culture needed to make the transformation succeed).

In a different organization, the members of a management team in a professional services company placed themselves at the beginning of the second curve and then drew several more curves out to the right, representing more leaps ahead in the future. They felt that their work should always be on the cutting edge. They would jump from the beginning of one curve to the beginning of another as soon as a new one appeared on the horizon. They would never "ride the curve all the way up into maturity." They would be the pioneers in their field.

For the members of this group, the life cycle S-curves helped them define their vision. The view that they were pioneers meant that they needed to build an organization that had the capability to find and evaluate new curves and to leap to them quickly. These managers would redefine the way they did business every two to three years, and their people had to be ready for the continual shifts.

Managing the Leap

Transformation is tough. Though it is easy to draw the two curves on paper, living through the transformational time on the job is often a dramatic experience that provokes a great deal of emotion. Laszlo Gyorffy, one of our colleagues who works with many groups facing this magnitude of change, drew the diagram in Figure 7.3 to illustrate the experience.

Overlapping Curves

Accommodating various businesses at different phases of development within one enterprise can be a struggle unless these busi-

Figure 7.3. Living Through Transformation.

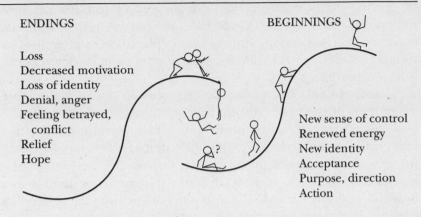

ENDINGS

Loss
Decreased motivation
Loss of identity
Denial, anger
Feeling betrayed,
    conflict
Relief
Hope

BEGINNINGS

New sense of control
Renewed energy
New identity
Acceptance
Purpose, direction
Action

nesses acknowledge that work related to both curves are needed during the transformational time. "Old-timers" often distrust and resent the "newcomers," working on "second curve" activities. They frequently view those working on the more entrepreneurial second curve as unreliable, flighty, not paying their way while using the dwindling resources of the old business and subjecting the enterprise to great risks. The newcomers, for their part, frequently devalue the old-timers, claiming that they are a "dying breed living in the past," the "culture guard" holding the enterprise back from its future. In reality, in a transformational time, both curves of the business life cycle must operate simultaneously.

The graphic image of the overlapping curves can be helpful to both old-timers and newcomers to resolve this transformational struggle. Newcomers must build the platform for the future enterprise before anyone can leap. Because their work is new and untried, they will need to take more risks and may generate a higher rate of failure. In fact, they may need to build several trial platforms before one succeeds. Although they do in fact put the resources of the traditional line of business at risk, they also hold the promise of the future. The newcomers can do this work of innovation best with backing and support from the rest of the enterprise. The discussion around the business life cycle curves often helps people working in the first-curve business to see that, looking forward into the changing industry environment, the current business is *already at risk* (otherwise a new curve would not be needed). Only the likely future decline of a traditional business impels the enterprise to take the risk of exploring how to innovate and evolve its way into the future. This explanation often helps old-timers understand why newcomers are operating under very different principles.

The traditional business on the first curve is naturally the more developed of the two. Though by itself it often cannot take the enterprise into the future, it often funds the development effort and preserves the strengths in the old systems and culture that help the new enterprise begin its movement up the new curve at a higher level. The new enterprise is not starting from scratch, as a brand-new entity devoid of history and infrastructure. It benefits from a well-built foundation that can give it a head start—if such a head start is strategically designed for the new enterprise. Under ideal circumstances, the people working on both the first and second curves acknowledge the value in the others being where they are. They decide together what must be maintained from the old culture and what risks are acceptable in the new. Under these conditions, people will generally find their way to the curve that suits their skills and temperament and can appreciate that others are working in different areas that are equally necessary for the success of the enterprise. They see the whole picture of the enterprise as it moves through time, rather than only the perspective from their own curve. They understand how together they can work from both curves to move the enterprise toward its future.

Managers from a high-tech defense-oriented company found the discussion about the overlapping curves helpful in resolving conflicts that had been brewing between their traditional business units and new ventures the company had recently launched. Similar to many companies in their industry, they were in the midst of shifting their business emphasis from defense contracting to consumer applications for their products. The two overlapping curves gave them an easy way to conceptualize the degree of discontinuity this represented in their business.

People in each area began to see why conditions were so different for the work related to the "old curve" and the "new curve." Whereas they had previously been oblivious to the need for these differences, each side had bitterly complained about and blamed the other for the natural difficulties inherent in transformational change. Once they could see why both had to exist simultaneously in their enterprise, they relaxed considerably. They realized that they were *supposed* to be different. One team member remarked to a member of the "other curve," "*Now* I understand why you act that way. Before I thought you were just plain stupid!" This was a fairly blunt statement, but it actually helped bring the two groups together. The comment led to a great deal of laughter and then some serious discussion, as many members admitted that they had carried similar assumptions and attitudes. Their understanding and increased acceptance of each other went a long way toward increasing their sense of belonging to one company and their ability to collaborate effectively when necessary.

Facing Decline

Many work groups, when confronting the life cycle curves, see a fairly threatening picture. As they look into the future, they do not see their business on the map—at least not in the way they had known it before. Some are tempted to turn away at this point, to ignore the revelation as just an exercise that can be forgotten in the fray of day-to-day operational pressures. Others look for ways to revitalize or prolong the current business. And many begin the hard work of creating a new business strategy and laying the foundations of the new organization that can carry the company into the future.

In the following example, hard times compelled workers in the fishing industry to examine the big picture and prepare for the future.

A group of fisheries faced a drop in fish prices from $2.40 per pound to 60 cents per pound. At this price, the business was not sustainable over the long term. Owners of boats and fleets, processors, and distributors began to argue over the best way to proceed and to look for someone to blame for the precipitous drop in prices. Their meetings were written up in the local press for being boisterous, full of finger-pointing, and unproductive.

The members of this group decided that they needed to devise a marketing campaign, to improve sales and drive up the demand (and the price) for their fish. As we examined their situation, it became clear that they were facing completely new conditions in their industry and that a marketing campaign would not see them through the changes ahead. When we questioned them more thoroughly about what they really thought they needed, one fisherwoman responded, "We need a miracle!"

Fisheries had typically been a relatively stable business. Work roles, family roles, and even communities had been built up around fishing. Men, and sometimes women, went out on large fishing vessels and spent days at sea in rough waters, to bring back tons of fish. They took great pride in their work. In fact, it was more than work; it was a way of life.

Recently, however, a new competitor had appeared in their industry. Japanese companies were beginning to farm fish in Chile. The idea of farming fish seemed somewhat silly to the rugged fishermen and women. They dismissed farmed fish disdainfully as "pretty fish." They believed that their ocean fish were far superior to farm fish—theirs were the real fish, the wild fish.

When we gathered data from customers, however, the view of farmed fish looked quite different. Farmed fish could be harvested every day. They were never placed at the bottom of a boat, buried below tons of other fish. They could be sent from the farm each day, direct to the markets and restaurants, without ever being frozen. Customers described these as "pretty fish" with a positive glow in their eyes, using the same expression that the fishermen and women had used with contempt.

The fishing industry was clearly facing a transformational time. Looking at their life cycle diagram, participants described themselves as the "last of the hunters and gatherers, facing the agricultural revolution." It was tough to compete. As it turned out, it was actually against the law to farm fish in the area where they lived and worked, a law that had originally been put in place to protect the local ocean fisheries. In a global marketplace, however, their local law could no longer protect them. Fisheries in other parts of the world were competing freely, while only they were constrained.

The people in the room working on the two business life cycle curves could clearly see their own curve—the hunting of wild fish—as a first-curve industry facing potential future decline, while the new curve—fish farming—had already progressed much farther than they had imagined earlier. Ocean-going fisheries were still the predominant mainstream industry, but it became clear that the second curve was growing rapidly. Seeing both curves simultaneously helped members in this group understand both the competition as well as the opportunities that lay ahead. Though their mood was very serious, most people in the room agreed that it was a relief to see the picture so clearly. Seeing the larger picture of what was occurring in their industry allowed them to stop blaming each other for the changes they were experiencing. For the first time in many months, all saw a common view and could begin to work together to address the real issues. It wasn't exactly a miracle, and it wasn't the picture they had all hoped they would find, but it was a good start to confronting their future together in a way that encouraged them to take realistic action.

Building the Second Curve in Time

Too often we have seen companies wait until their mainstream business is in decline before they start to build the next curve. They try to "prepare for the leap" by building new businesses (or radically different versions of their current business). However, once the mainstream business begins to plateau or decline, financial resources tighten up. Programs that return the lowest profits are often cut. Resources are pulled back into the parts of the company that generate the highest rate of return for the moment—almost always the traditional business. It is not hard to predict that when enterprises react to the first signs of decline by cutting out the new ventures designed to deliver their future, it creates a significant impediment to achieving a successful future. We have seen several work groups use the life cycle curves to take a more strategic look at their long-term business future, to look past the immediate current revenue or profit picture, and then to find and commit to developing the businesses that can serve as their second curve.

Managers from a high-tech company explained that their current product was slowly becoming obsolete as new products came on the market to replace it. They did not think their current business would end precipitously (as can happen in high-tech companies) and estimated that it had another three to five years to ride out the current curve. By that time, it needed to have established its new line of business.

When these managers worked through the life cycle curves, they noted two significant pieces of data. First, they had no vision for their long-term future. When they went to name the new curve, they had no clue what it would be. (The fisheries recognized the addition of fish farms as one key to their future; the members of this group, by contrast, had no idea of what would be the equivalent of fish farms for their industry.) They drew the second curve with a large question mark instead of a name.

Next, they recognized that they had a very poor track record with emerging new ventures. In fact, *none* had survived to date. As one member said, they always "killed the babies" when the parent company needed the resources. Typically, new ventures would get funding, but at the first sign of trouble, resources would be withdrawn and the start-up venture stopped.

Part of the difficulty was also related to an organizational problem. The company evaluated new ventures by the same criteria and rules as the established business, and of course, start-up projects, by their very nature, could never meet the same revenue and profit standards. It had been ten years since the company had begun its current mainstream business, and its managers had become entrenched in the systems and performance measures of the more mature business. But these very measures and organizational policies that were appropriate to the more mature traditional business were generally considered a burden for fledgling new ventures, representing excessive structure and expense.

Each of these pieces of information had been known previously, but putting them together on one diagram helped the managers see some important implications:

- Their current business curve had only a few years left in it.
- They needed to develop several new businesses soon, to have at least one or more "future curves" survive.
- They continually failed at creating new businesses because they killed off all new projects that could grow into a future mainstream business.

When the managers put these observations together, they realized that they would soon be in significant trouble unless they learned to grow their new ventures into new businesses that could succeed. This was a clear priority. The work with the life cycle model mobilized their energy, clarified the issues, and also pointed the way toward potential solutions. They were then able to articulate a business case that they could take to their senior management team to obtain the organizational and leadership changes needed to handle new ventures more productively.

Corporate Functions in Transformation

Because so many companies are facing pressures to improve quality and reduce costs in their primary business, many functions within the organization are being revolutionized. Whereas from the overall company viewpoint, these functions might be part of the organizational structure, for the work groups within the functions themselves, these changes are part of their core "business." For example, from the enterprisewide perspective, human resource policies are part of the organization structure. However, from the perspective of the HR department itself, these policies are its business (its task in the STEP framework of Chapter Four). HR policies and procedures comprise the core product offered to customers— the rest of the enterprise that HR serves.

As the information systems department mentioned earlier illustrates, functional departments in transition can use the business life cycle curves to chart the changes they face in their key tasks.

The Transformation of Human Resources

Human resources is one corporate function in particular that is undergoing dramatic transformation in its business. As many of their parent companies struggle with mastering intense global competition and typically want to cut personnel costs while increasing productivity and innovation, these new demands directly affect the HR departments. Many traditional HR tasks are being questioned, and new potential services and resources needed under these dynamic conditions are still being defined.

HR divisions that we have worked with have found the life cycle curves extremely useful to clarify their leap from a "transaction-based" centralized function to a service designed to add increased value to line managers and business units during times of rapid change. Although some departments are moving rapidly into the "second curve" of HR activities, many still see themselves at the point of the leap from the first curve. Still others have described themselves as "a little lost, between curves." Working with the two curves encourages HR staff members to begin discussions and to plan more clearly which roles may be left behind, to see which roles are emerging as essential for the HR of the future, and to understand the defining differences between the ways of working that the two curves represent.

For example, in many companies, the central corporate HR function is shrinking as many traditional HR tasks are shifted to line managers, outsourced, or automated. As companies remove layers of management and work to give more "empowerment" and decision-making responsibility to managers at the front line, many managers are taking back human resource management responsibilities. HR staff in these cases typically move out of the role of handling HR transactions *for* managers while shifting into training and consulting roles designed to ensure that managers can handle the tasks themselves. In effect, many HR staff are working themselves out of their traditional roles.

Outsourcing is also playing a part in redefining the corporate HR function. Many companies are finding that tasks previously handled in-house (such as recruiting, benefits management, or training) can sometimes be done more efficiently by outside specialty firms. As outside experts increasingly offer high-quality services for a fraction of the internal cost, many companies are choosing to outsource the HR activities not directly tied to the core competencies of their business. The corporate function then moves from the provider role into the new role of contracting with and managing the outside suppliers.

Emerging technology is redefining HR's business as well, by offering employees and managers direct access to basic HR information. Traditional HR transactions are being automated through a rich new assortment of information systems (such as multimedia HR kiosks, on-line systems, or company "Intranets"). There is a move toward "employee access" and "employee self-sufficiency," where employees can manage much of their own HR data (updating employee information, such as changes of address or new dependents; checking benefits or company policies; completing career assessments; registering for training courses; matching self-assessed skills to new job postings; and even applying for new positions on-line). Many traditional HR roles are going the way of bank teller positions after ATM machines were introduced. Once employees become the "owners" of their data, they typically prefer to manage it themselves. Just as in many other industries, they often do not need or want an HR "middleman" to connect them to the information or service they need.

A New Role for HR in the Dynamic Enterprise

As old definitions of the HR function are disappearing, new strategic HR roles are still being formulated. Particularly in companies where the business or industry is in the midst of transformation, HR staff are under pressure to ensure that people in the parent enterprise can make the needed changes in time. *HR staff are increasingly becoming the internal experts in creating Dynamic Enterprises.*

Many of the new HR roles closely resemble previous roles but have a dramatically increased focus on preparing the enterprise for dynamic change and shifting strategy, rather than for maintaining stable job categories and work roles. For example, HR is increasing its role in supporting shared strategic thinking, planning, and communication throughout the enterprise; in helping to design the organization structures and HR policies that can be most responsive to shifts in strategy as they occur; in enabling the workforce to have the right skills in the right places when needs are changing rapidly; in supporting leadership development and coaching for change leaders; in supporting team start-ups for new project teams and departments; and in contributing to the performance support for large-scale change initiatives.

As HR moves into the role of ongoing strategy support, change agent, and change support for the rest of the enterprise, one of the first departments to change is most often the HR department itself. Most departments are finding that they were defined for the first curve, and moving to second-curve activities requires an entirely new organization within their own group before they can begin to change the rest of the company. The separate curves in the business life cycle model imply that this is a discontinuous change. The core business of HR is changing, and the type of organization within the department or division itself will need to change to support this new HR business.

As the environments change, the core business of many companies is changing, as the fisheries and defense-related technology company examples illustrate. In turn, as companies are under pressure to redefine themselves, the functions within them are feeling the same pressures. The HR example is only one corporate function of many to face fundamental change in its role within its parent company. Information services in many companies is undergoing a similar transformation, as is the purchasing and procurement function (see Chapter Four).

Organizational Life Cycles

Most leaders and members of enterprises are not versed in large group dynamics. Many have an intuitive grasp of how their organizations develop and spontaneously respond to their organization's developmental needs. Much of the time, intuition can suffice. The Enterprise Development model of organizational life cycles is included here for readers who want a simplified guide to understanding organizational dynamics and requirements that can help build an organization that is strong, vibrant, and aligned with the business side of the enterprise.

The organizational life cycle component of Enterprise Development is the most advanced element of the framework, but it is optional. Many enterprises we work with choose to use all of the other concepts and approaches of Enterprise Development—STEP, business life cycles, establishing alliances among the drivers for development, learning how to respond to the inevitable tests, and developing their own customized blueprint for implementation—but they do so without considering organizational life cycles. Whereas the other elements of Enterprise Development are crucial to the success of the overall endeavor, understanding the developmental phases of the organization is a handy extra tool in the Enterprise Development tool kit. We include it here because many groups who have chosen to use it have found it extremely helpful for a number of purposes:

- To predict which configurations of STEP would be most likely to succeed and which would most likely not succeed or would be very difficult to implement
- To understand the type of organization that could best support a business at each phase of the business life cycle
- To understand whether an organization could effectively use a given program or change initiative, given its life cycle stage
- To understand whether the current challenge meant that the organization should stay the same, should try to be more functional within its current phase of development, or should move to a new phase of development
- To clarify a troublesome spot where a work group had become stuck, helping the members see their way through to the next phase
- To understand the *specific* nature of the current changes and transitions their own work group was facing, rather than adopting a generic program for "transition management" or "change management," as if all transitions were the same

The Organizational Life Cycle Model

The organizational life cycle model (see Figure 7.4) is designed to help leaders and members of the enterprise understand the challenges their organization is facing in its development and the range of their own possible responses. Whenever a new developmental need arises—and emerging needs are almost always experienced with considerable discomfort—the organization's leaders have a choice about whether and how to respond: Should they stay the course, change within the same developmental phase, or push the organization to a new level of development? The organizational life cycle model can provide guidelines for facing such developmental tests.

The Exploring Organization

The first level of development is the *Exploring* stage. When a work group or organization first forms, the main priority for its members is to figure out how things work. The organization's structure is often loose and informal: people seem to be making it up as they go. Often the core structure is the relationship of all members to a charismatic leader. Rules and expectations are ambiguous and always changing, leading people to be cautious and tentative as they try to figure out how to be accepted. People's primary need is to attain a level of safety and comfort with each other that will enable them to get the information and resources to do their jobs.

Because management often has not yet fully articulated the purpose of the Exploring Organization, few guidelines exist for dealing with problems that arise. Consequently, each problem must be addressed individually as a special case. As the organization grows in response to a successful business, or as tasks become more complex, the case-by-case approach can lead to full-blown crisis management. Planning and long-term thinking become both necessary and impossible. People start to feel like they are frantically running in place and develop an intense need to stabilize the organization and make it more predictable.

These difficulties present the organization with its first developmental turning point. At each turning point, the organization's leaders can choose among three options: (1) ignore the emerging need and change nothing, which most likely will lead to *impairment;*

Figure 7.4. Organizational Life Cycle Model.

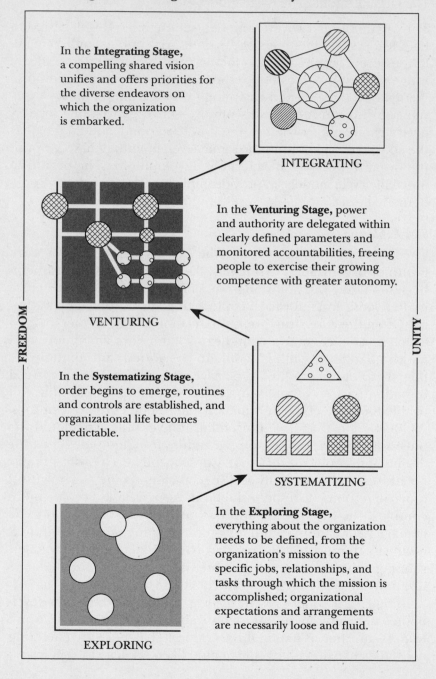

In the **Integrating Stage,** a compelling shared vision unifies and offers priorities for the diverse endeavors on which the organization is embarked.

INTEGRATING

In the **Venturing Stage,** power and authority are delegated within clearly defined parameters and monitored accountabilities, freeing people to exercise their growing competence with greater autonomy.

VENTURING

In the **Systematizing Stage,** order begins to emerge, routines and controls are established, and organizational life becomes predictable.

SYSTEMATIZING

In the **Exploring Stage,** everything about the organization needs to be defined, from the organization's mission to the specific jobs, relationships, and tasks through which the mission is accomplished; organizational expectations and arrangements are necessarily loose and fluid.

EXPLORING

FREEDOM

UNITY

(2) if it is found that the current organization form will continue to be appropriate to support the function of the business for the foreseeable future, the emerging needs can be addressed by implementing necessary fixes and improvements, but otherwise remaining basically the same kind of organization *(adaptation);* and (3) if the current organization is found to be inadequate for supporting the business, an organization will need to be developed that will support the emerging business functions in entirely new ways *(transformation).*

When the Exploring Organization ignores the rising need for order in a growing business and instead remains in firefighting mode, its freshness and optimism may gradually erode, leading to a hand-to-mouth, burnout-prone Chaotic Organization (see Figure 7.5). We have seen numerous start-up firms—buoyed by the early success of a brilliant product—follow this Chaotic route when their leaders, fearful of losing creativity and control, start acting in ways that undermine their own progress. These leaders find themselves and their organizations struggling, unable to stabilize work processes and develop an infrastructure capable of implementing a business strategy that will carry the enterprise beyond its early successes.

The members of an Exploring Organization can also make a reasoned choice that the business environment continues to demand them to present quick, flexible, one-of-a-kind solutions—in which case they may adapt into a Responsive Organization, an opportunity-driven organization with the flexible, informal—but reliable—organizational support systems needed to let people succeed with ever-changing possibilities.

The Systematizing Organization

The leaders and members of an Exploring Organization may recognize that the future of their enterprise does not lie in quick customized responses to immediate demands but in planned and reproducible approaches to business challenges. In this case, they may respond to the need for order by choosing to move the organization into the second developmental stage, *Systematizing.* In this stage, the organization establishes stable organizational structures and clear roles, accountabilities, policies, and procedures. Relationships to people in formal roles take the place of the previously

Figure 7.5. The Exploring Organization.

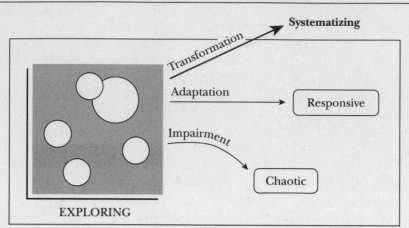

more personal relationship with the charismatic leader. People experience the competence, stability, and trust that comes from knowing exactly what is expected of them, what they can expect from others, and what they need to do to succeed. The organization settles down into maintaining productive routines.

At first, the establishment of predictability and routine is a relief, but once people master their carefully defined jobs, they may become restless. Particularly as the business begins to look to expand its horizons, the very policies and procedures that once made people feel competent and secure begin to get in the way, preventing them from taking initiative or responding intelligently to the demands and opportunities of unique and new situations. The need emerges for greater freedom and autonomy, presenting the second developmental turning point for the organization.

If the need for autonomy is ignored or stifled, the risk is for the enterprise to evolve into a Rigid Organization—the classic bureaucracy that keeps the focus on control long after it has served the useful purpose of settling the organization (see Figure 7.6). People spend their energy politicking and vying for control rather than getting work done. Policies and organizational structures may consume huge amounts of time and resources and often support nothing more than the continued existence of more policies and structures. Form supports form, rather than form supporting function.

Figure 7.6. The Systematizing Organization.

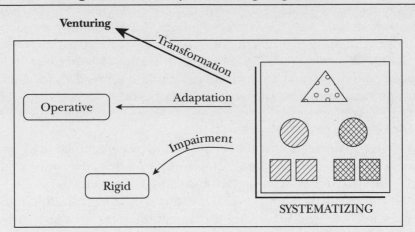

However, the company's members and leaders may instead consciously determine that its business mission is in harmony with a highly systematized approach (as is true for companies such as Federal Express and McDonald's) and may focus on designing structures that support the actual business needs of the company. The organization can address employee needs for autonomy by choosing adaptation and continuous improvement, becoming an Operative Organization. Clear roles and performance criteria are defined, creative attention is paid to employee involvement and motivation, and outstanding performance is recognized and publicly acknowledged.

The transition from Rigid to Operative was exemplified in the successful turnaround that took place in what became the New United Motors Manufacturing Inc. (NUMMI) plant in Fremont, California. When General Motors was running the factory, it functioned within the constraints of a typical Rigid Organization, with frequent flare-ups between workers and management. Absenteeism was among the highest of any GM plant, production per employee was the lowest, and defects were extremely high. As occurs with many Rigid Organizations, the factory lumbered along inefficiently until the operating costs finally grew too high and the plant was shut down. Several years later, with the same union in the same factory, GM and Toyota created NUMMI, in which the

Toyota production system was introduced. Toyota's philosophy and systems—such as just-in-time production, *kaizen* (continuous improvement), and *jidoka* ("stop the line") for eliminating all waste and streamlining manufacturing processes—are perhaps the most "operative" in the world. With a new Operative Organization, the plant not only turned around its problems but set records for quality, production per employee, and high morale.

The Venturing Organization

Businesses whose product or service requires a great deal of ongoing, multidimensional change and innovation may determine that the enterprise has most to gain by giving fuller rein to people's skill and creativity. They move to transform their organization into the third type, the Venturing Organization. The basic structure established during the Systematizing stage remains a strong foundation, but the organization begins to investigate ways to create freedom within that structure. During this stage, people begin to feel a sense of clarity about the aims of the organization and have the permission and ability to make unique individual contributions. The core structure of the organization is determined less by hierarchies of control than by processes of authorization that define boundaries and expected results, such as project management systems and procedures.

During the current period of economic restructuring, several of our clients from well-established, tradition-bound industries (such as oil, defense, and health care) have learned to revitalize their organizations. While building on established core competencies, new ventures within the organization are authorized to break out of Operative or Rigid levels of functioning, gaining the freedom to act associated with Venturing. The facilities development division described in Chapter Four successfully delivered a sixfold increase in productivity based on a bold and radical transformation from *rigid systemization* to *empowered venturing*. To the delight of their customers, they overhauled their operations and collectively redesigned the entire organization, increasing the use of cross-functional, self-directed teams.

At the Venturing level of development, the organization begins to recognize differences among its members and put this diversity to good use. The emphasis shifts from implementing procedures to achieving goals and objectives. With increasing role differentiation and delegation of significant responsibilities, people develop the ability to think independently and, paradoxically, the capacity for true teamwork—where groups become more than the sum of their parts.

Increased autonomy frees people to take initiative within clearly developed constraints. As more and more people accept this challenge, a new set of pressures begins to build. The organization may find itself moving in many directions at once without clear priorities to tie the directions together. People may begin to work at cross-purposes, energetically throwing themselves into projects that are not fully authorized or are redundant or overlapping. Rivalries develop, and leadership becomes distracted by the embarrassment of riches, finding it difficult to give any one project the support it needs to bear fruit. A need emerges both for an overall sense of purpose and for clear boundaries on authority and independence that will allow members of the organization to start pulling in the same direction. The organization has reached its third developmental turning point.

The organization can choose to ignore the emerging need for clear priorities and boundaries, in which case autonomy begins to runs amuck, ushering in the Reckless Organization (see Figure 7.7). In the Reckless Organization, people are sent off to work on projects without the clarity that would prevent them from making poor investments of time and energy, from performing disconnected or redundant work. "Empowerment" programs often fail at just this point, leading to increased frustration and cynicism as individuals and teams pursue overlapping or contradictory tasks. Team members often become disgruntled when they are first given the freedom to work independently, only to be told later, "I didn't mean you were supposed to do that!" When support is given with unclear parameters or when authorization is only partial, the support or authorization is often pulled back at the most inopportune times.

The Reckless Organization creates a serious risk to the spirit and work culture of its people and the effort they bring to their work (or to other organizational changes) from then on. People begin to burn out when they first feel hopeful and excited and pour great deals of energy and passion into their work but later cannot gather the real support needed to make their efforts pay

Figure 7.7. The Venturing Organization.

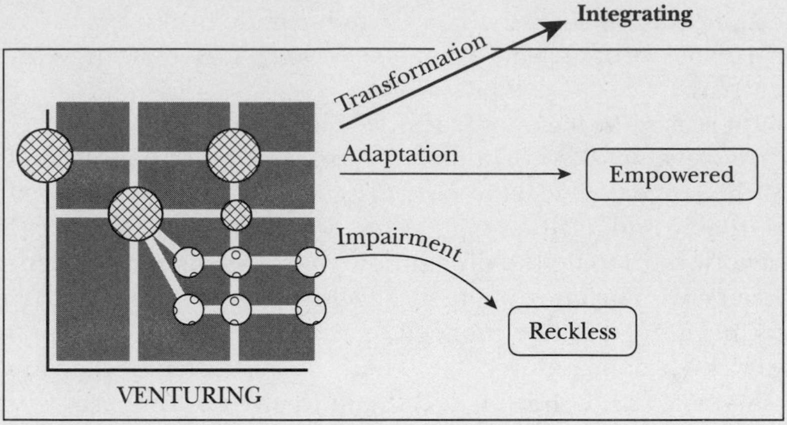

off. Shortsighted, me-first attitudes become the norm, and the organization limits its ability to develop the kind of synergy needed to stand out in its field. It also risks moral and ethical bankruptcy. Its people no longer believe in the charges given to them to make independent decisions or to work creatively.

Again, it may be appropriate for the enterprise to maintain its capacity for flexibility in response to its business environment and consciously adapt into an authorized or Empowered Organization. The Empowered Organization addresses the need for direction and coordination through organizational structures, policies, and communication networks designed to support complex projects. Matrix reporting structures, contingency planning, formal project reviews, regular status reports, and procedures for client involvement may be among the methods employed. Clear parameters must be given to the individuals and teams to be "empowered." The message is, "Within these boundaries, you are fully authorized to act creatively and independently," where the boundaries include such information as project scope, time, budget, communication needs, and the types and timing of agreements needed from others for continued authorization. The initial clarity is intended to enable subsequent freedom and independence. When empowerment, independence, and creativity are essential for the business to thrive, the Venturing structure is designed to make sure that these are coordinated enough, and realistic enough, that they will actually survive. "Empowerment" is not just a program in a Venturing Organization—it actually exists.

The Integrating Organization

If it is determined that the organization's mission is significantly greater than the sum of its individual projects, the enterprise may be transformed to the fourth level of development, *Integrating*. Once people have achieved a level of success and mastery in their work, a new need often begins to emerge. People want something more. Once they feel successful and competent, people often encounter a deep longing for *meaningful* work.

In the Integrating stage, the organization addresses the need for a larger purpose by articulating a vision or strategic intent and long-term goals to inspire and guide all efforts. People begin to consider the meaning of their activities in relation to this larger context beyond the success of their department or company, and they use their skills and autonomy in service of this deeper goal. They are motivated less by a desire to exercise their own competence than by a desire for fulfillment, and they take a long-term strategic approach to the achievement of their desired ends—ends that are frequently values-based. The core structure of the Integrating Organization ties all endeavors into the realization of a meaningful shared vision. The South African company described in Chapter Five, which included the renewal of South Africa as an African nation in its vision, took a significant step in the direction of becoming an Integrating Organization.

Eventually, the organization must recognize that people do not live on their convictions alone. The symbols and the culture of enthusiasm can begin to feel heady and esoteric, making it difficult to communicate with the "uninitiated" outside the organization—which can include clients and other key stakeholders. This emerging discomfort and sense of being out of touch with the supporting community brings the organization to the fourth developmental turning point.

If the organization chooses to ignore this emerging need to reconnect with its supporting community and external environment, it risks becoming an Overzealous Organization (see Figure 7.8). Separated from the demands of the external environment

Figure 7.8. The Overzealous Organization.

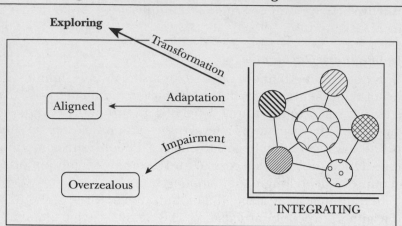

and from a sense of responsibility to any interests other than those of their own enterprise and internal values, people may lose their sense of the proper balance between means and ends. They feel exempt from the standards by which most human activity is judged, even to the point of believing themselves above the law. Such an organization can become practically delusional because all organizations are dependent on environmental support and interaction. The Overzealous Organization risks a disastrous fall.

If it is recognized that the scope and complexity of the projects of the enterprise are such that it can never accomplish its mission without close, ongoing partnerships with clients, community, and other key stakeholders, it can choose to address this need by adapting into an Aligned Organization. Relationships with outside parties are then built into the organization's structure through advisory panels, parallel project teams from client organizations, consultants, and other formalized relationships with resources outside the organization. The Aligned Organization integrates its most deeply held values into its work with and for the outside world.

Figure 7.9 shows how all the organizational life cycle stages are represented within the Enterprise Development model.

The need to reconnect with the external environment, the client, and the supporting community may bring the organization full circle in its transformation to once again become an Exploring

Figure 7.9. The Phases of Organizational Life Cycles.

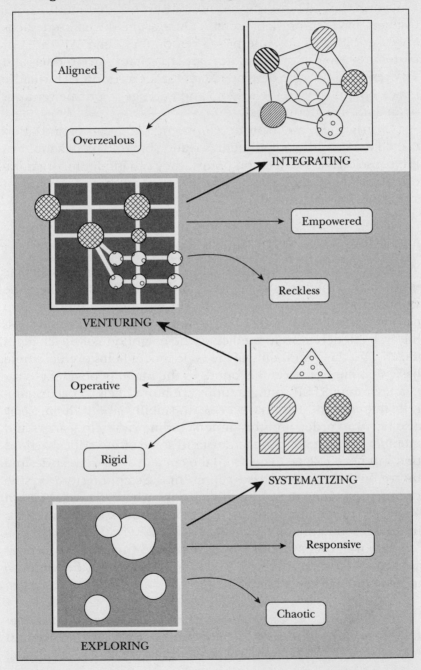

Organization. The members of the organization go through a deep transformation, discovering a sense of purpose that may be quite distinct from their previous identity. Once again, the basic questions are asked: What is this enterprise's reason for being? Who are our customers? How favorable is the marketplace for our products and services? And thus the developed organization revisits its formative issues, equipped with the wisdom and courage to pursue ventures of an entirely different kind.

Clearly, there are many developmental paths an organization can take. When the organization's leadership and its stakeholders are conscious of the decision points, they can guide the organization to make the choices that fit best with its business environment and its own capabilities.

Applications of the Organizational Life Cycle Model

Whereas vision helps members of the enterprise see where they must go, and the analysis of current and past STEP helps them see where they are and have been, the developmental models help clarify the qualitative nature of the steps in between. The business life cycle model assists in predicting the magnitude of the changes ahead, and the organizational life cycle model helps predict where basic steppingstones can be found. In the range of possibilities for change, some STEP configurations are more likely to occur naturally than others. They have a certain stability about them. They also occur in order, and this understanding can help leaders and members of the enterprise understand some of the critical actions they will need to take to get from the current state to their desired future. In this way, the phases represent the steppingstones or the resting spots along the pathway of change, where the organization may need to stabilize long enough to build the systems and skills inherent in that phase.

As work groups attempt to move toward their most appropriate organizational life cycle phase, it is important for them to understand five key principles.

1. *The phases are sequential. Each phase must be completed successfully before moving to the next.* We have found that organizations must move through the phases one by one. Phases cannot be skipped.

This fact is important to know when an enterprise observes that it is in one phase and needs to be more than one step ahead from its current state. Many organizational change programs fail at just this point because they do not build in the middle steps. Even though the organization may want to go from Chaotic to Operative or from Operative to Integrating, it may have to stabilize at the phases in between until the skills from those phases have been adequately internalized.

A familiar example of work groups that try to skip organizational phases (one that we have seen many times) is that of a young start-up company or project team that wants to move from Chaotic to the Empowered phase of Venturing. Such a team typically has a culture of moving quickly, of setting ambitious deadlines and meeting them. However, with success and recent growth, this team has moved from the positive Responsive phase into the more dysfunctional Chaotic mode, with a growing number of breakdowns beginning to occur. When members of the enterprise first see the organizational life cycle model, they look at the Venturing phase, apply their typical ambition, and decide, "We need to be *there*." Given their culture of quick delivery, they want to be there *now!*

However, when the members of this work group begin their development process, they find that they are not yet ready to move decision making into Empowered teams. In fact, their people rarely work as effective teams at all, much less Empowered ones. They often do not have clear parameters for their roles, the extent of their decision-making authority, budgets and resources, or linkages to other Aligned teams. Their lack of structure, clear definition, and shared agreements actually inhibits their ability to venture successfully.

The organizational life cycle model shows many of the steps that need to be taken on the way from chaos to empowerment in the Venturing phase. First, an organization at the Chaotic level of functioning must adapt to become Responsive. It has to become fully functional at its current Exploring phase of development, to internalize the developmental tasks of this phase before moving on to the next one. Tasks required might include clarifying the identity and direction of the company, healing the conflicts that have already occurred in key working relationships, and reducing internal rivalries.

The organization then needs to move successfully through the systemization phase and master the tasks of that phase as well, including the creation of systems for growth—the financial, legal, communications, human resource, and decision-making policies and systems that teams need to function effectively. Only then could an organization that was already dysfunctional at the earliest phases of development truly expect to launch Empowered teams. Venturing-phase teams depend on the earlier systemization—they succeed by acting freely, within clearly defined parameters.

If the stable foundation is not in place, the effort to move from Chaotic to Venturing will eventually falter. Again and again, we see teams undermined when they attempt to take Empowered actions. If the organization is still operating at the Chaotic level, one leader will launch a team while another will dismantle it. Or the team will be only *partially authorized,* a very risky condition that often leads to the response, "Oh! We didn't think you would do it *that* way!" Funding or authorization is withdrawn, and team members end up more frustrated than before. Ultimately, the whole process must wait until the proper supports have been put in place.

2. *Enterprises may not need to complete all phases.* The organizational phase that fits the task is the best phase for an enterprise—form follows function. Not all enterprises need to aim to become Integrating Organizations, but those that move to Integrating need to complete all the previous phases in sequence. For example, for a manufacturing company in a stable market, with a successful, well-defined product and with people who have the skills to carry out the required task, *Operative* can be exactly the right developmental phase. This type of organization does not need to push itself to move into another phase, although it must stay vigilant about making sure it does not slip into the more dysfunctional Rigid phase.

3. *The quality of each of the transitions is different.* Whereas many managers of change or transition programs train people in the generic skills required for functioning successfully in times of change, changes inherent in each phase—and the skills needed to navigate those changes—in fact differ significantly. The characteristics of those changes are predictable, and this information can be very helpful to the individuals implementing the changes and living through the transitions.

The roles of both leaders and stakeholders in the enterprise change dramatically from one phase to the next. People at all levels in the organization can begin to see which roles they may have to let go of and which new behaviors they must practice. For example, an organization moving from the Exploring to the Systematizing phase often loses much of its spontaneity and enthusiasm as it moves toward standardization and predictability. People must let go of the loosely defined business objectives that allowed people to make decisions based on personal preference or because something "felt right." Leaders may no longer be chosen because of their popularity or their ability to sell a given idea to others. During systematization, people need to work together to define the business objectives in a logical and consistent manner, and they must put the systems in place that assist them to select leaders based on competence for the task. Understanding how and why these new behaviors and actions are needed can help people manage the changes they require much more successfully.

4. *Shifts between phases can be powerful, moving members into a vastly different culture and a new set of expectations.* Each phase has a distinctly different character to it—different tasks and a different dominant culture. Working in an early Exploring Organization feels very different from working in a fully established systematized organization. The organization is concentrating on different developmental needs in each phase, and people who are successful, who are the "stars" in one phase, are not necessarily the most successful in another. People look to their leaders for different qualities in each phase as well. The company may produce the same product or deliver the same service, but the seat of real power may be quite different. What captures people's interest and enthusiasm is generally quite different. The changes from phase to phase, and even from one form to another within a given phase, can feel enormous to the people moving through them.

5. *People can navigate a transition better when they understand the specific nature of the transition.* Recall William Bridges's distinction between change and transition described in Chapter Four. Bridges defined *change* as the events that occur in the business and *transition* as the emotional reaction that occurs within the people. In a conversation about the organizational life cycles, Bridges told us that he liked the developmental model because it helped distinguish the

type of change or transition people were facing. Understanding the type of change could clarify the specific nature of the transition, and this would in turn help people deal with the transition more successfully.

This has been borne out in our experience: people more easily absorb, accept, adjust to, and work creatively with changes they understand. When members in a relatively young technology company realized that the "good old days" of the energetic and spontaneous "anything goes" early days of the start-up were beginning to give way to standard policies and procedures, they helped this change succeed when they were given the opportunity to understand that it had to occur and why. They began to realize that the old spontaneity had already been slipping into more chaotic and unfocused behavior and that the originally enthusiastic culture was beginning to turn negative.

As the members of this group examined their organizational development, they realized that *growth* was forcing change, not the personal whim of a malicious new leader (as they had suspected earlier). They were able to redefine the size, scope, and boundary of their business and create an organization that would fit. Given their vision for growth, keeping their early start-up culture was no longer an option. Understanding that their choice was between chaos and systemization, they actually began to long for the stability and predictability that systemization promised. They understood the reasons for letting go of their old culture, the nature of the transition ahead, what new actions were required of them, and why this change was necessary to move forward to a vision they had helped create.

Matching the Change to the Developmental Phase

When members of the enterprise are clear about their organization or work group's current developmental capabilities and understand where on the continuum it needs to be, it also helps them understand what changes will best help move the organization to the optimum place on the continuum. Once the characteristics of different developmental phases are understood, it is easier to see where many of the popular organizational interventions fit on the continuum (for example, total quality management, empowerment, self-managed work teams, or transition management). Even though a specific organizational change may be quite popular and may have many success stories to its credit, it may not be the best intervention for a given organization at its particular life cycle phase. For example, when members analyze their enterprise from the perspective of business and organizational life cycles, they can learn to understand when in the developmental life cycle self-managed work teams are most likely to succeed. (Such teams are in fact best created at a fairly mature stage of development. If clear priorities, policies, systems, and trust levels are not stable from earlier developmental phases, self-managed teams are likely to fail.)

Another common example occurs when members of a business unit are encouraged to act as innovative entrepreneurs, and yet the organization around them remains structured as a rigid bureaucracy. With proper analysis of the business and organizational life cycles, members of the enterprise begin to see quite clearly that the entire organization needs to be entrepreneurial, not just its people, and that the organization may have to move to a new form, more loosely structured, to succeed in the new effort.

Combining Business and Organizational Life Cycles

Because an enterprise is made up of both a business and an organization, an equivalent stage exists in the organization for every stage of the business life cycle (see Figure 7.10). Obviously, an enterprise is most effective when the business and the organization are developmentally aligned, that is, when one doesn't significantly lag behind the other. In fact, the enterprise will encounter a great deal of difficulty if its organization is not adequately matched to meet the challenges faced by the business in the particular phase of its life cycle.

The idea of aligning the business and organizational phases helped one oil industry supplier understand that its organization had become decoupled from its business. During the 1980s, the company had grown tremendously and had anticipated continued growth. In the 1990s, however, as oil companies streamlined contracts with suppliers, this particular supplier realized that it had placed people in roles to handle complexity and growth that had never

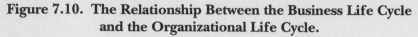

**Figure 7.10. The Relationship Between the Business Life Cycle
and the Organizational Life Cycle.**

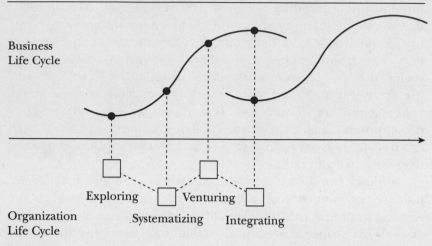

materialized. They had built the organization ahead of the business, and the business never caught up. It was time to retrench, to align the organization with the real needs of the company in the current and very near future.

The managers of a growing high-tech company, by contrast, recognized that they had the opposite problem: their business was ahead of the organization.

This company had grown to annual revenues of almost $1 billion using systems, policies, and procedures carried over from its start-up days. All individuals in the company made decisions their own way. When someone asked a question about the best way to get something done, the answer depended on whom they asked. The mixed messages were beginning to compromise everyone's work.

When these managers learned about the organizational life cycle model, they all had strong negative reactions to the Systematizing phase. Although they agreed that they needed more systems and more uniform work processes, to them the idea of *systematizing* was equivalent to becoming ossified, *rigid*. In their minds, installing routine processes signaled the end to the dynamism of their enterprise—they equated routine with bureaucracy and ultimately with the death of their business. Even though they knew they needed to systematize their organization and realized that the lack of shared systems was becoming a bottleneck constraining business performance, they were so fearful of systemization that they avoided it at all cost.

The organizational life cycle model helped these managers see that positive systemization (a new concept to them) was possible. They did not have to systematize in the way the traditional companies had in earlier times (work environments many had left to come to this company). Instead, they recognized that they could systematize in a way most appropriate to their current business. Because their business was based on constant innovation and creativity, they could build the systems that supported large groups of people to join new projects quickly and to share information rapidly across organizational boundaries. They felt great relief in seeing that routine systems and procedures could be designed to support the very parts of the business they most valued and enjoyed.

The developmental model presented here is just that, a model. Actual organizations and their various units never exhibit pure manifestations of the phases described. Instead, one finds general approximations of the outlined conditions. Yet understanding the developmental phases promotes clarity not only of the current state but also of the journey ahead. This clarity can be the essential added ingredient that enables leaders and organization members to make choices that will help their enterprise fulfill its potential, instead of becoming stifled and stagnant. A developmental model not only helps leaders make the right choices about the direction of the overall enterprise but also helps groups within the organization respect each other's differences in style and appreciate the varying needs and priorities that underlie those differences.

Chapter Eight

Mobilizing the Three Essential Drivers for Change

In these situations of high intensity and high complexity, the primary job of senior management becomes to lead the company through discontinuous change. Change is not merely one of the issues on the CEO's agenda, it is the CEO's agenda.
DAVID NADLER AND MICHAEL TUSHMAN,
"Types of Organizational Change: From Incremental Improvement to Discontinuous Transformation"

Over the course of our work during the past fifteen years with companies and institutions, teams, and venture partners who wanted to enact large-scale, complex change in response to a rapidly shifting environment, we have seen how difficult it can be to turn blueprints into reality. The members of one change team for a large manufacturing company humorously characterized this quite well in large cartoon maps of their change process. In their map, the vision ahead was clear, and their starting points were well-defined and agreed to. However, as team members looked to the process of change itself, they realized they had quite a task ahead to move a group that seemed unconsciously committed to being "stuck in the mud." The arrow representing the change on their Enterprise Development map emerged as a swamp, full of alligators and snakes, as well as cannons and a full assortment of hidden weapons aimed at one group or another. Leaders, meanwhile, were shown sitting safely on the sidelines in director's chairs, shouting with bullhorns into the fray, "You can do it!" or "Try this!" The plan to reach the vision was neatly drawn, but the change process that lay ahead was seen as a pit of known and unknown perils.

Plans are needed for effective change to occur, with the right balance of inspiration and down-to-earth truth telling, but ultimately, it is *people* who implement the plans. There is no such entity as "the enterprise" without its people. A Dynamic Enterprise is one whose *people* can view the external environment, understand and create the new strategies required, and actualize the changes in their day-to-day decisions and actions. What determines whether the people actually create a Dynamic Enterprise? What motivates them (and gives them the skills) to cross the swamp to get to the other side? What drives change forward?

The Three Drivers of Change

As indicated in Chapter Three, we have identified three key drivers of change for the Dynamic Enterprise: leadership, stakeholders, and performance support. For ongoing complex change efforts to succeed, it is essential that all three groups are linked in a powerful alliance for change (see Figure 8.1). Key leaders and stakeholders who must implement the new actions, and performance support—persons whose role is to coordinate and support the change—must all be linked in ongoing communication with each other. Without these three groups working together to further the development or change, it will not occur. As many people who have tried to institute change in their businesses or organizations well know, the likelihood of failure is high. Large groups can find many ways to stall development, and there are many ways to fail. After years of experience in working with groups who have wanted to take shortcuts, we have found this assertion to be consistently true: large-scale, complex change will not succeed without a strong working alliance among key leaders, stakeholders, and performance support.

Figure 8.1. The Three Essential Drivers of Change.

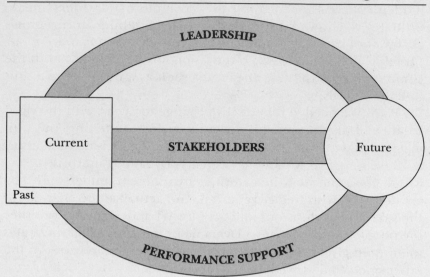

Leadership

The creation of a Dynamic Enterprise requires the commitment of the leaders. Whether the enterprise is a company, a department, or a project team, leaders must understand and help clarify for others how the external environment is changing, what this implies for the enterprise, a visionary future that can meet the challenge of change, and a plan for how to get there. Leaders do not have to be the first to see this picture or to put it all together, but ultimately, they must be the ones who take a stand for this future.

When a major change is first announced, the stakeholders who hear the message most often "look up," to see how their leaders react to the message. Innumerable times, one of the first questions we hear is, "But where does Leader X stand on this?" People do not want to take the risk to join a change that will later be seen as a failed project. They want to know that their leaders fully support them. We have worked with several change teams who knew that this was not the case. If we took a straw poll at any time to survey team members' most honest impressions, a large majority typically responded that when push came to shove, they fully expected their leaders would back down from the proposed new ways of working. They predicted that old ways would prevail, and every day, as they went about their work, they felt that their days were numbered because they would be identified with an unsuccessful effort. Many thought they would be moved out of their department, or out of the company altogether, because their very presence would be a humiliating reminder of a failed change. This is not a good way to build an inspired team for change!

Leaders as Developers

The creation of the Dynamic Enterprise places a new demand on the role of leaders. Leaders must become committed not only to the performance of the current core business tasks but also to the ongoing development of their enterprise. Ongoing development of the enterprise becomes an essential part of the leaders' work, not an optional task to be done in the spaces between the "real work."

To practice developmental leadership, leaders must hold and represent the vision. They stand for the future of the enterprise. They must also be able to see the current enterprise clearly and honestly so that stakeholders do not withhold or try to hide the real data about the current situation. Finally, they represent the commitment to change, and whatever unique forms of development are required.

In the book *Discontinuous Change* (Nadler, Shaw, Walton, and Associates, 1995), David Nadler and Michael Tushman describe how the role of leadership varies in relation to the complexity and intensity of the change. For low-intensity changes in relatively simple teams or organizations, standard management processes are generally sufficient to handle the change process. Existing meetings and communication pathways between employees and managers can carry the messages and enable them to take the actions needed for the change. As either intensity or complexity increases, change best occurs through delegation and with the assistance of a transition management team. Senior leaders manage as usual, while a transition team is delegated the responsibility to design and manage the specific change. However, when *both* intensity and complexity of the change are high, the primary task of the leader becomes to take an active role in ensuring that the change occurs.

Daryl Conner underscores this point in his book *Managing at the Speed of Change* (1994) as he describes how the person in authority has to be actively involved in the change. Employees who are expected to participate in change will rarely respond to change agents or support staff who have been given responsibility for a change if the employees' immediate superiors do not directly sanction the change or the support personnel. Conner differentiates between "sponsors," the individuals or groups that have the power to authorize the change; "advocates," individuals who want to achieve a change but lack the formal authority to enact it; "agents," the individuals who plan and carry out the change process; and "targets," the individuals who must actually change. Difficulties arise when advocates or agents try to get targets to change when the sponsors (leaders) are not fully on board. Conner writes, "Sponsors cannot pass on sanctioning power to people who do not hold that status with the targets. Having agents tell targets who don't report to them what to do almost always fails" (p. 109).

We have found this to be a very helpful description of what occurs when we have worked with leaders who wanted to delegate the responsibility for a critical and strategic change. Enterprises pay a high price when senior leaders are kept out of the change process. Stakeholders watch their leaders closely to see if they encourage and sanction the changes taking place. Events and announcements introducing change will not be taken seriously if key leaders are not present. Such events are not considered as truly "blessed" by the leaders unless the leaders themselves are present and unless they repeatedly reinforce the messages about change through both words and actions.

Leaders must become aware of their stakeholders' expectations of them. They need to know how symbolic acts and concrete actions signal to stakeholders whether leaders are truly behind the changes taking place. The following examples illustrate that members of various enterprises watch their leaders' behavior for predictions about change process viability.

When the leader of a customer focus and culture change initiative in a community hospital walked through one of the kickoff events without talking to anyone and went directly into his office, closing the door behind him, it symbolized that the new "collaborative, team-oriented culture" was off to a rocky start. Almost everyone noticed—and heard a message the leader never expected to send.

————

The members of a work process redesign team in a company where we were working as external consultants offered to buy us dinner using their own personal money "at the most expensive restaurant in town" if only we could get their senior leadership team to meet with them to listen to their concerns about the overall progress of the redesign efforts. After two months of trying, they had been unable to get a single senior leader to meet with them, and they were getting desperate. They were also getting demoralized about the probability for success for their the planned redesign, as they judged—correctly—that it did not have enough management attention to support major change.

————

The members of another team were so frustrated with the lack of senior managers' involvement that when they finally had a meeting together, they made name cards by pasting managers' pictures onto empty milk cartons, to symbolize the "missing executives."

The Visible Leader

In the most successful Dynamic Enterprises, which are able to implement large-scale and complex change on an ongoing basis, the leaders are visibly involved in change each step of the way. They may delegate the tactical, day-to-day operations of design and implementation, but it is clear that they embrace the change. These leaders see it as their job to make sure that the necessary people are engaged and that changes occur as planned.

Julian Darley, president of BP Exploration Alaska in the early 1990s, led a major organizationwide transformation. As the company faced profound changes, he described feeling that he "couldn't be there enough." He was needed everywhere at once. BP Exploration was the biggest producer of crude oil in the United States, and employees thought it was performing well. However, in the early 1990s, the world of oil production was shifting dramatically. Production costs were up, and oil prices and yields were down. As the leaders of BP Exploration looked into the future, they could see that the company could no longer succeed using business methods that had made it successful in the past. Radical transformation in business processes and work culture was needed at a time when employees did not yet feel the pinch of potential difficulties. It was the leader's job to make the future visible.

Being seen as a visible leader committed to change presented its own set of challenges. Darley recognized that not only did the company need to change but he had to change his own leadership style as well, to fit the needs of the changing organization. The company needed employees and managers to take charge of the change in their areas, to be innovative about finding solutions, and to be accountable for the results. In meetings, managers would often wait for Darley to jump in and make an executive decision. Given the old culture, this was a familiar role for him, but he knew that his role had to change if his managers were going to step up to their new responsibilities. He was there to set out and clarify the challenge for managers and their teams and then to encourage *them* to generate the best solution. He described how he personally initiated and kicked off workshops and team meetings designed to tackle the challenges and then he would leave. He would return later, when the walls were covered with flip charts, to hear the results. In this way, team members realized that he truly wanted and needed them to explore new ideas and would personally ensure that these ideas were put to use. Darley had learned to negotiate the fine line between standing for the future while still enabling the people closest to the work to design and implement it so that they would embrace it as their own.

Building a Network of Leaders

Most often, large-scale and complex change must be led by more than a single leader alone. There are typically numerous leaders, at various levels within the organization, who influence the success of a given development. We have seen initiatives—even when powerfully backed by a president or CEO—get undermined by board members, leaders from a parent company, or other leaders within the same company. For these reasons, it is crucial that all leaders who can influence a given development, including those who may have veto power, ultimately be committed to the future vision and the changes proposed.

Alva Wheatley was vice president of facilities development at Kaiser Permanente Medical Center, Northern California Region, when she led the participatory restructuring of her organization. This reorganization resulted in a sixfold increase in productivity within six months of implementation, while adding only three new jobs to the overall workforce.

To succeed, she worked early on to build a powerful network of leaders. Wheatley's change team identified each area of the larger company that could have an impact on the success of the intended change. Wheatley herself then went out to the field to enroll each of the identified leaders. In one-on-one conversations and larger local meetings, she generated a level of understanding, excitement, and commitment to the project and elicited the support that was vital from other leaders throughout the large health care corporation.Wheatley first secured the commitment and strong support of Wayne Moon, then regional manager for Kaiser Permanente's Northern California Region. Moon's support in turn encouraged Wheatley to take a spirited and at times even aggressive approach to gain rapid senior leadership commitment to the complete redesign and turnaround of facilities development. Wheatley actively engaged with other leaders and got them behind her team's method of change. For the facilities development reorganization to succeed, numerous other divisions and departments would have to collaborate differently (for example, as facilities development redesigned its purchasing practices, the purchasing department would have to reorganize many of its own practices).

Wheatley and the network of leaders throughout the enterprise helped people understand the changes that were planned, the rationale for the new actions proposed, and the new roles that would be required from them. Other department leaders held their people accountable for delivering promised actions and results. Ultimately, leaders from finance, auditing, procurement, organization development, human resources, and corporate planning were brought on board, as well as the medical and administrative leaders from each of the sixteen hospitals and medical centers in the region. Each department or facility knew how it fit into the larger change and committed to the actions its members would need to take.

Wheatley worked with other VPs to convince them that she not only needed support from their divisions but also needed much higher performance than usual during the transition. Human resources, for example, helped write two hundred job descriptions in one week (rather than the twelve weeks this would normally have required at that time). Other departments too joined in the spirit, energy, and high performance required for the change. This rapid and far-reaching change was possible only with the support of many leaders and many teams working together.

We have seen change efforts of similar scope fall apart several months into a project when a previously unenrolled senior leader did not fully sign on to the change process. In one case, after six months of highly committed work by large numbers of people, a senior leader from the parent company stopped the project. Change team members, along with the rest of the workforce, which had been actively involved in all elements of the project (from assessment to visioning to redesign), were left skeptical and cynical about any future possibilities for change.

One leader alone can rarely lead a multidimensional complex change effort. It is essential to know where all the leaders stand who are crucial to a project before investing large amounts of time, resources, and energy. All key leaders involved must be pulling in the same direction for the changes to succeed.

Providing Clear Parameters and Tools for Change

Leaders must signal how big a change is required. Does the leader expect stakeholders or change team members to design improvements in existing work processes or to pursue incremental problem solving, or does the change require a rethinking of the fundamental strategies and core work processes? Is the change a transformational leap to a new curve? How much creativity or "blue-sky thinking" is encouraged—or allowed? Most employees will look to their formal leaders (the leaders to whom they report) to offer definitions, even if some other leader has been designated team leader, project manager, or "change czar."

Each of the leaders described in these examples provided leadership not only for motivation and inspiration but also for direction and clarity about the change. Stakeholders had a clear vision of the future, an understanding of what was required and why, a realistic assessment of the current situation, and a good sense of the expectations for the change process.

In addition, the leaders not only *motivated* their stakeholders to change but also provided the tools and structure for the change process that *enabled* stakeholders to change. These leaders put a competent *change organization* in place, one that included steering councils, specific change teams, and means to engage the larger group of stakeholders who would implement or support the changes. (We provide more details on this later in this chapter.) Councils and team members were regularly provided with information they needed to be successful (such as assessment data, benchmarking data, or industry trends), as well as training in team skills or particular change methodologies if needed (such as cost-modeling tools, partnering, change management, or project management skills). Team members working on a range of changes were given specific parameters for time lines, budgets, working or reporting relationships for the change project itself, and expected results. Within the given parameters of the change they were working on, team members were then encouraged to act innovatively and creatively to deliver the actual designs and ideas needed to reach the goals.

Stakeholders

The stakeholders of an enterprise are predominantly its employees but may also include others who can influence the future direction of the enterprise, such as strategic partners, suppliers, legislators, community members, and key customers. Some stakeholder groups will have more influence than others, and some may be included more than others in particular phases of the development process. Employees are usually the largest and most important stakeholder group, but ultimately *all* stakeholders will influence the development effort. To the extent that they all participate in the development process, their influence becomes an integral part of the effort.

Ultimately, it is the stakeholders who enact or inhibit the development of the enterprise. In many ways, the stakeholders are the *real drivers* of the development process. If they do not support it, change does not occur. The stakeholders cannot remain passive. They have much to do in the development process: they must act as the key designers and implementers of the changes ahead; they must be involved every step of the way. Stakeholders are also the ones who actually live through the transitions; they have to let go of old practices and learn new ways of doing their work. They are the ones who ultimately enact the repairs, improvements, and transformations.

Stakeholders are a diverse lot who may need to get to know other members of their own group and learn how the various groups fit into the whole system. They need to understand who all the other stakeholders are and how to formulate plans and make decisions in ways that are best for each group and the enterprise overall. Getting this overview of the entire stakeholder community is often a developmental task in itself.

> In a health care institution trying to reduce wasteful expenses, departments typically made cuts in their own budgets without considering the effects on other departments. When their company began an Enterprise Development effort, the stakeholders began to see themselves as a larger network. They became more aware of the impact of their decisions on others in their group. In one case, they learned that when they had cut costs by 5 percent (a change they had been extremely proud of), their cuts had caused an increase in costs in a neighboring department that were five times larger than their savings! As they began to understand their connections to the other stakeholders, they readily joined with them to redistribute the accounting for their budgets and developed tools for "program budgeting." Their new solution actually raised the costs in the first department slightly but decreased the costs in the second by a much greater percentage. This ultimately delivered better service to patients and employer groups at lower overall cost to the larger enterprise.

No Secrets

Stakeholders are generally very smart—they have good instincts and are not easily fooled. Secrets rarely exist for long in any enterprise. Everyone generally knows what is taking place, even when the information officially communicated tells a different story. For this reason, it is important for leaders to communicate honestly and openly with stakeholders and for stakeholders to do the same with each other.

Stakeholders carry powerful information of their own. When they are given important business information freely and openly, they most often respond by sharing their own crucial data (which leaders are often not aware they have). In one enterprise, the managers did not want to tell employees of impending layoffs because they were afraid employees would quit once they were told. In fact, employees had already learned of the layoffs, and withholding the information only strengthened their distrust of their managers and put them into an adversarial relationship. In another division, where the managers did share information freely with employees, the employees gave managers data on their own intuitions about the shaky loyalty of a key customer group, and as a result, they were able to work together to save this key account before the customer went elsewhere.

Engaging Stakeholders

Stakeholders in many of today's enterprises tend to be hypercritical. Given an ambiguous situation, they rarely give leaders or other stakeholders the benefit of the doubt. They will often have serious (and valid) concerns about particular changes occurring, and if they do not know the details of what is happening, they tend to assume the worst. Given this tendency, leaders and other stakeholders must communicate very clearly—and often. A development process that involves substantial change will rarely be welcomed with open arms. An expectation must be built into the development effort that allows for stakeholders to be suspicious and distrustful of change, since distrust almost always occurs. The members of each group of stakeholders will need a slightly different approach from leaders for them to take the development effort seriously, to believe that it is something other than their leaders "trying to get them to do more while getting paid less." Transforming each group of stakeholders from a potentially suspicious group expecting to be exploited into powerful participants in the development of their enterprise requires artfulness on the part of those carrying out the development process.

"Tell Them Early, Tell Them Often, Tell It All"

Margaret Jordan, a vice president brought into Southern California Edison to transform its corporate health care division, provides a clear example of how powerfully a leader can engage initially suspicious and critical stakeholders and help them become capable of far-reaching change (for further details, see Jordan, 1996). For more than seventy years, Edison had provided in-house health care to employees and retirees in one of the best-known self-administered corporate health care systems in the United States. Over the years, the utility had built up eight medical clinics, a pharmacy, laboratory services, and a self-administered, self-insured health benefits program. It employed almost three hundred health care professionals to serve over fifty-five thousand employees, retirees, and family members.

At the start of the 1990s, like many other large employers, Edison's health care costs were increasing rapidly. Under the direction of its previous administration, Edison made dramatic changes to its health benefit program to control these costs, but at the price of alienating its major unions and many of its other employees. By the mid 1990s, it became clear that further changes would be required to continue to reduce costs, and a formal negotiated agreement with the union would be necessary.

Jordan's charge was clear, although not easy. She had to determine if the company's health care system needed to be redefined and, if so, to lead the necessary changes. She had to accomplish this assessment and change in the face of major distrust from both union and nonunion leaders. To have even a chance for success, she had to turn their distrust into collaboration.

In short order, Jordan recognized that Edison's Health Care Program (its health benefit plan, direct delivery system, and the department itself) needed to be fundamentally changed. Edison needed to move out of the insurance and health care delivery business and instead become an organization capable of negotiating and managing contracts with external companies that could provide health care services more efficiently than the utility could itself. To pursue these solutions, Jordan first had to gain support and negotiate clear agreements with the unions about changes in health benefits. They needed to understand the reasons behind the changes and lend their wholehearted support.

As the work progressed, it became apparent that the new function would require fewer than 25 percent of the current workforce. However, Jordan also knew that the only way she could accomplish this massive transformation would be with the help of the very employees whose lives would be turned upside down.

Jordan described her charge as "asking employees to help build a house that most of them would not live in." She did not try to hide the fact that almost all of the people involved in the change effort would either lose their current job or stay employed in a workplace environment completely different from the one they were accustomed to. Even her own job would be short-lived: she would be designing herself out of a role as well.

Jordan succeeded at her transformation effort while facing some of the toughest challenges of change. She explains that although the department lost some employees before the transformation was complete, "the majority of employees took the challenge to stay and participate in an exciting enterprise rebirth." How did Jordan and her transition teams accomplish this change? How was an initially skeptical group of stakeholders turned into a team capable of orchestrating and implementing a complex transformation, even while they knew their own jobs were disappearing?

Jordan believed in the power of clear and honest information about a compelling need for change to help engage large numbers of stakeholders. Jordan's key motto was "Tell them early, tell them often, tell them all." She believed that all stakeholders—employees in the Health Care Program as well as employees and retirees who would be affected by the changes—should be treated respectfully, as adults, and given as much information about the changes ahead as possible. In addition, she outlined a series of four principles for the change teams to follow in engaging stakeholders into the change effort:

- Communication with all employees will be open, direct, candid, and factual.
- Employees will be involved in the transition process whenever possible.
- Employees will be encouraged to look at their situation realistically and be helped to take charge of their own future by making decisions based on objective criteria.
- Each individual will be treated with dignity and grace.

These principles guided all actions taken. Communication occurred constantly through every conceivable venue: large group meetings, department and ad hoc gatherings, e-mail, phones, one-on-one meetings, memos, and newsletters. In short, if a path to communication existed, it was used.

All employees were encouraged to participate in facilitated problem solving and design meetings. Self-assessment, personal development, and career counseling services were made available in parallel with the broader organizational change initiatives. In this way, while people were helping develop the future organization, they were also gaining skills and confidence for building their own future.

People were consistently supported where they had the most significant needs: if it was information they wanted, they got information; if it was support, that's what they received; if they needed a particular action to be taken, that action was initiated.

The Futures Forum

Because many stakeholders may need to understand and quickly support a given development effort, there is often insufficient time to begin a change at the top and have it "cascade down" or to begin at the front lines and have the message travel up and across.

the organization. Sometimes hundreds or even thousands of people must be involved in changes in the enterprise. Everyone needs to see the new conditions at once and give input into future designs and plans. Each of the leaders described in this chapter at some point used town hall meetings, "all hands" meetings, or facilitated large group events to get significant numbers of stakeholders engaged very quickly.

In our practice, we have used the Futures Forum, an interactive meeting designed to enable eighty to two hundred fifty people, representing a cross section of key stakeholder and leadership groups, to build an Enterprise Development map for the changes they face together. Because key stakeholder groups are represented at the event, the information generated represents a wide breadth of knowledge available in the enterprise. Stakeholder groups get to know each other very quickly. They learn which groups affect their own work, as well as which ones depend on them. Decisions and plans are also much more likely to be implemented, as they already contain input from the full range of stakeholders. In addition, representatives from work groups present can take the ideas generated at the forum back to their own departments or teams and transform ideas into action more quickly.

Similar to the Enterprise Development Futures Forum, there are many tools and methodologies emerging for conducting interactive events for large groups of stakeholders (for a summary of these methods, see Bunker and Alban, 1996). Though each approach has a slightly different structure and delivers somewhat different benefits or perspectives to the change process, all focus on the advantage of "getting the whole system in the room." Steps are usually built in to the meeting process that allow key groups to interact, as well as work in their homogeneous subgroups to integrate the input.

Performance Support

Performance support provides the processes and infrastructure needed to enable stakeholders and leaders actually to *perform* to the vision. The concept of performance support is still new and unfamiliar to many who are working to create a Dynamic Enterprise capable of managing continuous change. However, the role is indispensable when executing large-scale change. The existence of performance support to track and enable development efforts has often made the difference between an enterprise that succeeds in implementing needed change and one that abandons its efforts partway through, as soon as resistance crops up. When people get busy with the day-to-day operational pressures of the enterprise, performance support often keeps the change alive and ensures that everyone gets back to it.

Some work groups call this function *change support* or *transition support*. The members serve the same function as the team we prefer to call *performance support* to reflect the fact that *performance* is the primary objective of the Dynamic Enterprise. The capability of quickly and smoothly designing and implementing change is not for the sake of change itself. The Dynamic Enterprise changes only to achieve higher levels of performance in response to changing conditions in the business environment.

The Role of Performance Support

Performance support is usually provided by teams composed of members from key stakeholder groups, often with trainers, consultants, or support staff (internal, external, or a combination of both) who are knowledgeable about large-scale change and development. It is their job to support stakeholders and leaders to achieve the desired new levels of performance.

Performance to a new vision and strategy typically demands that stakeholders work in different ways, that they let go of old practices and work styles. Stakeholders must think and act in new ways. They often must simultaneously learn new skills, work with departments or functions they have never worked with before, communicate differently, make decisions that were previously made by others, take on new responsibilities, learn new technologies, and even handle their conflicts and emotions differently. Yet people do not readily adopt new ways of working, even when they are asked to make only minor changes. People do not simply change when asked. People change when they are given support to change. They need good reasons, clear information, encouragement, and the necessary tools and assistance.

The aim of the performance support function is to enable competent performance by stakeholders. The work of performance support is to ensure that stakeholders have the support and resources they need to move from their current state and capabilities and, step by step, develop the new skills and behaviors required by the new vision. Ultimately, performance support's role is to assist the stakeholders and leaders to bring the vision to life.

Large-scale change efforts inevitably experience breakdowns at multiple points in the implementation process. Although comprehensive planning can ward off some of those breakdowns, change never proceeds exactly as planned. All the details and unique reactions of various stakeholder groups can never be foretold and designed into the change process. One group may need further training before its members can begin to take the required new actions; another team's members may need emotional support before they are willing to let go of their old work habits. A third group may be willing to work with other stakeholder groups but not know the members of those groups or how to contact them. Others just "get busy" and cancel a meeting scheduled to work on the new vision. The performance support team is the group of people who coordinate these details and can connect stakeholders with the resources they need. They catch the breakdowns and attend to them. Performance support team members maintain an overview of all aspects of the change process and help keep it on track. Ensuring successful development is their job.

A New Function

Much has been written and a great deal of common knowledge is available about the role of leadership in large-scale change, as well as the need for stakeholder participation, ownership, and empowerment. Much less is known about the role of change management or performance support. The idea of a performance support team as a full-time function is still relatively new. Just as the advent of rapidly emerging new information technologies led to a growth of information technology capabilities in many enterprises and institutions, the recognition of ongoing change and development as an integral part of the Dynamic Enterprise must lead to the provision of an ongoing capability for strategic change as well. When performance guided by a constantly shifting future vision is seen as a core task of an institution, necessary for survival in a dynamic marketplace, the effective management of change and an ongoing change support function become essential elements of its process and structure.

A Multidimensional Function

The role of the performance support team is multidimensional. Let's take a closer look at some of performance support's responsibilities.

Change Management Expertise

Performance support team members are usually drawn from line organizations and are trained to become change and development specialists in the context of their change support team assignment. They become knowledgeable about developmental dynamics in both the business and the organization. They play a central role in the design, planning, implementation, monitoring, and communication aspects of the development process. They guide leaders and stakeholders in Enterprise Development and change, supporting them to think strategically, systematically, and developmentally. They may benchmark how other institutions develop, set visions, and align performance with strategy. When members of the enterprise wonder how they can best accomplish changes they need to achieve within their own unit, the performance support team can facilitate them through this process.

Organizational Systems Design

Performance support team members act as innovators for the change process. Because many team members come from stakeholder groups and from the line organization, they retain their understanding of the stakeholders' current culture and practices, but at the same time, they are asked to be one step ahead. For example, many performance support teams work with their human resource departments to ensure that reward and recognition systems promote movement toward the envisioned future. They work with the information technology departments to create or install communication systems that allow new teams to work together or new networks to form. They may work with the finance groups to determine how business units that produce major cost savings are rewarded for those savings. (In many efforts, departments that succeed in decreasing their costs often have their budgets reduced the following year. Thus they are punished for their good work and end up with less money available for innovative projects they may have wanted to undertake.) The performance support team keeps current with the latest social and technical tools and practices that enable large systems to change more rapidly and more effectively.

It is not the role of performance support to implement these new practices themselves but rather to facilitate key leaders and stakeholder groups to develop the systems as needed.

Facilitating Engagement, Collaboration, and Participation

The performance support team helps promote engagement and solidify relationships between leaders and stakeholder groups, as well as between stakeholder groups with each other. They support participation, linking, collaboration, and relationship building among all who need to engage with one another for the vision to become a reality. For example, managers may need to develop relationships with key customer groups, leaders with local community leaders, or one group of stakeholders with another. The performance support team can help them to build these key relationships by clarifying the alliances needed, scheduling events, facilitating meetings, or helping secure whatever resources each unique situation requires.

Coordination and Project Management

The performance support team is responsible for the overall coordination and project management of the change effort. Team members have insight into the range of needs and activities taking place throughout the institution. They are sensitive to seeing if one area has been left out of the process or if redundant efforts are occurring that could be combined. They monitor calendars of scheduled events to make sure that activities and changes occur within the appropriate time frames. However, this team is not a centralized planning body, as tasks specific to the change efforts within a given area should be assumed and carried out by the stakeholders closest to the work. The performance support group serves as a resource for the stakeholders, providing an overview of all the activities in other areas of the enterprise.

Communication and Visibility

Performance support team members play a key role in keeping the overall development process visible and helping stakeholders connect to other members of the institution in ways that can move the process forward. The performance support team may keep development wall maps visible for all, create on-line "dashboards" or bulletin boards, or collect case studies of successes and failures that help stakeholders learn from one another's work. Some groups put out newsletters or hold regular, informal meetings to focus on what is working best and what has not worked well and needs to be adjusted.

Information Clearinghouse and Referral Center

The performance support team acts as the clearinghouse for information on the development process and keeps stakeholders and leaders connected to each other in ways that help them be more productive. The team is often a knowledgeable databank or referral source. When members in the institution have questions or need a particular type of expertise, the performance support team can generally help them find others inside or outside the enterprise who can help them with the challenge at hand.

Administrative Logistics

The performance support team manages the many practical, logistical details of the development process. The team "gets it on the schedule" and "makes it all happen" by coordinating and scheduling key meetings; facilitating meetings or workshops for groups that need to do in-depth work together; arranging necessary events, presentations, and activities (if stakeholders request help with them); and helping to produce or distribute materials.

Providing Trustworthy Emotional Support

Sometimes a new vision creates a crisis. People may be moved out of roles they have had for an entire career or are placed into new roles they had never expected for themselves. They need to learn new skills, new technologies, or new ways to work, often with colleagues they don't yet know. People may be experiencing many losses as well—of territory, long-built expertise, the predictability and stability of their work environment, identity, and the future they expected. In times of such significant change, many people will quite naturally and appropriately require emotional support to let go of the old and make the leap to new practices and behaviors. They may need a sounding board to help determine what to keep of the old ways and what to let go, or they may need coaching or guidance in the new culture. They may also need a place to bring legitimate grievances or criticisms of the development process, as well as a place to contribute their own knowledge.

Catching Breakdowns

One of the most important roles of the performance support team is to catch the inevitable breakdowns and help get the development effort back on track. This role may determine whether the change effort succeeds or not. We have seen many enterprises that attempted to work toward a new vision and yet had no process in place to catch the breakdowns. They expected simply to outline the new expectations and then wait for everyone to meet them. Everyone assumed that managers would "manage to the vision," and as a result, the vision would be actualized. Experience has taught us that in the midst of complex change, this simple, linear process rarely occurs. The development effort is kept on track only when performance support teams work hand in hand with strong leadership—especially when we consider the demands of the daily business routine experienced by members of an institution.

Transforming Negativity into Momentum for Change

Some stakeholders will readily appreciate a new change process. They have been hoping for it and waiting for it, often for a long time. Their general outlook on life is optimistic, and they expect change to happen as planned. Unfortunately, this group may be in the minority. Most stakeholders will be skeptical of any new change initiative. They have seen numerous change programs come and go. Some programs worked for a while, but most were abandoned before they were fully implemented. Therefore, particularly at the beginning of a new change process, many stakeholders may be reserved and cautious. Many have complaints and grievances they have held in for years, and when a large systemwide vision and development process is initiated, all of these critical ideas and negative feelings naturally rise to the surface.

Sounds tough! Just when an institution is willing to face its future and when it needs all of its stakeholders to use their best intelligence to design and implement an enterprise that can survive in a rapidly changing marketplace and external environment, the very worst complaints and deepest feelings begin to bubble to the surface. As members of the institution initiate an exciting improvement process, or perhaps even revolutionary change, people bring up the grievances (both petty and substantial) that they have held on to for years. Many such complaints are not expressed formally but surface in the grapevine or in hallway conversation. It may seem unfair to raise these issues just at the time the enterprise is trying to change, but the phenomenon occurs very often. The way leaders and the performance support team work together to face these emerging criticisms and complaints will have a strong influence on the course of the entire development effort.

Stakeholders are much more likely to bring up these issues with performance support team members than with their leaders, and the performance support team can bring significant value to connecting the stakeholders with the leadership. Let's look at two examples of how performance support members performed this important role.

A global firm had recently reorganized to become more flexible and quick to respond to changes and had set up weekly video teleconferences with the executive leadership so that people could communicate with them directly from the various locations of the company. However, people were resentful of the changes and did not trust their leaders. No one asked questions in the teleconferences, and the conferences were eventually discontinued. In one location where no performance support team had been set up, people started an underground e-mail network, complaining about the teleconferences and eventually about other issues as well. The tone of the messages was quite negative, as most writers voiced resentment at how terrible everything was. The leaders in this location assumed an authoritarian stance; to squelch the growing negativity, they made it impossible to send e-mail messages anonymously and blocked access to the electronic bulletin board completely. However, the negative feelings did not go away; they continued to grow in backroom conversations.

In another location in the same company, a performance support team had been put in place. The same e-mail phenomenon began to develop. The reactions that the performance support team members observed made sense because they themselves were part of the stakeholder community. They understood the existing distrust of the leaders. They saw the anonymous e-mail complaints as a sign of a vibrant and energetic group discussion, and they wanted to capture this energy for the change process. They arranged to bring the leaders into direct dialogue via e-mail. In this way, the conversations that people had withheld in the more public video teleconference settings could now occur anonymously. The development process was not easy or smooth, but it got the real issues on the table, and leaders and stakeholders began to address them in authentic ways. Face-to-face meetings soon followed, and more people began to attend. After several months, the tone of the e-mail messages and conversations began to shift, and more and more of the stakeholders joined in the development process with increased interest and trust.

———————

Charlie Rickard, the head of Alva Wheatley's performance support team at Kaiser Permanente (described earlier in this chapter), directed the team that enabled the facilities development division to make such rapid change. When Wheatley committed to undertake transformational change in a short time frame, she knew that the pieces had to fall into place at exactly the right time. The change process had to be managed, just as a construction project did. When meetings were necessary, the logistics were handled and events happened as scheduled. When assessment or benchmarking data were needed to design the future organization, performance support would gather the information or expertise and get it to where it was needed. Employees were given support to assess their work skills and to find roles in the new organization where they could put their knowledge and talents to use, even if these differed from the skills they used in their previous positions.

The performance support team also managed communications about the changes as they occurred. Particularly at the beginning, many details were still unknown. However, the performance support team distributed whatever information was available, as soon as it was available. All members kept their eyes and ears open, in both formal feedback sessions and informal ones. They stayed in touch with the active grapevine throughout the division and the larger company. Rickard described how they kept the change process vibrant and alive by publishing all the feedback, both positive and negative. "If something was in the rumor mill, we put it in the newsletter." If the concern was legitimate, they addressed it. If it wasn't, they gave the accurate information. People affected by the changes knew that their concerns were being addressed. The team's quick response to identified difficulties and to correcting misinformation and assuaging unfounded fears helped stakeholders develop trust in the team and in the change process overall.

Linking the Three Drivers for Development

As depicted schematically in Figure 8.1, it is important that the three drivers—leaders, stakeholders, and performance support—be aligned with one another. Each driver needs clear communication and ongoing support and authorization for planned actions. The three groups must work well together. Leaders must give clear and consistent signals that the performance support and stakeholder groups are authorized, sponsored, and encouraged to do what they are doing. Likewise, the performance support team must believe in and support the leaders as well as the stakeholders.

A test of the effectiveness of the linkages of these alliances that we see quite often occurs when stakeholders go to the performance support team to complain about the leaders, rather than going to the leadership directly. The performance support members are often pulled to side with stakeholders because they generally come out of the stakeholder group. They can be tempted to try to gain popularity and very subtly (or sometimes not so subtly) undermine the credibility of the leadership. It is important that at such junctures the performance support members balance the different pulls for supporting the stakeholders and supporting the leaders. The key role of performance support in this case is not to pit work groups and leaders against each other from an adversarial either-or perspective but to support the *two* groups as they work out their issues. Performance support members must communicate to stakeholders both that the stakeholders' issues are legitimate and that the leaders are to be trusted in their leadership role. The performance support team's role is crucial in these cases for ensuring that the three driver groups stay linked and working toward the same objectives throughout the development process.

> In the Kaiser Permanente project, Wheatley as a leader, Rickard as the head of performance support, and other performance support members made a powerful team for responding to urgent change. Wheatley continued to keep her core performance support team intact when she took on new roles and projects (while adding members from the new work groups as well). This combined leadership–performance support team alliance became recognized for being able to bring out major transformations or to kick off new corporate initiatives. Wheatley described being criticized regularly for taking along "her team," in an era when individual performance was the norm, but she found that the working alliance that had been built between leader and performance support was a valuable part of managing major changes more quickly and smoothly. It had taken time to learn how to manage change together and to nurture and fine-tune their working relationships. This was not something that could be dismantled and re-created later on without significant delay. Over time, she and her team became recognized as an effective leadership–performance support team that could be called on to help tackle some of the company's toughest challenges.

Tests

The Dynamic Enterprise moves forward through a process of *testing*. Each of the three drivers for development—leadership, stakeholders, and performance support—are tested in unique ways, and the way they respond to these tests tells the members of the enterprise whether to take the new actions required for the vision. If any one group fails its tests, the needed development will not occur, and the enterprise will not reach its hoped-for vision.

Imagine an enterprise poised to kick off the implementation of a change. Leaders and members have generally learned and accomplished a great deal by this time. They have worked hard together to create a shared picture of their enterprise and the challenges that lie ahead. They have taken a look at the whole system of the enterprise at different times in its history and learned where it has been, where it is now, and where it needs to go. They have examined the forces coming from the external environment, the market pressures, changing technology, and the changing expectations of their customers. They have recognized the forces pushing for change—from the external environment, from their business tasks, and from the internal needs of the organization itself.

Leaders and members of the enterprise have also identified critical business issues affecting the enterprise. They have identified the *pushes* from the stakeholder community: they discovered that customers and other stakeholders want something *now*—they are impatient, yearning for something. Participants now understand those needs, desires, and opportunities. They also have views about the developments going on in the internal environment, about the changes in the mission and changes in the focus of the leadership. All those forces are pushing the enterprise forward from where it is today.

In addition, participants have developed formulations about the *pulls* on their enterprise toward the future vision. The future environment contains strong pulls toward new opportunities. Participants have learned to clarify those pulls, to use them as the catalytic forces for capitalizing on the opportunities offered by the future. They have created a vision of how the enterprise can best respond to the emerging opportunities. They have agreed on changes in the ways things will be done, on potentially new organizational structures, and on new working relationships and expectations that are quite different from those of today.

All of this work was done to enable the people of the enterprise—its stakeholders—to have the clarity they needed to leave old roles behind and to commit themselves to the new roles and actions necessary to reach the future vision. These shared understandings enable them to feel empowered, to experience a sense of control that comes from clarity, and to have a sense of confidence in the new direction, rather than being mystified by ambiguity and complexity.

The picture of the needed change has been drawn for all to see, often literally drawn in visual images on large wall maps. The direction is clear. Confidence abounds as leaders and members alike expect the vision to be implemented. *But will it be?*

A new challenge emerges: the picture is now clearer than ever, but it is still only a picture, an internalized image, a vision of what the enterprise could become. Now comes the challenge of actually getting there, of doing all the things required—enacting behaviors that may be altogether new and previously unknown. It is now time to create the changes. It is also the time for tests.

The Fuel for Converting Plans into Action: Tests and Responses

When the enterprise embarks on a planned journey toward a changed future, members engage in a number of testing behaviors to check what will be required of them if they are to function successfully in the emerging enterprise. They also check the sincerity of their leaders' involvement and commitment and the capabilities of performance support:

- What will the picture really look like in implementation?
- What behaviors will be validated and rewarded, and what others will be disallowed?
- What responsibilities will be placed on people?
- What skills will be required?
- Do the leaders mean what they say?
- Are the leaders really committed to change?
- Is the support for change stable and reliable?
- Are the stakeholders willing to team up with others to participate in change?

To find answers to these questions—and regain a sense of clarity and conviction about the enterprise and their place in it, as well as to solidify their commitment to change—the people of the enterprise listen to what they are told, but then they *test* with their behavior.

People will test—and watch for the response, not always consciously. They will then act on the message implied in the response. For example, if the leaders are tested to see if they mean what they say and their response implies that their actions don't align with their words, the stakeholders won't feel compelled to change their own behavior either. Stakeholders may likewise change only their words, just as they saw their leaders do. Some may consciously and somewhat maliciously take this route, but for many others the response is unconscious. Their failure to take new actions will occur in the natural course of many split-second decisions that are made during the workday, and they may not even realize that they are continuing to act in the old ways.

Because the phenomenon of testing and the often unconscious modeling of the responses is so powerful, it is important for leaders, stakeholders, and performance support members to expect these tests and to be prepared for them.

Stakeholders test each of the driver groups (including other stakeholders) in specific ways related to their role in the development process:

- Leadership must pass tests of commitment.
- Stakeholders must pass tests of responsibility.
- Performance support must pass tests of competence (can they enable *stakeholder* competence?).

Figure 8.2 shows how these tests are illustrated on the Enterprise Development framework.

Figure 8.2. The Three Drivers and Their Leadership Tests.

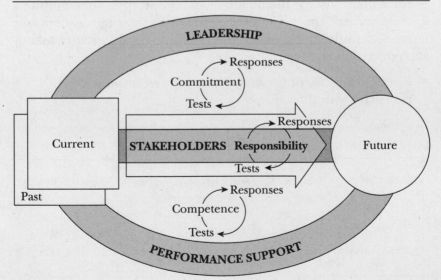

Figure 8.3. Failed Test.

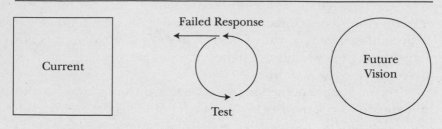

In Figures 8.3 and 8.4, the arrows represent tests from the stakeholders toward each driver group and the response to the stakeholders. If the test is failed, stakeholders withdraw their energies and resources from the change effort. Failed tests typically push the development back toward the current conditions. But when tests are passed, stakeholders become more strongly committed. Successful tests tend to energize the stakeholders. The stakeholders take increased responsibility for the new actions, and they are supported and enabled to be competent at their new roles. Successfully passing the tests drives change forward.

How Leadership Is Tested

When a plan calls for the members of an enterprise to commit to a new direction, they will quite naturally observe their leaders and check for confirmation before they begin to act differently, asking such questions as these:

• Is the leadership of the enterprise aligned with the new plan, with the vision?

Figure 8.4. Successful Response.

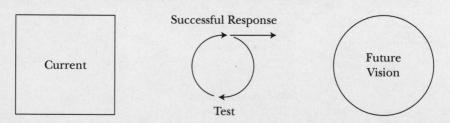

- Are the leaders committed to changing *themselves* in ways required by the plan?
- Are leaders behaving in ways that demonstrate their commitment to the emerging enterprise?

Stakeholders will test the leadership for *commitment*. Members will watch their leaders very closely for signals that either reinforce or contradict the expressed direction of the enterprise. They will challenge and test their leaders around expectations set by the new vision.

Stakeholders will internalize their own commitment to the vision and begin to translate that commitment into action only when they have experienced commitment firsthand in the behaviors of their leaders. They will test—and watch. If the leaders fail their tests, the members of the enterprise typically withdraw their own commitment, and the enterprise will most likely not succeed in going where it is planning to go.

A powerful feature of testing the leaders is the pervasive hope that they fail the tests because people often wish to preserve the status quo, no matter how compelling the new vision. People have settled into the comfort that comes from familiarity, and some fear the unknown. If leaders fail their tests, relief and disappointment mix into corporate cynicism and blame. If things are not perfect, at least they are known. With this attitude often comes "just enough" performance, actions that are enough to *look like* they are in the direction of the vision but that are not actually enough to make substantial changes happen.

But human beings also thrive on discovery and mastery. Many desire growth. They aim to do better. They crave learning and creativity. This side of human nature hopes for leaders to pass the tests. Seeing commitment in action, through leaders' behavior and symbolically powerful acts, engenders hope, commitment, and courage to move in directions that are as yet unknown. This type of energy promotes breakthrough actions that are necessary for achieving the desired future.

In the Southern California Edison example earlier in this chapter, Margaret Jordan understood that stakeholders needed to test her as a leader. In one of the "all hands" meetings called to give information about the upcoming changes and to elicit stakeholder's input, Jordan asked department members for their questions about changes they faced. No one responded. There were no questions. This was a moment where many other leaders might have heaved a sigh of relief and moved on to the next topic. However, Jordan recognized this as a test. She *knew* that people had questions, and she wanted to give them accurate and realistic answers. She understood the great cost of people holding on to their concerns and assumptions and was unwilling to let the moment go by, thus wasting a powerful development opportunity. She asked everyone to write down questions they had and then called a break so that she could read them and organize her responses.

After the break, Jordan answered the questions one by one. It turned out that there were indeed a number of questions that she had previously heard murmured in the halls, as well as straightforward requests for information that people needed to know to do a good job in designing the changes ahead. She answered each question with great authenticity and forthrightness. Her response to their previous silence signaled to stakeholders that she really did want them actively involved, that she would in fact require their full participation. She would not tolerate a stance of passive standing back and waiting. They needed to know what was ahead because they all had a great deal of work to do together.

The questions actually presented another test for Jordan as well. Toward the end of the question-and-answer session, which by now had become quite animated, Jordan told the group that two of the written questions had actually been hostile comments directed toward other department members. Jordan did not read these comments to the group but rather encouraged the individuals who had written them to think their reactions through and consider how they might be related to the change. If their comments stemmed from an emotional response, she encouraged them to reflect on their own feelings, take a walk, talk to a friend, or come talk to her so that she could help find a way to make the changes easier or more workable for them. Blaming each other would not help anyone move forward. Conversely, if there were actual work issues to be addressed with other group members, they needed to be approached as serious work-related concerns. She encouraged all participants to take responsibility and "work their issues." Perhaps they might talk with a neutral third party (such as a performance support facilitator) to plan how to resolve their concerns.

Jordan's response let her people know that blaming would not be tolerated. They needed to work together through this emotional time. She was respectful of people's natural and understandable emotional responses to these significant changes and offered support they needed so that they could take a more productive approach to the impending change. It was a moving moment in the group and one remembered throughout the change process.

By the time Jordan returned to her office, e-mail had already begun arriving. People expressed appreciation for her forthrightness and for her setting a standard for collaborative and productive work. They were energized by the meeting and were ready to go to work. This outpouring of energy is a typical sign of a leader's successful response to a test. A successful test mobilizes energy and spirit in service of the work.

In reality, leaders will not pass all tests. Even excellent leaders watching out for tests will miss some here and there. If failed tests are caught after the fact, the effects can often still be turned around.

In a major reorganization in a manufacturing plant, a number of people needed to change jobs and reporting relationships. Everyone understood the reasons for these changes and accepted the new strategy. However, when it was time for people actually to take up their new work roles, one manager who was also an old friend of the vice president in charge of the initiative called him up "to cash in his chips." The manager cajoled his friend, "You can't do this to me. I've worked here for twenty-two years. Remember all the times I've supported you." This was a test. The vice president could have stuck to the plan, explained the need for the change, and worked with the manager to find a way to make the change easier. Instead, in the words of other group members, "he caved in." The vice president told the manager he didn't have to move to the new position.

This event was soon known throughout the organization and seemed to take the wind out of the sails for the change effort. Other team members assumed that the leader was not really committed, and in what was a very political work environment, they were not about to hang their professional reputations on a halfhearted initiative that they expected would never be fully implemented.

When the leader became aware of how visible his behavior had been and what a strong impact it had made, he realized that he had failed a crucial test that put the entire change effort at risk. In truth, he was strongly committed to the change and was unwilling to see it fail. He believed that the change was essential for the survival of the company. Knowing that this test was critical, he also understood that he had to go back and repair the situation—on two fronts. First, he had to work with his long-term friend and colleague to help him understand how important it was for him to support the new change. He worked with this manager to find a way to reshape his new role, to make it acceptable to him while still supporting the new work process and organization. The manager could not be exempt from the needed changes.

Second, the leader went back to the stakeholder group and acknowledged his role in the previous difficulties and announced the new resolution. This was another test that offered him a new opportunity to demonstrate his commitment to the change. His open acknowledgment of his struggle and his own learning actually turned out to be a powerful motivator for his team, as they saw in real time that both professional and personal change was required. Stakeholders heard the message.

How Stakeholders Are Tested

Ultimately, the enterprise is its people. Whether or not they fulfill the promise of their enterprise is in large part determined by their sense of involvement in it. The test of the stakeholders is related to their willingness and courage to take *responsibility* for the planned developments. Whereas the test of the leaders is "upward," this test of the stakeholders is "inward." Stakeholders, in effect, test one another. They test their willingness to follow, to initiate, to participate in a way that allows all stakeholders to express their authority, courage, talents, and spirit in service of the overall enterprise. Stakeholder tests are crucial because it is ultimately the common spirit, the common effort of the entire community of stakeholders, that drives the enterprise to its successful future.

To pass stakeholder tests, full and *responsible* engagement is required. Effective self-testing requires a new discipline for the members of an enterprise, discipline that replaces the controls from the traditional chain-of-command structures. Enterprises will always encounter some difficulties in progressing toward a challenging vision. A typical stakeholder test is whether stakeholders can question their own role and responsibility in these difficulties or whether they finger-point and place the blame elsewhere. If they acknowledge only awkward moments caused by the failures of leaders or other departments, they will fail the test of stakeholder responsibility. They will not be able to question their own role and ultimately will not be able to change.

The unleashing of the total intelligence of the enterprise comes from everyone's shared actions for the benefit of the whole. If stakeholders act only in service of their own personal or departmental interests, that choice can jeopardize the development of the overall enterprise. Most of today's complex visions require that stakeholders balance various responsibilities—to themselves, to their departments or functions, and to the whole system. If a particular seemingly appropriate action helps the reputation or fiscal health of one division but does so at the detriment of another division, the overall enterprise has not been advanced. The stakeholder test of responsibility requires that stakeholders recognize and accept their multiple responsibilities and be able to chart the best course to keep them all in balance.

One utility company faced difficulties that arose when its stakeholders failed their tests. The utility was launching a major reengineering effort to improve service and cut costs in the face of upcoming deregulation and the massively increased competition predicted to lie ahead. Leaders were attempting to transform their organization to become process-driven and had identified six core processes that crossed functional department boundaries. Six reengineering teams began to look at how each process could be improved. Meanwhile, the CEO had recently warned that the company needed to cut over $100 million annually from its budget to meet the projected competitive pressures.

Reengineering teams had spent several weeks designing new processes and costing out the savings. When they reunited for the first time, bringing all six teams together to integrate and design the overall change process, they discovered that the suggested changes were not as far-reaching as they had hoped. While the project manager glowed about the results, managers complained that they had only "rearranged the dirty laundry on the clothesline." They felt that they had reproduced the results from the prior year's problem-solving efforts and that none of the suggestions were new. Even worse, the results produced savings of less than $20 million, far short of the CEO's goals. During the course of the day's work, the six managers were quite animated about the shortcomings of their efforts. This was the first time all teams had sat down together and the first time they realized how much distance they still had to cover. They were motivated to go back to the drawing board as a group and look for farther-reaching changes that might yield the results the company needed.

The project manager in this case had a different agenda, however. The reengineering effort was on a schedule that he was held accountable to uphold. The teams were scheduled to present their findings to the vice presidents of the company in three days. He was ready to accept the recommendations for change as presented and wanted managers to begin prioritizing which ones to implement first. He didn't seem to mind that the changes were not enough to save the company—the project was on a schedule.

The managers, though, insisted that the changes were inadequate and that they could and must do better. They believed that a delay of several weeks to look for more transformational changes was justified, with so much of the company's viability at stake.

The test for this stakeholder group came at the end of the meeting— actually five minutes past the end of the meeting. The project leader had set up a matrix on which to rank the changes and determine which would be implemented first. He asked each manager to give numerical rankings to the proposed changes in various categories and tallied the totals to determine the order of implementation. The next steps in the plan would be for this group of managers to present "their findings" to the senior leaders in a meeting scheduled early the following week. The project leader would prepare the charts, and the managers would present the work to the vice presidents of the company.

The managers clearly didn't believe this was the right approach, but they were under strong pressure to comply with the project leader. Five minutes after the daylong meeting was scheduled to end, the project leader took a poll to make sure everyone was on board. He went around the room and asked each manager individually, "OK with you?" Even though the managers had spent the entire day trying to explain that it was *not* OK, that they thought they could do better, that they *wanted* to do better, none of them was willing to step forward at this late moment. One by one, the managers gave their OK.

To other reengineering team members who were observing this meeting, this was a powerful example of a failed test by a critical stakeholder group. No manager was willing to take a stand with the project leader, to work on the many significant disagreements with his approach, even though the entire management group was opposed to his plan. Other change team members described this as typical in this organization: no one wanted to make waves or to be identified as rocking the boat. Managers withheld their real beliefs and, along with them, their energy and enthusiasm for change.

The following week, the managers presented the material to the vice presidents as if it were their own. The program was accepted, but it never became a change effort with much spirit or innovation. It did not meet the needs of the enterprise, and even though many people recognized its inadequacies as they pursued implementation, no one took responsibility for dealing with and resolving the situation.

Stakeholder tests are not easy or trivial. When failed, they jeopardize the success of the development effort and sometimes of the enterprise itself. When dealt with successfully, they add energy to the change process and energize others who will face tests as well. Stakeholder testing tends to have a "snowball effect" that magnifies either failure or success as stakeholders model themselves after those who responded before them.

How Performance Support Is Tested

Another test is "down," in the direction of performance support. Stakeholders and leaders, in effect, "look down" to see if there will be ground under their feet. They check to see if they will be supported to learn new skills and capabilities and take the new actions the vision requires. Typical stakeholder tests attempt to answer such questions as these:

- Does a foundation exist for moving forward?
- Is the development effort grounded in stable support for the changes that need to occur?
- Does performance support have the ability to enable the required stakeholder competence?

Performance support members are tested for their ability to promote needed *competence in the stakeholders.* When change is planned and implemented, people always experience the insecurity of the new, of the unknown. They are uncertain of their skills and abilities to perform to new requirements. They typically look for support from within the enterprise to learn the needed skills and new behaviors.

Whether or not people feel this kind of support determines to what degree they will let go of previous performance and behavior patterns. People feel more secure when they know that support exists for learning and that they will be trained in the new skills necessary to succeed in a future they do not yet understand. They feel more comfortable with change when they have an avenue for dealing with the emotions associated with change and transition and are also assured that they will be rewarded for the success of their new behaviors.

The ability to provide effective support requires competent, sensitive staff. Effective performance support staff are people committed to providing support in the areas described. The team may include professionals with change management or organization design expertise but must also have people who come from the ranks of the organization, have earned their credibility in the line organizations, and have taken a temporary assignment to benefit their enterprise in a time of change.

When the performance support function is discounted or not fully authorized or supported by leadership, it often cannot become a competent service to the stakeholders. This almost guarantees that the test for competent performance support will be failed.

In a manufacturing company, senior executives recognized that in order to support the various change initiatives, they needed to rearrange the way they managed their time. The performance support team was asked to assist them with time management training and to reorganize executives' calendars as well. Although they had requested this intervention, when it came time to participate, many senior executives failed to show up or to honor commitments they had made. Because senior executives treated the performance support team so cavalierly, no one else in the company took the team seriously either. As a result, the team could not manage and support the larger change process. It had no credibility with stakeholders, and few of the events the team organized were well attended or had much impact.

In a small community hospital, the significant nature of the intended changes made it clear that there was a need for three full-time performance support staff. Because resources were tight, the leaders chose three of the most problematic individuals, using the change initiative to "put them out to pasture." Most stakeholders knew this was the case and hence did not trust or even use performance support. It was perceived as an irrelevant function.

In an engineering company, a very busy office assistant and two line managers were "freed up" for the change effort, but they were not replaced in their regular roles. Soon all three were struggling to do two full-time jobs and could do neither very effectively. Performance support tasks were the first to go when schedules became busy, and several months later, little progress had been made on the changes planned.

In each of these cases, performance support itself could not act as an effective function, fulfilling the critical roles of administering, supporting, and monitoring change. Because the members were not allowed to be a competent team, they failed the test of enabling stakeholders to become competent in their own new roles.

Ten Tests for the Dynamic Enterprise

In addition to the tests of leaders, stakeholders, and performance support, tests must be passed for each other element of the Enterprise Development framework. After learning about the concept of tests, a member of the enterprise may at times experience the vague sense that he or she is being tested but may not be sure what the test is about. Here we provide a list of ten tests that must be passed for effectively developing the Dynamic Enterprise. Each test corresponds to one component of the Enterprise Development framework.

The first six tests occur at each juncture of the development process as outlined in the Enterprise Development framework (see Chapter Three). Tests 7, 8, and 9 are the tests just described for the three drivers of change. The last test will be described in Chapter Nine.

1. Do the members have a shared view of the forces affecting the enterprise from the external environment?
2. Do the members have a shared vision of the ideal future enterprise, which includes the dynamics of the whole enterprise system (future STEP)?
3. Do the members have a shared view of the past and current conditions of the enterprise system (past and current STEP)?
4. Do the members have a shared view of the development path (arrow)?

5. Do the members have a shared view of where the business is on the business life cycles curves and where it must go? (How large is the business change?)
6. Do the members have a shared view of where the organization is in the organizational life cycles phases and where it must go? (How must the organization develop?)
7. Are leaders committed to the changes required to reach the future vision?
8. Do stakeholders accept responsibility for these changes?
9. Does performance support exist that can enable the leaders and stakeholders to be competent to change and to accomplish the new tasks needed in the future?
10. Can the enterprise translate strategies and plans into performance? Does it have the ability to implement change?

At each new stage of change, one group of stakeholders or another will throw out a challenge: "Is this serious?" "Do we really need to do this?" "Do the key leaders agree?" Each phase of the process will be tested many times before stakeholders move forward. If early tests are responded to successfully and stakeholders begin to gain a level of trust and confidence, they will test less often. Change begins to feel easier—moving with its own momentum, on track.

Part Three

From Strategy to Performance

Chapter Nine

Creating the Enterprise Development Workplan

Too many times in organizational change,
when all is said and done, more is said than done.
NICHOLAS IMPARATO AND OREN HARARI,
Jumping the Curve

How do leaders and stakeholders accomplish the work of Enterprise Development, the work of creating and maintaining the Dynamic Enterprise? What concrete steps do they actually need to take? The first recognition of dramatically needed change sometimes begins with the convictions of a single individual or small group. How do these originators expand their ideas into a recognition shared throughout the enterprise? How do they enlist others to help them develop their ideas into a shared strategy, to design these strategies into day-to-day actions and routines, and ultimately to see the ideas emerge as new practices that are widely embraced throughout the enterprise? What is the path from insight to action for the Dynamic Enterprise?

The Enterprise Development Workplan answers these questions by providing a basic outline for turning strategy into performance. The workplan presents an outline for planning, guiding, monitoring, and mapping dynamic change. The goal of the workplan is to transform the Enterprise Development map into more than a map. A map alone is not much help to an enterprise facing rapidly shifting internal and external conditions. The Dynamic

Enterprise must have the added capability to translate the information on the map into performance.

Ultimately, the Dynamic Enterprise needs to be able to implement changes in each of the STEP categories (see Chapter Four). It should have the following capabilities:

- To create awareness about and build vital connections with the *external environment* (including industry trends, customers, competitors, suppliers, resources, culture, regulatory groups, as well as emerging threats and possibilities)
- To set strategic *task* directions and priorities based on an understanding of the external environment and internal capabilities, to redesign business processes as needed, and to clarify the individual and team performance required
- To configure the organization *structure* and systems to support these business processes and required performance
- To prepare *people*—individuals and teams—to deliver the needed business results
- To align the company's *internal environment,* its culture, values, and work styles, to ensure the enterprise has an ongoing ability to deliver the best products and services to its external environment

Each of these areas of change needs to be defined at the broad, conceptual, visionary level and then "drilled down" to the more detailed operational level. Each needs to be translated into specific roles, policies, and procedures in ways that clarify who does what on a daily basis. Given the realities of time and resource pressures, no single development effort covers all the details required for the perfect implementation. Depending on its size, scope, available resources, and time line, each implementation will pursue its priorities from a "menu" of these implementation steps.

Principles of Implementation

A high-level overview of what needs to be done in implementation seems relatively routine and obvious. Most people know what they need to do to implement change—or could sit down and figure it out fairly quickly, using some version of "plan, do, check." Implementation is a fairly straightforward and logical process. It is not hard to figure out what to do—the tricky part is figuring out how to get people to take the steps they know they need to take. How does one get a network of people (who are busily engaged in productive work already) to shift their priorities and attention, to commit to a new development or change effort, and to follow it through to completion?

Not surprisingly, when we begin to work on implementation, a common response we hear is, "We already know how to do that—our team knows how to implement." In fact, many companies already use implementation processes or project management models, and some have extensive information systems to manage these as well. Many have existing frameworks and language for launching, implementing, and monitoring complex projects. Even in enterprises where everyone agrees that prior implementation efforts have failed, most stakeholders assume that they already know what they *should* have done; they just didn't do it. But it is not because they didn't know what to do. The change programs themselves are rarely seen as deficient. The implementation programs are typically seen as logical and workable—it's just that people didn't use them. (It's like a diet that is a good way to lose weight. The diet itself works perfectly well, and the person knows all about how to use it, but it still doesn't work if it's never put into practice.)

We have found that a few principles of implementation make it much more likely that all the phases of change will be completed as initially planned. Although the steps to implementation are logical and straightforward, paying attention to a small number of critical principles in the *process* of implementation make it more likely that each phase will be completed.

Based on these principles, *the Enterprise Development Workplan adds two phases at the starting point of implementation that are not often seen in traditional change management models: Initial Engagement and Building the Foundations for Development.* These two phases emphasize engaging the essential people and support needed to drive the rest of the change process. In essence, the workplan adds engaging and building the political power base and the support resources needed for a change before embarking on the subsequent implementation steps.

Principle 1: The Three Drivers Provide the Dynamic Force for Implementation

The three drivers—leaders, stakeholders, and performance support—all have to work effectively together to drive change forward. If any one of these groups is not fully engaged in its vital role in moving the enterprise or is not linked effectively with the other two groups, realistic implementation is at risk (see Chapter Eight for more detail on each of these groups and their role in implementation).

Furthermore, *the drivers' role must be built in at the earliest possible point in implementation.* To ensure that these roles are established from the beginning of implementation, we recommend starting with the *Initial Engagement* phase, designed to put the leader–performance support alliance firmly in place from the earliest days of change. This first phase begins by giving the individuals or team members initiating a change a "once over lightly" view of the entire process that lies ahead of them. (These change initiators may or may not be formal leaders of the enterprise.)

Once the initiators have stabilized their view of the needed changes, they may then choose to "expand the circle," to bring in others to help them think through, brainstorm, or troubleshoot their ideas. They establish an expanded group of "thinking partners." We have seen individual leaders who want to bring in their peers or staff members who report to them. Some team members want to bring in the rest of their team. Sometimes individuals or groups prefer to bring in people whom they trust, who can act as sounding boards, or who can test out or expand on their ideas.

Saving the detailed work for later (and for a group with wider participation from the larger enterprise), this first group of project initiators and their thinking partners work through the entire Enterprise Development map at the overview level. They begin to see the most general direction of where they are going, where they are starting, and what is required to make the change succeed.

Once they are able to design a first-draft overview of the change process needed, the initial set of thinkers can identify a second group—their "change partners," the people they need to have on board to help them succeed. They begin to identify and enroll the leaders who will need to authorize, clarify, and lead the changes going forward. (If they can't gain leaders' real commitment, they may choose to stop at this point or at least be aware of the fact that they are proceeding under extremely tenuous conditions.) These early planners must next decide who their key stakeholders are and develop a first-draft overview of the kinds of performance support they will need (see Chapter Eight for a more detailed discussion of performance support).

The next step in this phase is to select and enroll performance support team members and to link them with the leaders. *A competent leader–performance support alliance provides the driving force for all the steps of implementation ahead.* Regardless of how the initial ideas for change originated, this leader–performance support alliance is an essential early ingredient for the success of the subsequent phases of implementation. This alliance brings into partnership people who are indispensable for educating, motivating, and supporting stakeholders to commit to and complete the rest of the phases.

Principle 2: Forget Change Rollout: Stakeholders Must Be "Enrolled"

When leaders or teams create a vision or set a strategic direction and then try to communicate it to others, they face an uphill climb. Dynamic change is rarely "rolled out" effectively or "cascaded" through an organization, no matter how artful the process. Change management literature in recent years has documented extensively the need for participation and involvement. Stakeholders want to contribute, to bring their own expertise, ideas, and experience into the new vision of the future. Stakeholders, both those who must implement change and those affected by it, must be "enrolled" in the change process. They are the ones whose day-to-day actions make change happen (or not happen) and are often the best experts at designing the specific actions that are needed. Rather than having an authority figure tell them how the future will look (while they dig in their heels and turn every shift into a slow, labor-intensive, and painful process), "enrollment" means that stakeholders are active designers and implementers of their future enterprise. Stakeholders "sign up" to create the future.

In the second phase, *Building the Foundations for Development,* the leaders and performance support team members begin to identify the key stakeholder groups that are needed to design and implement the changes ahead and begin to plan how to engage these groups. They inform their key stakeholder groups that they are beginning a process of change and let them know as much as possible about what lies ahead. Finally, depending on the scope of the change (this is obviously different for a change involving five people than for one involving five thousand), they plan and begin to build the working relationships, networks, teams, communication systems, support, and follow-up processes that will enable stakeholders to engage in all the following phases of implementation.

By the end of this phase, the essential "movers and shakers" in the enterprise—the individuals in both formal and informal positions who are needed to make the changes occur—have seen an overview of all that lies ahead. In addition, they have participated in creating the outline of the rest of the workplan and have decided how they will move the larger group of stakeholders through these phases. They have developed a change management plan.

Part of the power of developing the workplan itself at this stage is not just for the content of the plan but for the fact that key individuals and teams have looked at these plans together and decided whether they are ready to move forward. At this point, while they don't yet know all the details that will emerge later, they do have a clear idea about the magnitude and type of change they are advocating. They understand the commitment (and often the levels of personal change) that will be required from them. They won't be surprised in midstream.

People who are action-oriented may want to jump right in, start on the logical steps, and forget about these two phases at the beginning. However, for a complex change—one in which failure or delay might have dire consequences or in which implementation will not be easy—these first two phases can be decisive. They build in political support and change capability as the "launching platform" to energize and drive the rest of the change. They provide the means to "go slow to go fast."

Principle 3: Frame the Challenges and Let People Create Their Own Maps to the Future

After initiating a new direction, the individual or team does not have to "tell and sell" this direction to others. Rather, the initiators can offer a blank Enterprise Development framework as a planning tool and let others *discover* the direction on their own. We have worked with CEOs who created their own vision and clarified changes essential to their enterprise and then led their executive teams or board members through the exercise of creating their own map without filling it in for them. Managers have led their teams, or vice versa. Work groups have sat down with other groups to design their collaborative work together, without one team showing the other how to fill in the map. We have found that when individuals or teams present an open Enterprise Development map to others and simultaneously provide much of the up-front data about the external environment and internal requirements, the new participants create a map with about 90 percent overlap. The remaining 10 percent of differences are often helpful and enlightening and provide valuable data. In cases where other teams come up with an entirely different picture, there are usually important reasons why this is the case, and the first team needs to understand why others' picture of the future looks so different.

Using the Enterprise Development map effectively requires that the necessary strategic information be shared freely with whoever is creating the map. Enterprise Development is based on the assumption that all teams—not just the CEO and top management—need access to information about the outside business environment and industry trends. When people working on the front lines of an organization receive vital information about the status of the overall business and its potential opportunities and challenges in the future, they can typically create a map of their own future enterprise that links with the maps of other teams and the larger institution as a whole. For example, leaders may need to provide information or financial data up front that stakeholders may not have easy access to, such as "Our funding sources are being cut by 50 percent this year," "Forty percent of our customers are telling us they want a total enterprise solution, customized for their business and delivered to them fully formed," "Our suppliers have requested to know our most important quality concerns so that they can focus their own quality production and service," or "Overall, we show good numbers for customer growth, but we have a serious problem with customer retention—five customers are leaving for every six new customers we get."

When given a structure that frames the relevant information and guides them to ask the next questions, people do not have to be told what the big-picture trends imply for their team or department or how they might need to shift their roles to fit into the larger picture. They can discover it for themselves and are then more likely to own the picture they have created. They are generally quite adept at designing their unique contribution to the future and usually see it in far richer detail than the individuals at the top of the organization.

Next, we present a brief outline of the Enterprise Development Workplan (the *what* of implementation) and then describe several additional implementation principles that run through all the phases (the *how*, the dynamics of implementation common to all phases, that encourage stakeholders to complete the implementation process).

Overview of the Enterprise Development Workplan

The Enterprise Development Workplan describes implementation in a step-by-step sequence of phases (see Figure 9.1). It serves as an outline for planning, monitoring, and mapping dynamic and large-scale change. Although the phases are shown in the approximate sequence in which they take place, in reality they rarely occur in such a linear progression. Phases can occur in parallel or in an iterative process that moves back and forth between one phase and another. The actual development process is shaped by the unique and often unpredictable interactions of the members of the enterprise with each other, as well as with the external world that changes around them in the midst of their development process. Because neither the target vision nor the environment around them nor the organization itself holds still while everyone is trying to change, the workplan should be applied with flexibility in mind.

Each organization or team creates its own customized workplan. At each step of the way, organization members supply content from

Figure 9.1. The Six Phases of the Enterprise Development Workplan.

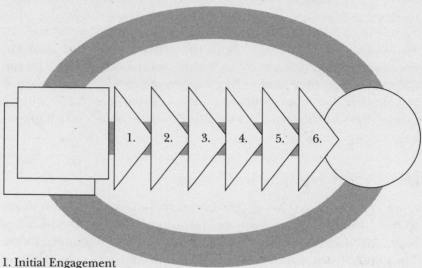

1. Initial Engagement
2. Foundations for Development
3. Vision and Strategy
4. Design
5. Change
6. Continuous Learning

their own situations. Customized workplans typically set out details for how each enterprise will implement the development process, including the key objectives, the scope of the process, who will be involved in each step, the time frame, budgets, how specific plans link to other plans or actions that are part of the development process, and the ultimate performance to be delivered.

In addition, workplans run along three tracks. There are three separate lines of workplan activity: what leaders will do in each phase, what actions stakeholders will take, and how performance support will keep the whole process coordinated and on course.

Phase 1: Initial Engagement

As described earlier, in the Initial Engagement phase, change initiators pull together the essential team needed to begin the change process and help this group understand the highest-priority issues in the enterprise. The initiators create a preliminary Enterprise Development map to clarify these issues using a systems-oriented, strategic perspective. This phase is an important opportunity for members of this group to establish effective working relationships with one another, to learn about the process of change they are undertaking, and to build commitment to the work ahead. The initial phase is a "once over lightly" approach in which key leaders, stakeholders, and performance support members clarify a high-level overview to think through the entire change effort from beginning to end.

Phase 2: Foundations for Development

Once committed to change, the members of the initial team begin to build the foundations for the development effort ahead. They begin high-level planning for change and transition management. They identify the primary work teams and alliances that will have to be involved, agree on the general workplan, begin to build the collaborative networks that will be required, and establish the communications vehicles for use throughout the work.

Phase 3: Vision and Strategy

This phase looks toward the future to create a compelling picture of the desired enterprise and the change strategy needed to reach it (see Chapters Five and Six for more details). Assessments of the company's external business environment and of its current business and organizational functioning help unfreeze old assumptions and develop a clear understanding of current realities. Critical gaps are identified between the present situation and the desired future. The result is an integrated set of strategies for addressing gaps and creating the desired future.

Phase 4: Design

Now that enterprise members know what they want to do, designated work teams begin to design specific activities and tasks for implementing the strategy. Work is assigned, standards and commitments for performance are negotiated, and issues that arise over the course of the transition are continuously addressed. The design work typically occurs in three subphases.

Phase 4a: Business Process Assessments

An initial review of key business processes is conducted. High-level performance indicators and measures are established. Necessary bridging actions are identified.

Phase 4b: Conceptual Design

Selected processes are assessed, comparisons to available benchmarks are made, and new processes are designed. Policy, infrastructure, and other systems requirements are identified, and cost-benefit analyses are conducted.

Phase 4c: Detailed Design

Necessary policies and procedures are defined. Organization designs, including new job descriptions, roles and responsibilities, policies, and systems and technology requirements, are developed, reviewed, and authorized. Prototypes are drafted and tested. If needed, migration paths are clarified and decided, and specific transition plans are completed for the changes designed.

It is important to note that this phase is rarely planned by a central design committee. The individuals and teams closest to the work typically complete the detailed design of the new work processes, roles, and organizational changes required.

Phase 5: Change

During this phase, previous plans are put into practice. Transition events are conducted, followed by the introduction of restructured business processes, new procedures and measurements, new technology and information systems where needed, and new organizational arrangements. People begin work in their new roles.

Phase 6: Continuous Learning

The performance support team helps leaders and stakeholders build and implement systems and processes for ongoing evaluation and adjustment of the development process, to ensure that new systems work well together and produce the desired outcomes. They develop systems to catch and correct breakdowns and also work to build the corrections into the knowledge base of the enterprise, to prevent similar breakdowns in the future. Many groups at this time go on to establish lasting systems to support Continuous Learning.

Roles of the Three Drivers: Different Skills in Different Phases

Each of the drivers plays a unique role throughout all of the work-plan phases:

- *Leaders* steward the development process, commit needed resources and support, authorize changes, and model the new actions.
- *Stakeholders* make the changes happen. They design and implement the new business processes and organizational arrangements.
- The *performance support* team enables development to occur with the fewest obstacles. The team keeps the change process alive (in the face of competing demands) through coordination, facilitation, monitoring, and problem solving.

Because the activities in each implementation phase are so different, a range of skills and talents will be required at different times during implementation. This can present difficulties for leaders or change teams that want to stay in charge throughout the whole change process but realistically have the passion and skills for only one or two phases.

For example, Phase 1, Initial Engagement, requires vision, initiative, entrepreneurial spirit, and advocacy skills (to persuade others to join in a new idea or project). Phase 2, Building the Foundations for Development, requires political and interpersonal skills (to build the networks and alliances required for successful change), as well as skills in communication (personal as well as larger enterprise communication systems) and change management.

Phase 3, Vision, requires big-picture, longer-term, strategic thinking. It requires an ability and interest in thinking about the future and larger trends, as well as the ability to focus on the present. It requires courage to name unpleasant realities or future threats that no one else may be speaking about. It requires charisma, or a bit of poetry or inspiration to develop a "visionary" approach to the future and the path to get there.

Phase 4, Design, requires a substantial shift in skills from those required in earlier phases. Each subphase requires progressively more heads-down, focused attention to operational detail. It requires people who enjoy the step-by-step details of new processes, policies, and systems and who can create migration paths from the old to the new. Varying content expertise may be required, depending on whether the new designs entail changing core work processes, the organization chart, job descriptions, roles and responsibilities, leadership and management roles, incentive programs, HR policies, communication or meeting systems, selection processes, training and learning systems, teamwork processes, corporate identity, or group culture. The Design phase also typically requires people who have good team and interpersonal skills, as design work is often conducted by teams, in concert with multiple stakeholder groups who give input and review their designs.

Phase 5, Change, requires people who are action-oriented, who have a passion for moving from ideas to action. They must be willing to introduce new practices to others and to adjust these practices as needed until they work. This phase also requires people who are willing to change themselves. Leaders and performance support team members must be the first to model the new ways, even if this requires substantial change on their own part. Change leaders and performance support must also understand that they will be tested heavily in this phase, be open to being tested without getting defensive (see Chapter Eight), and be prepared to respond successfully to tests.

Phase 6, Continuous Learning, requires people who have monitoring and evaluating skills and enjoy using them. They must be skilled at designing and implementing measurements that can track implementation progress and ultimately progress toward performance objectives. In addition, this phase requires deftness at translating these evaluations into learning and at communicating them back to a wider audience. Designing systems and measurements to capture learning is sometimes a very different skill from transmitting this learning back out into the enterprise, in helping others to use the learning. Communicating learning to others may require educational skills and information systems design, in addition to skills for organizing the means to debrief problems and failures and to celebrate successes.

Obviously, no single leader or performance support team member will have the requisite skills in all six of these areas or even an interest in all of them. For example, in many change efforts, the leader is acknowledged throughout the enterprise as a visionary but takes no interest in the day-to-day realities of implementation. Other leaders are known for their operational excellence and attention to detail. Everyone respects their understanding of core business issues but doubts the quality of their long-range strategic thinking. These leaders may be missing the forest for the trees. Other leaders are skilled at both strategy and operations but cannot communicate their insights to others in a way that motivates action. In short, one individual leader or change team member can rarely do it all—but it all needs to be done. What does this tell us about implementation?

The workplan is a helpful guide precisely because it outlines the implementation phases from beginning to end. Part of the work in Phase 2, Building the Foundations for Development, is to design a change management plan that will ensure leadership commitment, stakeholder involvement, and performance support capability *throughout the entire implementation process.* If there is a phase that no one on the team likes or is capable of carrying out, the planners can discover this early (rather than waiting until they have reached that phase to discover that details mysteriously get lost, key information falls through the cracks, and the change effort "surprisingly" falls apart at that particular point). The individuals drafting the whole change process in Phase 2 can also use their knowledge of the multiple skills required to assemble diverse change teams or build a series of teams that will "pass the torch" from one to the other to make sure that all essential phases are completed.

Planned Change Versus Emergent Change

Debate is growing in the change management community as to whether change can be planned or controlled at all. The concern is that planned change comes out of our "old paradigm," traditional view of organizations. In industrial era thinking, organizations were considered static, mechanistic entities that could be moved only by human intervention. An emerging perspective on organizations is articulated well by Margaret Wheatley and Myron Kellner-Rodgers (1996). Organizations are considered more similar to biological organisms than to machines. Organizations are always changing and have the innate ability and the drive to self-organize. From this optimistic perspective, people in organizations will interact spontaneously to create complex, vibrant networks of information. They will discover and implement the changes that are needed. It is viewed as presumptuous for one group of individuals to think that they know more than others about what needs to change or that they need to direct this process at all. Trying to control and direct change will only kill the natural vitality that might have emerged. From this perspective, attempts at planned change appear somewhat arrogant and actually get in the way of creative, self-organized change.

Our own view of human behavior in organizations and people's capacity for spontaneous self-organization is not this optimistic, yet we find many of the ideas about emergent change extremely useful. If our businesses and institutions had the amount of time that geological and biological systems have taken to produce order out of chaos, we too could wait for change to emerge. However, within the time frame more familiar to our current institutions, chaos runs the risk of staying chaos, and what was order runs the risk of dissolving into chaos. Organization and new systems do not necessarily emerge just when they are needed, and it is messy and painful when we need order and it isn't there. Too often, people get blamed or fired; lives are disrupted; companies and institutions that have been successful in the past run into trouble.

The Need for Both Kinds of Change

The Dynamic Enterprise requires the capacity to plan and implement change as quickly as its external and internal conditions demand. Sometimes it cannot wait for change to emerge. However, planned change does not have to equate to a command-and-control, hierarchical, patriarchal change process. The Dynamic

Enterprise needs its people to create the rich, diverse, informal networks that keep emergent change alive, that bring into the change process ideas that could never be anticipated in the original plan. Planned change can and should consciously leave room for and encourage emergent change.

> A government agency was trying to identify the services its "customers" needed most. Managers wanted to redesign their work to increase quality and service in those areas while cutting costs elsewhere by reducing red tape, overheads, and redundancy. A lengthy hallway conversation between two staff members led to the idea that the agency should actually merge their two departments, to decrease the overlap between them and simultaneously provide more coordinated service to their shared customers. This was not a change specified in the original organization design or one designed by the managers, but it fit with the spirit and need of the larger change process. The employees began to design the merged department themselves and soon brought in coworkers to help them. As they worked together, they began to get more creative. They envisioned how the new department could not only cut costs but also be the first to put innovative ideas from the change process into practice (for example, by operating as a "paperless" department). They were inspired. When it was clear to them that their ideas could work, they offered a proposal to their managers and change teams. Ultimately, their "emergent change" was incorporated into the larger "planned change." In this best of both worlds, the Dynamic Enterprise can not only implement planned change effectively but also spontaneously create and implement complementary changes. When people understand where the enterprise is headed and why, they can join this development. As they naturally create informal networks and work groups, they can bring about spontaneous changes that further the spirit and direction of the enterprise strategy.

The Enterprise Development Map as a Tool for Integrating Planned and Emergent Change

The Enterprise Development map provides a tool for focused dialogue. People need to be able to talk to each other clearly about the changes they are creating together. Successful implementation occurs through hundreds of daily decisions, and people make their decisions on the basis of the information and understanding they have at the time. However, there are always an overwhelming number of issues to have conversations about. "Dialogue" could be held on any topic—that doesn't mean it would help the enterprise meet its objectives within the time required.

The Enterprise Development map gives stakeholders a larger picture of why change is required, of what kind of change is required, sometimes of the multiple changes occurring through-out the enterprise, and about their own unique role in this picture. They can see where they fit on the map, as well as where others belong. This tool makes it easier for people both to plan changes together and to invent solutions they need. By providing focus, a bit of structure, and a shared vision of the future, it helps them know which issues have priority and deserve their attention.

In every Enterprise Development map, many constraints or parameters are given—even for CEOs or board members. Require-ments imposed by a number of external or internal sources may appear as givens on a particular map (such as the marketplace, funding sources, another team's priorities, a customer's deadlines, or a competitor's actions, to name just a few). However, within these constraints, each team has a wide range of freedom to cre-ate its own local enterprise vision, strategy, and change map. Teams can identify their own issues and design how to get to the future. They design a change process that makes sense to them. They know where they are in their implementation process and how the change is progressing. Most important, they know why they are doing what they are doing, and they can explain it to others. For those who find graphic tools helpful, they can draw the story they are describing and point out where they are on the map.

This map (and accompanying understanding or story) can then serve as a tool for focused dialogue, a description that can be shared and negotiated with others. For example:

- In times of change, employees can use their Enterprise Development map in discussions with their managers to negotiate a new performance contract or to identify their role in a larger development or the new deliverables they will be responsible for.
- Team members can begin dialogue with other teams to understand their interlinked roles and the new responsibilities that will be required of each.

- When one team finds a need for a change in its own group, it can make sure that other teams that will be affected understand the new plans and join in the development process if needed.
- Strategic partners (inside or outside the enterprise) can create shared maps to ensure that they are seeing the future in compatible ways, they understand each other's strategies and priorities, they understand what each group will do to change and that new designs for their own unit link with the designs of the others.
- Teams that need to collaborate can make sure that the leaders from each group work together effectively and that each group receives adequate support for change.
- Teams can create a shared map with their customers and suppliers, to understand the most important requirements for increasing value throughout the supply network.

Spontaneous, emergent change is more likely to be productive when people have tools for developing strategies and implementing change. When people working together have information about the larger picture of their environment that makes change essential, when they understand why change is needed, they can see what is most urgently required. When they understand which changes are linked to others, they can figure out whom to contact, where and when dialogue would be most helpful, and whom to connect with to build collaborative plans for the future.

Warm-Up Time

For all the change we are experiencing now in our businesses and institutions, more change and bigger change seems to lie ahead. We see for-profit businesses, nonprofit institutions, and government agencies facing a remarkably similar and wide range of change. Many are redefining the fundamental products or services they provide, while others are working to improve them (or pursuing both approaches at once). Many are redesigning the core business processes through which they produce or deliver products and services, to find a way simultaneously to increase quality and to cut costs. In addition, we are seeing an explosion of experimentation in new organizational forms in support of these changes in the way of doing business: flatter organizations, outsourcing previously central functions, partnership arrangements with new groups (including competitors), virtual organizations, a multitude of new kinds of teams (including cross-functional teams, problem-solving teams, change teams, and self-managed work teams), and new alliances, networks, and associations. As boundaries shift, functions that were inside companies move to the outside, and functions that were outside are often moving inside (such as suppliers or distributors who deliver their goods to the point of service and then keep the goods stocked as needed, replacing previously internal functions). New information technologies and new business practices seem likely to keep this list expanding.

This is the time for work groups to master the skills of the Dynamic Enterprise. It is time to develop expertise in finding direction in the midst of apparent chaos, in defining and refining strategy, and in continuous change implementation. There is already enough change in our work environments to justify the investment of time and resources for developing this competence. There is still time to practice learning these skills. The Enterprise Development framework offers six tools for the Dynamic Enterprise: seeing the whole system of the enterprise, creating a shared future, seeing the past and current enterprise honestly and accurately, understanding the nature of the change, mobilizing and aligning the three drivers of change, and implementing the change. No enterprise learns all of these skills at once. Some skills will already be present. Other skills will come quite naturally to an enterprise, while still others will be more of a stretch from its current operations and culture. The tougher skills (which can be different for each setting) will require much determination to master. Over time, the enterprise will become more and more "dynamic" as its experience and proficiency with each step progresses.

This is the time to learn. As change progresses ever more rapidly and profoundly, strategy and change management are becoming essential disciplines for our times. In the past ten years, many businesses and institutions have undergone more fundamental and fast-paced change than they had experienced in the previous fifty years (if their industry even existed fifty years ago). Yet leaders and stakeholders across a wide range of industries and institutions tell us that they foresee more change ahead of us than behind us.

This is the warm-up time, the time for practice. Bigger changes lie ahead.

Epilogue
Looking into the Deep Future

There are good reasons for suggesting that the modern
age has ended. Many things indicate that we are going
through a transitional period, when it seems that
something is on the way out and something else is
painfully being born. It is as if something were crumbling,
decaying and exhausting itself, while something else,
still indistinct, were arising from the rubble.
VACLAV HAVEL, PRESIDENT OF THE CZECH REPUBLIC

The Dynamic Enterprise must keep its eye on the future. Actually, it must learn to have "double vision." The Dynamic Enterprise must simultaneously have both a clear view of the most compelling and urgent current needs and how to respond to these and the means to search out those changes that are not yet entirely clear, that are still around the next curve.

As we look into the future, we see very disturbing trends. In fact, these trends are here now, but we so widely ignore them in the world of business that it is often easier to imagine them by looking into the future. We expect the future to look different, so we seem more open to new ideas as we look ahead. If we look closer, we often find that these future trends are already present now.

Working with business and nonprofit groups across a wide range of industries and functions, we have found that the current condition is already different from the way our prevailing work culture traditionally defines it. We all seem to share an unspoken

245

agreement to leave certain types of information off our strategic maps. We are like the South African work group (described in Chapter Five), which first tried to examine its business as if it were operating in a part of the world with a stable, peaceful society surrounding it. Group members initially tried to ignore the fact that their country was facing a potentially bloody revolution and did not add this to their business strategy map because it did not fit in with the traditionally acknowledged business variables. They wanted to go about business as usual, yet it was only when they included all the data in their Enterprise Development map that they could find their most powerful solutions. Many people in their company felt fearful about the impending but rarely spoke about it at work. The anxiety about what would happen to their country, their economy, their jobs, and their homes and families greatly influenced people's decisions, company morale, and business potential. But because their anxiety was mostly unspoken, it remained unexamined, unconscious. When the company's managers added these powerful but previously unacknowledged fears and possibilities to their map, they developed a vision that became a vital and moving force within the company.

The Dynamic Enterprise must put the toughest data on the map.

Typically, when companies look at the external environment around them to add to their Enterprise Development maps, they look at the traditional categories for businesses and organizations: customers, competitors, suppliers, government regulations, new technologies, resources, and culture. However, in our experience, most for-profit businesses and nonprofit institutions restrict the type of material that is included in these categories. In particular, even in the face of increasingly available data telling us that this is an area of growing impact, we leave the natural world and resources off our strategic maps. The natural world is not typically considered part of the world of business or work. And if natural systems are considered outside and separate from the work world, they aren't taken seriously and aren't added to the Enterprise Development maps (or any other strategic planning, visioning, or change management models).

However, as discussed in Chapter Four in connection with the enterprise STEP Model, it is precisely the areas that have been ignored that often contain many of the most important issues. These overlooked areas often carry the greatest room for improvement because attention has been directed elsewhere for so long.

Every day, news items warn about the deteriorating state of our natural environment. We read and hear about a growing ozone hole, global warming, climate shifts, melting polar ice caps, loss of forests and rain forests, and massive species extinctions, while our own population and levels of consumption continue to rise exponentially.

Some of the reports are so frightening that they are hard to attend to (25 percent of mammal species are already endangered; one-third of all species living today will become extinct within the next ten years). What do we do with this kind of information?

We are all like the fishermen facing the advent of fish farming. We are the blacksmith seeing the first horseless carriages in town. The town isn't full of cars yet, we don't yet have massive freeways and traffic jams (can we even imagine that these will come about?)— we are just seeing a few more cars each month. But the world is still full of horses and carriages as it has been for ages, isn't it? People will still need plenty of saddles, feed, and horseshoes, right?

How can we learn to see the emerging data? How can we learn to put it on our maps so that we can begin to think about these vital issues, to plan them into our future business and organizational strategies?

It is easier to ignore data about emerging environmental destruction, to just not pay attention, because there is little in our current lives that tells us we must pay attention. As we look around our everyday environment, we can't see the ozone hole or feel global warming. People continue to go to work, the world economy functions separately from these trends, and performance evaluations for most jobs are based on criteria that have nothing to do with these news items. The world around us appears to be functioning adequately.

However, data continue to emerge, and more and more business and world leaders are beginning to address these issues. Vice President Al Gore wrote about what he calls "the global ecological crisis," in his book *Earth in the Balance* (1992). He summarizes research on how our growing human population is affecting our air, water, soil, climate, and food production, affecting virtually every aspect of the ecosystem that supports life as we know it. In moving and powerful descriptions, Gore links these separate problems together to show that they are symptoms of an underlying fundamental dysfunction in the way our civilization (businesses and institutions included) views the natural world, in how we use resources and discard waste. We are upsetting the very balance in the earth's ecosystems on which we and many other species depend.

Peter Ward, professor of geological sciences, adjunct professor of zoology, and curator of paleontology at the University of Washington in Seattle, studies catastrophic extinctions that have occurred throughout our planet's history. He describes the first major wave of extinction, which occurred 250 million years ago and wiped out 90 percent of the species then living on the earth. A second great mass extinction took place 65 million years ago and killed 50 percent of the species (including the last of the dinosaurs). His current research, and that of many other scientists, finds that more and more locations studied already show an increasing loss of native species due to the multiple intrusions of human intervention. Ward concludes that we are in the midst of another cataclysmic wave of extinction and that unless we take proactive measures now, loss of species will likely increase exponentially in the next fifty years (Ward, 1994).

We are clearly in the midst of a crisis—not one experienced yet in our day to day lives but one on which we have enough data to be identified by those who study the issues. Paul Hawken, a businessman, relates these deteriorating conditions in our natural environment not just to "human intervention" in general but to our work world in particular. He gives perhaps the bluntest and most succinct indictment of business's role in this decline. After first detailing a list of natural resources that are on the verge of depletion from the effects of our farming and business practices, Hawken (1993) states, "Quite simply, our business practices are destroying life on earth. Given current corporate practices, not one wildlife reserve, wilderness, or indigenous culture will survive the global market economy. We know that every natural system on the planet is disintegrating" (p. 3).

It's hard to follow statements like these. They need silence afterward, to let the concepts sink in. (Put the book down; go take a walk; think about this.) What do you do if you believe even a portion of what Gore, Ward, Hawken, and many others say?

We are living at a critical moment in time. Our generation—the twenty to seventy-year-olds in the workplace now—face important decisions that affect the well-being of generations far into the future. To the generations before us, the data was not quite so clear, not so compelling. For the generations that come after us, time may be too late—some changes may have passed critical thresholds, some may be irreversible. We are the generation at work that now has the data to put on the map. We are the generation with the choice.

Our businesses and institutions now hold much of the hope and possibilities for finding solutions to these enormous challenges. A few pioneers in the business world are beginning to address these important issues. It is not clear whether they will prevail, whether enough other companies will face these challenges in time, but a new wave of change has started. Taichi Kiuchi, chairman and CEO of Mitsubishi Electric America, now also serves as the chairman of the Future 500, a network of leaders from business, technology, science, and the environment devoted to achieving a "Factor Four improvement in productivity." They seek to achieve a fourfold increase in value from each unit of productive resource used (including energy, materials, purchases, labor, and capital).

Mitsubishi Electric recently received an award for its joint venture with the Japanese government to take back millions of electric and electronic products through a new series of "remanufacturing plants." The company is working on a Design for the Environment initiative to develop electronic products that can be disassembled into safe, reusable, high-value, low-waste components (Kiuchi, 1996, pp. 1–3).

Ray Anderson, CEO of Interface, an $800 million company that is the world's largest carpet tile manufacturer, frequently describes how profoundly moved he was after reading Hawken's *The Ecology of Commerce* and realized that he had to redefine his company fundamentally. He made a vow that Interface would become a leader in industrial ecology. Anderson began to promote systems to redesign Interface as a "restorative enterprise," a company that would not only stop contributing to natural destruction but would work to put back more into natural systems than it took out. He began a program for the company's twenty-two manufacturing plants worldwide to "reduce, reuse, reclaim, recycle, and redesign" (Lawrence, 1996).

In addition, Interface began to lease its carpets to customers, rather than selling them. As carpet tiles wore out, the company replaced them and took the used tiles back (rather than leaving customers to dispose of them). Their guiding principle was that once resources were brought into the company, Interface owned those materials for life. The company committed to an approach of lifetime stewardship for resources that continually forces it to learn more about the best use and reuse of its materials.

In a recent *Harvard Business Review* article, Stuart Hart (1997), a professor of corporate strategy at the University of Michigan Business School, describes companies that have saved millions of dollars through recycling and reusing materials and energy. However, Hart asserts that the real potential in sustainable business lies in the opportunity for immense revenue growth that still lies ahead and that sustainable development is "one of the biggest opportunities in the history of commerce" (p. 71). He makes the case that because the planet is "stressed beyond what biologists refer to as its carrying capacity," the transition to sustainable business will be inevitable. Sustainable business practices have traditionally been framed in terms of reducing risk and cutting costs rather than developing new products and technology, and Hart observes that "as a result, most companies fail to recognize opportunities of potentially staggering proportions." He continues, "The more we learn about the challenges of sustainability, the clearer it is that we are poised at the threshold of a historic moment in which many of the world's industries may be transformed" (pp. 66–67).

Robert Shapiro, chairman and CEO of Monsanto Company, similarly believes that the global marketplace is going to want sustainable products because our planet's resources have limits and "we're beginning to hit them" (Magretta, 1997, p. 82). Because the issues are so complex, Monsanto does not yet have clear solutions for sustainable development. Shapiro cautions, "No one—not the most sophisticated thinker in the world—can describe a sustainable world with 10 billion to 12 billion people. . . . But we can't sit around waiting for the finished blueprint." He describes how Monsanto is launching an open-ended, exploratory process to confront these issues: "We're trying to invent some new businesses around the concept of sustainability. We may not even know exactly what those businesses will look like, but we're willing to place some bets because the world cannot avoid needing sustainability in the long run" (p. 81).

Shapiro also refers to the effect of involving people in the work of finding globally sustainable solutions to some of our toughest problems: He describes how people "know at a visceral level that we're headed for trouble and would love to find a way to do something about it." When asked how he gets people in his company involved in this effort, he responded, "It's not hard. You talk for three minutes, and people light up and say, 'Where do we start?'" (Magretta, 1997, p. 84). Clearly, many people are ready, and waiting, to join their enterprises in beginning these deep transformations.

A Role for the Dynamic Enterprise

Many more businesses and institutions are likely to join the search for ways to slow the decline of natural resources on which we all depend. Many more customers are likely to demand this in the products and services they buy. If these market trends alone don't produce change quickly enough, regulations and tax policies will likely emerge to require sustainable business practices. What other choices do we have?

We believe that Dynamic Enterprises—companies and institutions large and small that have learned to be responsive to the chaotic forces of change in their environments—will be the ones best equipped to face these critical challenges in the future. The global ecological problems we will face together are complex and interlinked. They will require fundamental rethinking of many current business practices, areas where many people and companies have deeply ingrained traditions and financial interests. This will not be easy, but it will demand solutions nonetheless.

Our hope is that today's Dynamic Enterprises are preparing for the future through their practice with the traditional business problems they currently face. They are learning to notice and chart external pressures and demands. They are learning to redefine their industries and institutions around these new demands, to restructure and rearrange basic business processes when needed.

They can design and implement new organization structures, policies, and procedures. People can nimbly move into new jobs with new performance criteria. They can build teams and work cultures needed to get to their future. They can be simultaneously visionary and realistic about implementation. Their leaders know how to drive change forward, and they know how to deliver the support needed for real change. Their people can work together, collaborate across boundaries, have relevant dialogue, have conversations that matter.

Dynamic Enterprises are practicing on the current business challenges of improving quality and service; on working as global companies; on decreasing waste and cutting costs; on pairing up with customers and suppliers to improve sourcing practices and to add value up and down the supply chain; on moving some functions outside the organization; and on forming new partnerships and alliances that bring other functions closer in. The Dynamic Enterprise is proficient at changing its practices and boundaries as needed.

Expanded Environment, Deep Future

Work groups that have used the Enterprise Development framework and map to chart their future business strategies and implementation plans can apply the same tools to emerging environmental and social issues as well. We have recently begun to use these tools with groups in sessions we call Millennium Strategy Workshops to help groups clarify their own thinking about these difficult issues and to begin to plan their response. We find that only two modifications are required in the Enterprise Development process. First, when filling in the map, the external environment is looked at from a larger system's perspective than we typically examine in most business and institutional planning. The natural environment and resources are added to the map, and often the social or cultural environment as well, to give a picture of the larger system affecting the enterprise. We call this bigger picture the *expanded external environment.*

Second, the future is looked at from a longer-term perspective. We often call this longer-term perspective the *"deep future"* (see Figure E.1). It is not uncommon for companies and teams we work

Figure E.1. The Expanded External Environment and the Deep Future.

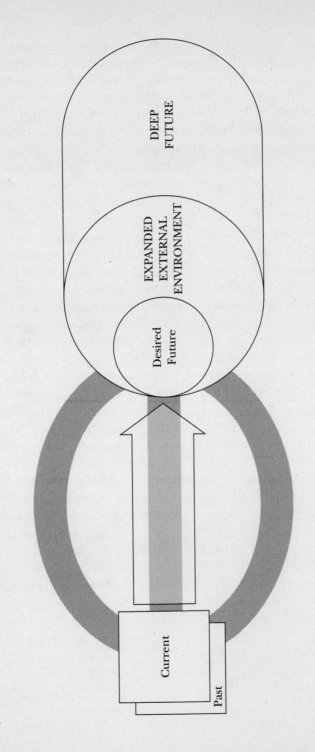

with to map the near future, the future that goes to the end of the current business year or perhaps one to three years out for companies that want to think "long-term." For the deep future, groups may easily think ten years ahead and sometimes twenty-five years or even longer. Of course, we don't actually believe we can foresee the future this far ahead, but the scenario planning for the deep future generally leads to valuable insights. It changes the perspective of what we expect to encounter in the future and can help bring to light critical business forces that in fact are already present.

For "millennium strategy planning," the Enterprise Development framework begins as an open map as usual. It isn't necessary to offer data about the external environment (as described in the beginning of this epilogue). Although people may not be conversant with the specifics, the general environmental and social trends are common knowledge. Most people already know the scope of the challenges ahead—they just don't know they are supposed to connect these to their work lives. Simply giving the instructions (or permission) to include the expanded external environment on the Enterprise Development map, as well as direction to consider the deep future, is generally enough to produce a very different kind of map. People in the enterprise begin to look forward, to consider the very real and critical forces affecting their enterprises that they might not otherwise include in their planning. They begin to generate a new view of their future. They can use the same creative energy and capacity for seeing the connections between the forces affecting their enterprises that they have used for their more traditional business and organizational development. They can use the same tools to begin to think longer-term, to begin to tackle the toughest challenges we must face in the future.

We offer Enterprise Development and the concept of the Dynamic Enterprise as additional tools in the tool kit to help businesses and institutions meet these larger challenges that lie ahead.

References

Axelrod, D. "Getting Everyone Involved: How One Organization Involved Its Employees, Supervisors, and Managers in Redesigning the Organization." *Journal of Applied Behavioral Science*, 1992, *28*(4), 499–509.

Bergquist, W. *The Postmodern Organization: Mastering the Art of Irreversible Change*. San Francisco: Jossey-Bass, 1993.

Bridges, W. *Managing Transitions*. Reading, MA: Addison Wesley Longman, 1981.

Bridges, W. *Surviving Corporate Transitions: Rational Management in a World of Mergers, Start-Ups, Takeovers, Layoffs, Divestitures, Deregulation and New Technologies*. Mill Valley, CA: William Bridges & Associates, 1988.

Bunker, B., and Alban, B. *Large Group Intervention: Engaging the Whole System for Rapid Change*. San Francisco: Jossey-Bass, 1996.

Conner, D. *Managing at the Speed of Change: How Resilient Managers Succeed and Prosper Where Others Fail*. New York: Villard Books, 1994.

Dannemiller, K. and Jacobs, R.W. "Changing the Way Organizations Change: A Revolution in Common Sense." *Journal of Applied Behavioral Science*, 1992, *28*(4), 480–498.

Davis, S., and Davidson, B. *2020 Vision*. New York: Simon & Schuster, 1991.

Drucker, P. *The Practice of Management*. New York: HarperCollins, 1982.

Emir, R., and Butterfield, B. "Co-Creation at Work: Connecting to Each Other and to the Whole." In J. Renesch (Ed.), *The Conscious Organization: Multiple Perspectives of Organizational Transformation*. San Francisco: New Leaders Press, 1997.

Gore, A. *Earth in the Balance: Ecology and the Human Spirit*. Boston: Houghton Mifflin, 1992.

Grove, A. *Only the Paranoid Survive*. New York: Currency Doubleday, 1996.

Hamel, G., and Prahalad, C. K. "Strategic Intent." *Harvard Business Review*, May-June 1989, pp. 63–76.

Hamel, G., and Prahalad, C. K. *Competing for the Future*. Boston: Harvard Business School Press, 1994.

Handy, C. *The Age of Unreason*. Boston: Harvard Business School Press, 1990.

Hanna, D. *Designing Organizations for High Performance.* Reading, MA: Addison Wesley Longman, 1988.

Hart, S. "Beyond Greening: Strategies for a Sustainable World." *Harvard Business Review,* January-February 1997, pp. 66–76.

Havel, V. *1996 Final Report.* San Francisco: State of the World Forum, 1997.

Hawken, P. *The Ecology of Commerce: A Declaration of Sustainability.* New York: HarperBusiness, 1993.

Imparato, N., and Harari, O. *Jumping the Curve: Innovation and Strategic Choice in an Age of Transition.* San Francisco: Jossey-Bass, 1994.

Jacobs, R. *Real-Time Strategic Change: How to Involve an Entire Organization in Fast and Far-Reaching Change.* San Francisco: Berrett-Koehler, 1994.

Jordan, M. "Communicating Change Through Employee Involvement." In P. Boland (Ed.), *Redesigning Health Care Delivery: A Practical Guide to Reengineering, Restructuring, and Renewal.* Berkeley, CA: Boland Health Care, 1996.

Kiuchi, T. *The Future 500: A Business Network for the New Economy.* Sacramento, CA: Global Futures Foundation, 1996.

Lawrence, M. "Business Head Turns to Sustainability," *Timeline,* September-October 1996, pp. 8–9.

Magretta, J. "Growth Through Global Sustainability: An Interview with Monsanto's CEO, Robert B. Shapiro." *Harvard Business Review,* January-February 1997, pp. 78–88.

Meyerson, M. "Everything I Though I Knew About Leadership Is Wrong." *Fast Company,* April-May 1996, pp. 71–80.

Moore, G. *Crossing the Chasm: Marketing and Selling High-Tech Products to Mainstream Customers.* New York: HarperBusiness, 1991.

Moore, G. *Inside the Tornado: Marketing Strategies from Silicon Valley's Cutting Edge.* New York: HarperBusiness, 1995.

Morrison, I. *The Second Curve: Managing the Velocity of Change.* New York: Ballantine, 1996.

Nadler, D. A., Shaw, R. B., Walton, A. E., and Associates. *Discontinuous Change: Leading Organizational Transformation.* San Francisco: Jossey-Bass, 1995.

Nadler, D. A., and Tushman, M. "Types of Organizational Change: From Incremental Improvement to Discontinuous Transformation." In D. A. Nadler, R. B. Shaw, A. E. Walton, and Associates, *Discontinuous Change: Leading Organizational Transformation.* San Francisco: Jossey-Bass, 1995.

Owen, H., *Open Space Technology: A User's Guide.* Potomac, MD: Abbott, 1992.

Pascale, R. *Managing on the Edge*. New York: Simon & Schuster, 1990.

Peterson, S., and Richmond, B. *I Think: The Visual Thinking Tool for the '90s*. Hanover, NH: High Performance Systems, 1993.

Pinchot, G., and Pinchot, E. *The End of Bureaucracy and the Rise of the Intelligent Organization*. San Francisco: Berrett-Koehler, 1994.

Senge, P. *The Fifth Discipline*. New York: Doubleday/Currency, 1990.

Schein, E. H. *Organizational Culture and Leadership* (2nd ed.). San Francisco: Jossey-Bass, 1992.

Stalk, G., Evans, P., and Shulman, L. "Competing on Capabilities: The New Rules of Corporate Strategy." *Harvard Business Review*, March-April 1992, pp. 57–70.

Ventura, M. *Shadow Dancing in the USA*. Los Angeles: Tarcher, 1985.

Ward, P. *The End of Evolution*. New York: Bantam Books, 1994.

Weisbord, M. R. *Productive Workplaces: Organizing and Managing for Dignity, Meaning, and Community*. San Francisco: Jossey-Bass, 1991.

Weisbord, M. R., and Janoff, S. *Future Search: An Action Guide to Finding Common Ground in Organizations and Communities*. San Francisco: Berrett-Koehler, 1995.

Wheatley, M. *Leadership and the New Science: Learning About Organization from an Orderly Universe*. San Francisco: Berrett-Koehler, 1992.

Wheatley, M., and Kellner-Rodgers, M. *A Simpler Way*. San Francisco: Berrett-Koehler, 1996.

Additional Reading

Adizes, I. *Corporate Lifecycles*. Upper Saddle River, NJ: Prentice Hall, 1988.

Beck, A. "Developmental Characteristics of the System-Forming Process." In J. Durkin (Ed.), *Living Groups: Group Psychotherapy and General System Theory*. New York: Brunner/Mazel, 1981.

Beer, M., and Eisenstat, R. *The Critical Path to Corporate Renewal*. Boston: Harvard Business School Press, 1990.

Bion, W. *Experiences in Groups*. New York: Basic Books, 1959.

Block, P. *Stewardship*. San Francisco: Berrett-Koehler, 1993.

Bradford, D., and Cohen, A. *Managing for Excellence*. New York: Wiley, 1987.

Champy, J., and Nohria, N. (Eds.). *Fast Forward: The Best Ideas on Managing Business Change*. Boston: Harvard Business Review, 1996.

Hesselbein, F., Goldsmith, M., and Beckhard, R. (Eds.). *The Leader of the Future*. San Francisco: Jossey-Bass, 1996.

Kotter, J. *Leading Change*. Boston: Harvard Business School Press, 1996.

Savage, C. *Fifth Generation Management*. Bedford, MA: Digital Press, 1990.

Schwartz, P. *The Art of the Long View: Planning for the Future in an Uncertain World*. New York: Doubleday, 1991.

Index